IMPERIUM

COLLECTING
MONSTERS

JOSHUA DYSART | DOUG BRAITHWAITE | DAVE SHARPE

CONTENTS

Collection Cover Art: Raúl Allén

Writer: Joshua Dysart
Artist: Doug Braithwaite
Colorists: Brian Reber with Ulises Arreola
Letterer: Dave Sharpe
Cover Artist: Rafael Albuquerque

Doug Braithwaite
Butch Guice
Trevor Hairsine
Kano
Tom Muller
Cary Nord

Editor: Alejandro Arbona
Editor-in-Chief: Warren Simons

VALIANT.

Peter Cuneo
Chairman

Dinesh Shamdasani
CEO & Chief Creative Officer

Gavin Cuneo
CFO and Head of Strategic Development

Fred Pierce
Publisher

Warren Simons
VP Editor-in-Chief

Walter Black
VP Operations

Hunter Gorinson
Director of Marketing,
Communications & Digital Media

Atom! Freeman
Matthew Klein
Andy Liegl
Sales Managers

Josh Johns
Digital Sales & Special Projects Manager

Travis Escarfullery
Jeff Walker
Production & Design Managers

Alejandro Arbona
Editor

Kyle Andrukiewicz
Tom Brennan
Associate Editors

Peter Stern
Publishing & Operations Manager

Chris Daniels
Marketing Coordinator

Ivan Cohen
Collection Editor

Steve Blackwell
Collection Designer

Rian Hughes/Device
Trade Dress & Book Design

Russell Brown
President, Consumer Products,
Promotions and Ad Sales

Jason Kothari
Vice Chairman

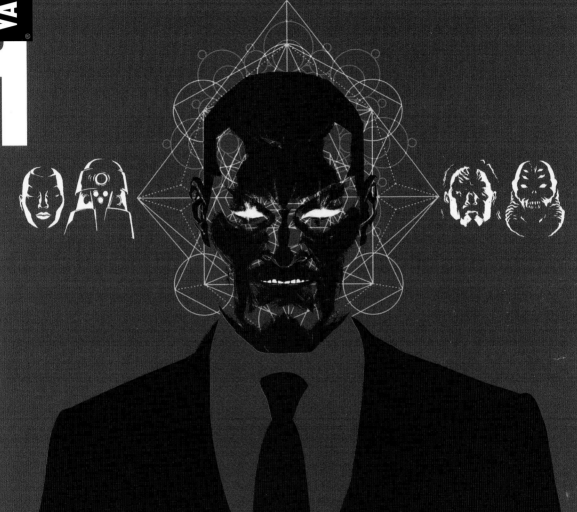

IMPERIUM

インピリアム

VALIANT

1

JOSHUA DYSART

DOUG BRAITHWAITE

インピリアム

IMPERIUM™

The story so far...

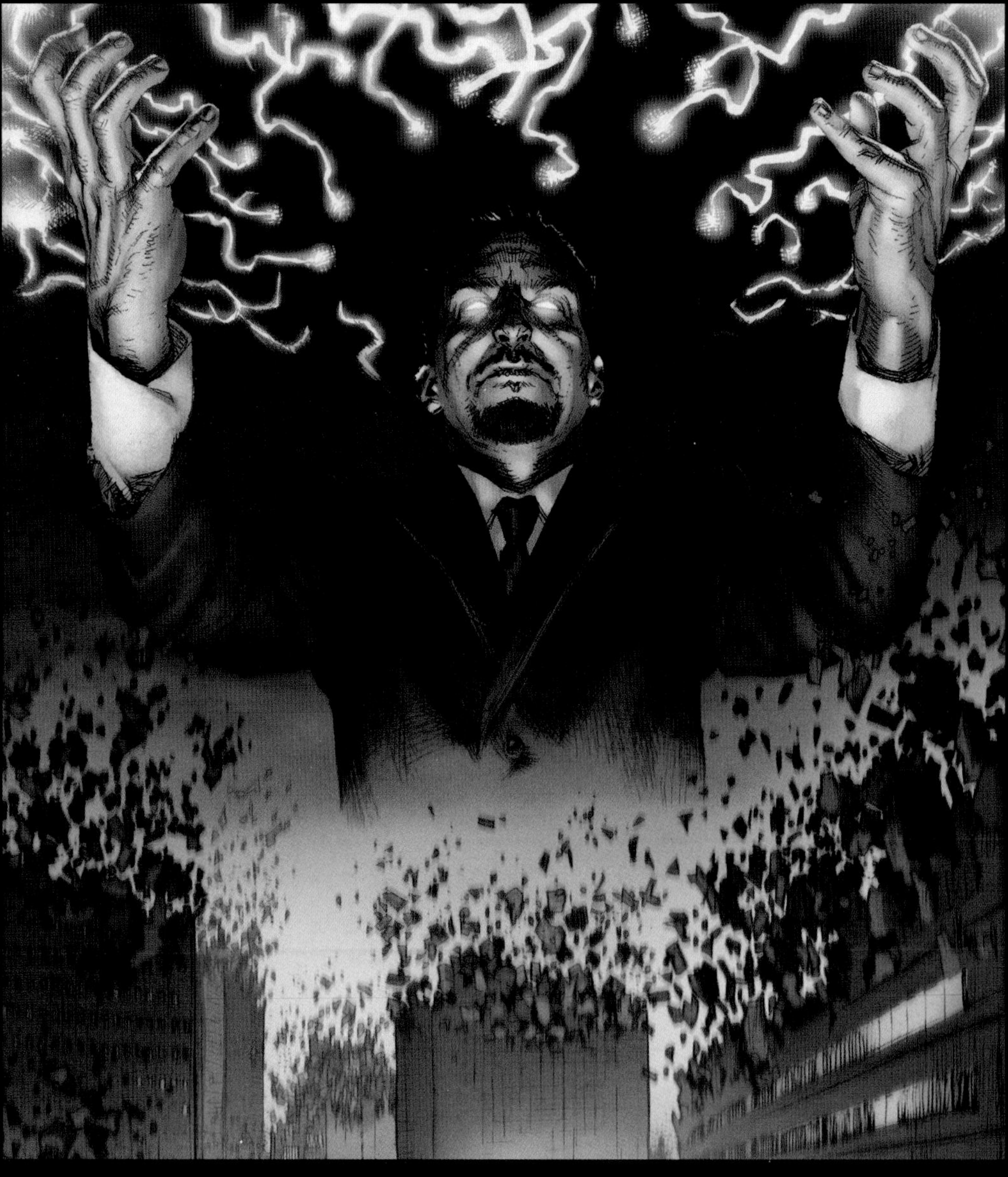

Toyo Harada is the world's most powerful psiot–a human gifted with mental abilities that unlock tremendous powers. With his top-secret Harbinger Foundation, Harada sought out and trained other psiots, to bring about world peace, cure disease, and end poverty and hunger...by any means necessary. But because Harada was willing to manipulate and kill anyone who stood in his way, a group of psiot renegades exposed him and brought down his global empire.

Now, with nothing to hide, nothing to lose, and no reason to work within the system anymore, Harada is waging open war to save the world. Backed by his loyal Foundation followers, Harada has conquered a small territory in Somalia, proclaiming it the Foundation Zone. But with the world's powers united against him, Harada will need deadlier and more dangerous assets than his students to make his dreams for a better world real...

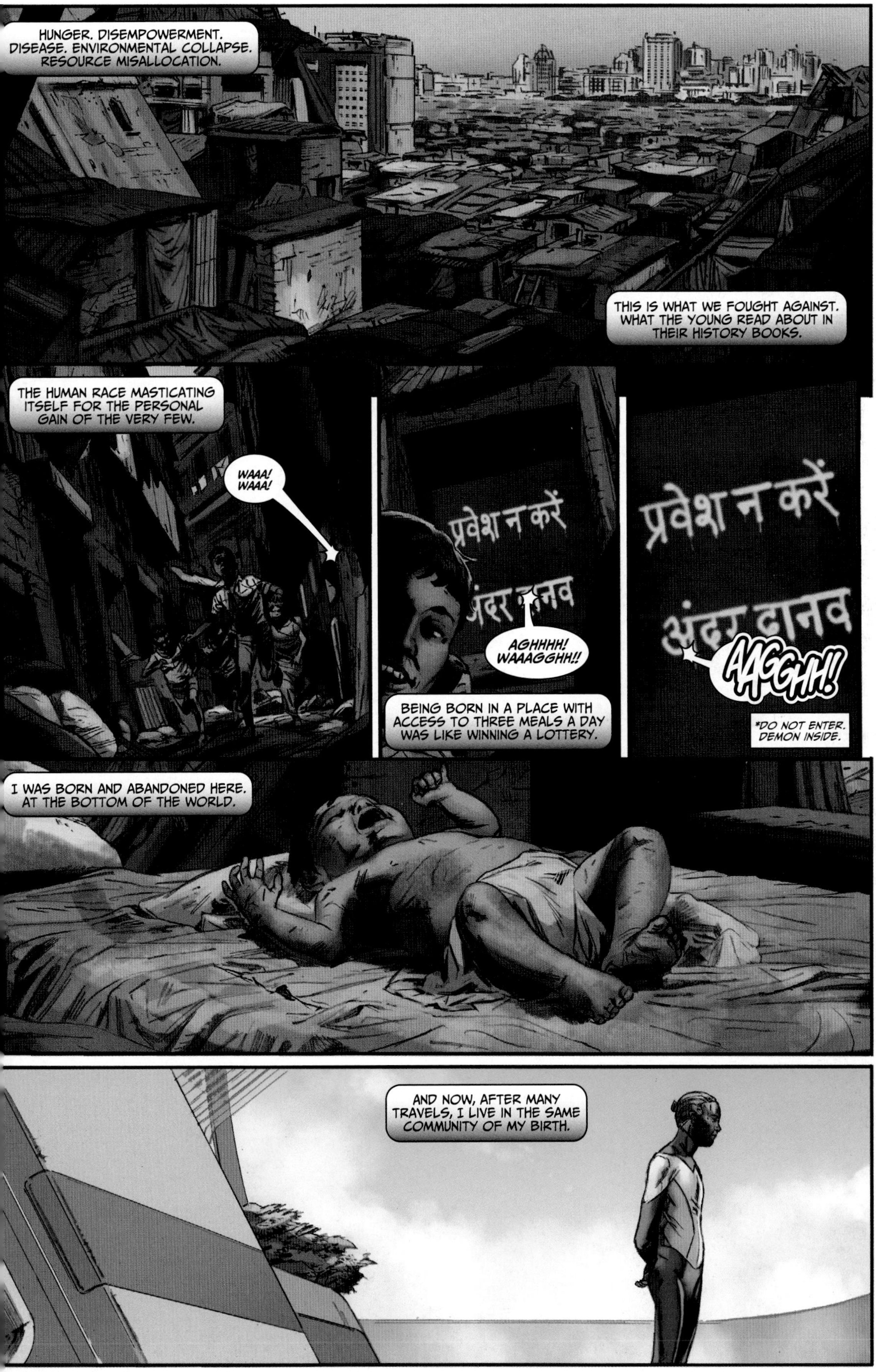

HUNGER. DISEMPOWERMENT. DISEASE. ENVIRONMENTAL COLLAPSE. RESOURCE MISALLOCATION.
THIS IS WHAT WE FOUGHT AGAINST. WHAT THE YOUNG READ ABOUT IN THEIR HISTORY BOOKS.
THE HUMAN RACE MASTICATING ITSELF FOR THE PERSONAL GAIN OF THE VERY FEW.
WAAA! WAAA!
प्रवेश न करें
अंदर दानव
AGHHHH! WAAAGGHH!!
BEING BORN IN A PLACE WITH ACCESS TO THREE MEALS A DAY WAS LIKE WINNING A LOTTERY.
प्रवेश न करें
अंदर दानव
AAGGHH!
*DO NOT ENTER. DEMON INSIDE.
I WAS BORN AND ABANDONED HERE. AT THE BOTTOM OF THE WORLD.
AND NOW, AFTER MANY TRAVELS, I LIVE IN THE SAME COMMUNITY OF MY BIRTH.

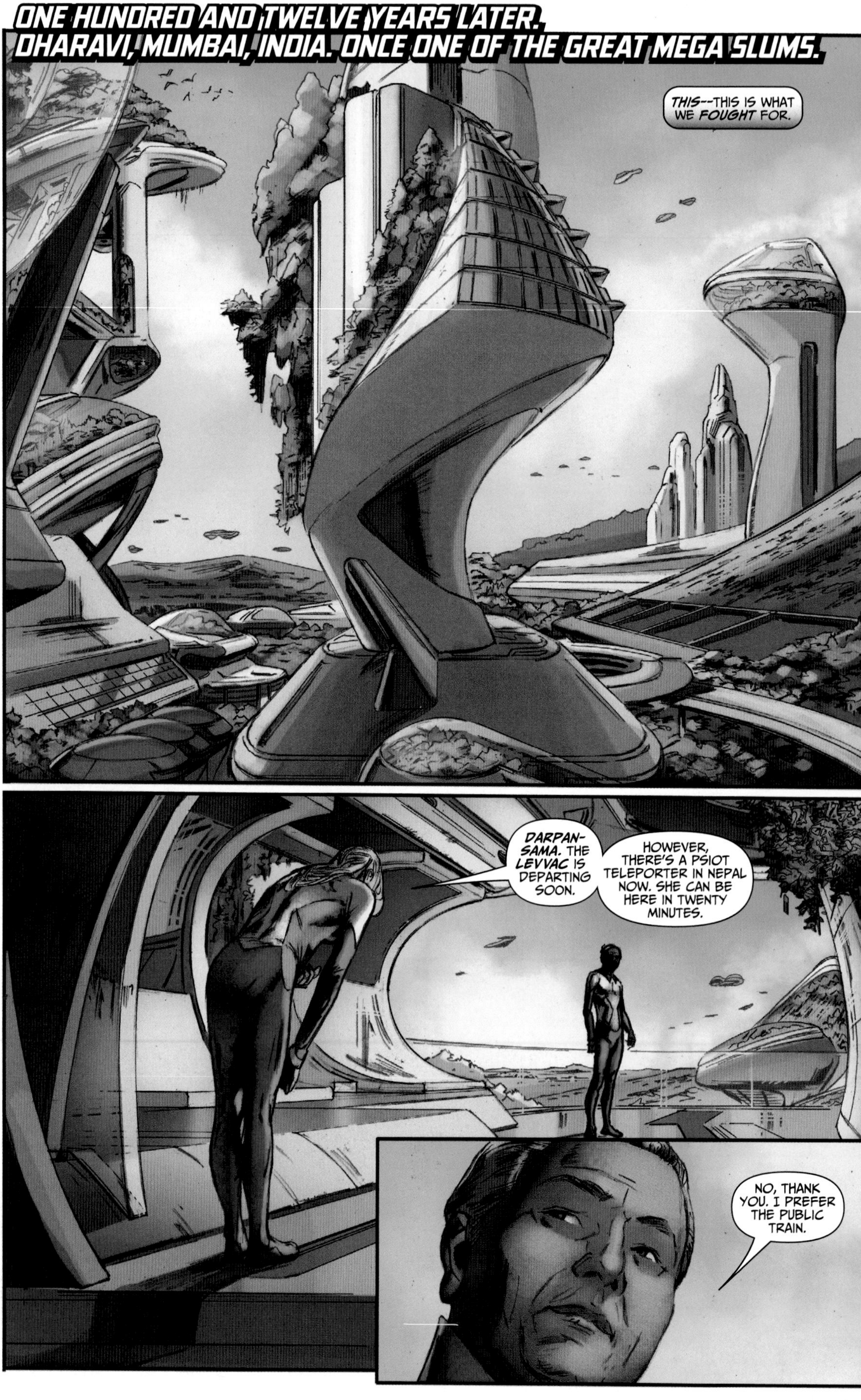
ONE HUNDRED AND TWELVE YEARS LATER.
DHARAVI, MUMBAI, INDIA. ONCE ONE OF THE GREAT MEGA SLUMS.
THIS--THIS IS WHAT WE FOUGHT FOR.
DARPAN-SAMA. THE LEVVAC IS DEPARTING SOON.
HOWEVER, THERE'S A PSIOT TELEPORTER IN NEPAL NOW. SHE CAN BE HERE IN TWENTY MINUTES.
NO, THANK YOU. I PREFER THE PUBLIC TRAIN.

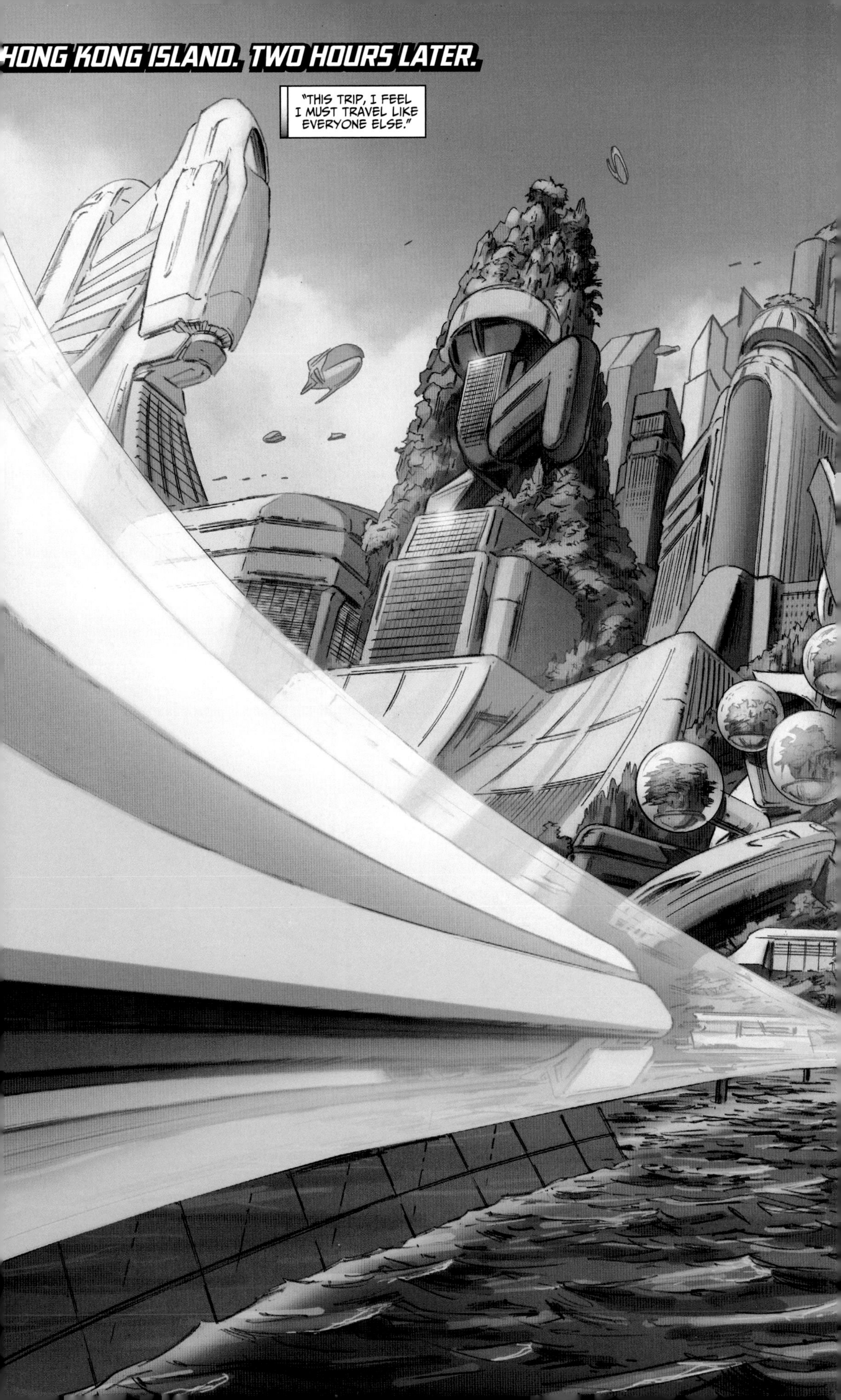
HONG KONG ISLAND. TWO HOURS LATER.
"THIS TRIP, I FEEL I MUST TRAVEL LIKE EVERYONE ELSE."

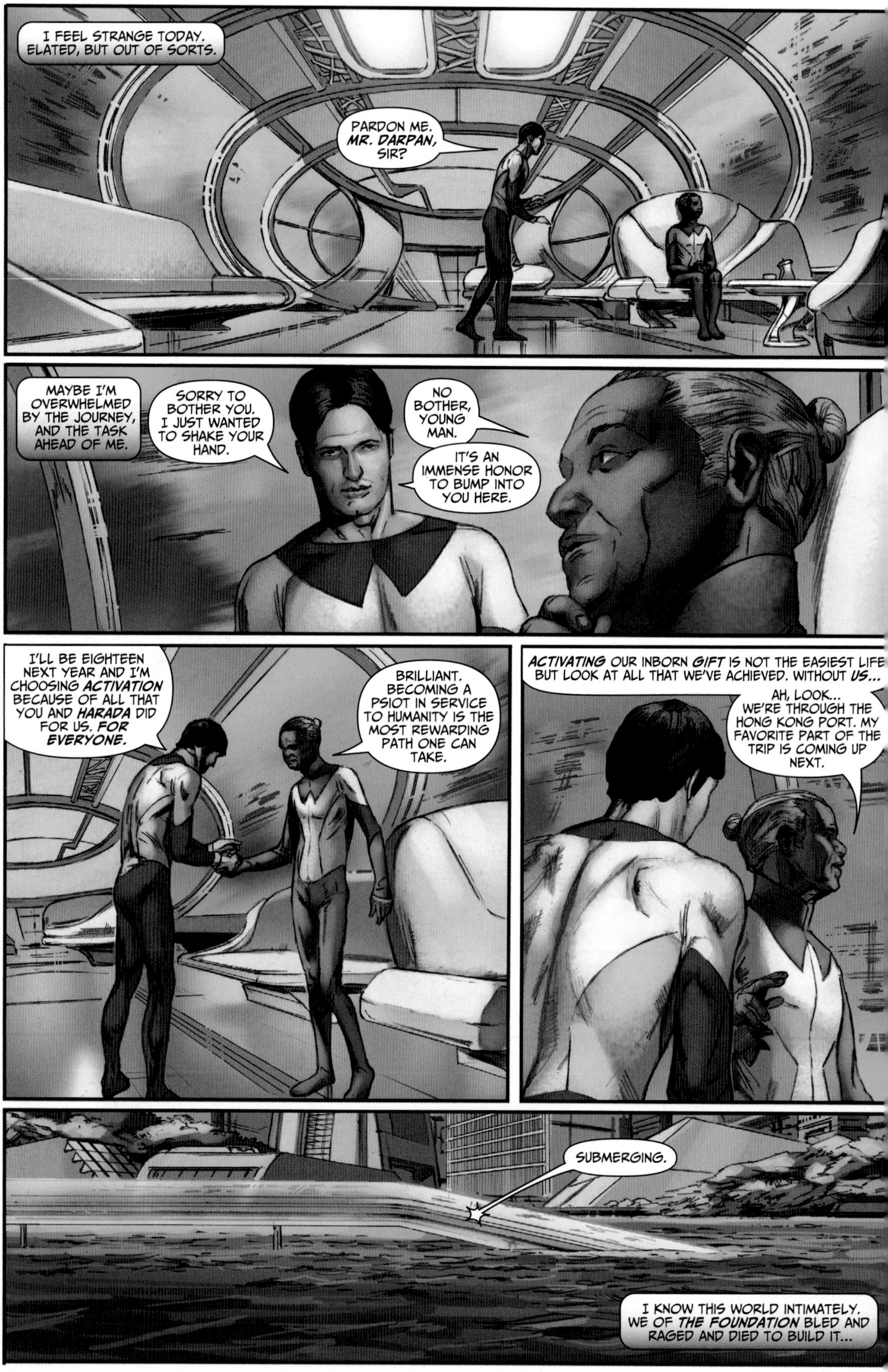
I FEEL STRANGE TODAY. ELATED, BUT OUT OF SORTS.
PARDON ME. MR. DARPAN, SIR?
MAYBE I'M OVERWHELMED BY THE JOURNEY, AND THE TASK AHEAD OF ME.
SORRY TO BOTHER YOU. I JUST WANTED TO SHAKE YOUR HAND.
NO BOTHER, YOUNG MAN.
IT'S AN IMMENSE HONOR TO BUMP INTO YOU HERE.
I'LL BE EIGHTEEN NEXT YEAR AND I'M CHOOSING ACTIVATION BECAUSE OF ALL THAT YOU AND HARADA DID FOR US. FOR EVERYONE.
BRILLIANT. BECOMING A PSIOT IN SERVICE TO HUMANITY IS THE MOST REWARDING PATH ONE CAN TAKE.
ACTIVATING OUR INBORN GIFT IS NOT THE EASIEST LIFE BUT LOOK AT ALL THAT WE'VE ACHIEVED. WITHOUT US...
AH, LOOK... WE'RE THROUGH THE HONG KONG PORT. MY FAVORITE PART OF THE TRIP IS COMING UP NEXT.
SUBMERGING.
I KNOW THIS WORLD INTIMATELY. WE OF THE FOUNDATION BLED AND RAGED AND DIED TO BUILD IT...

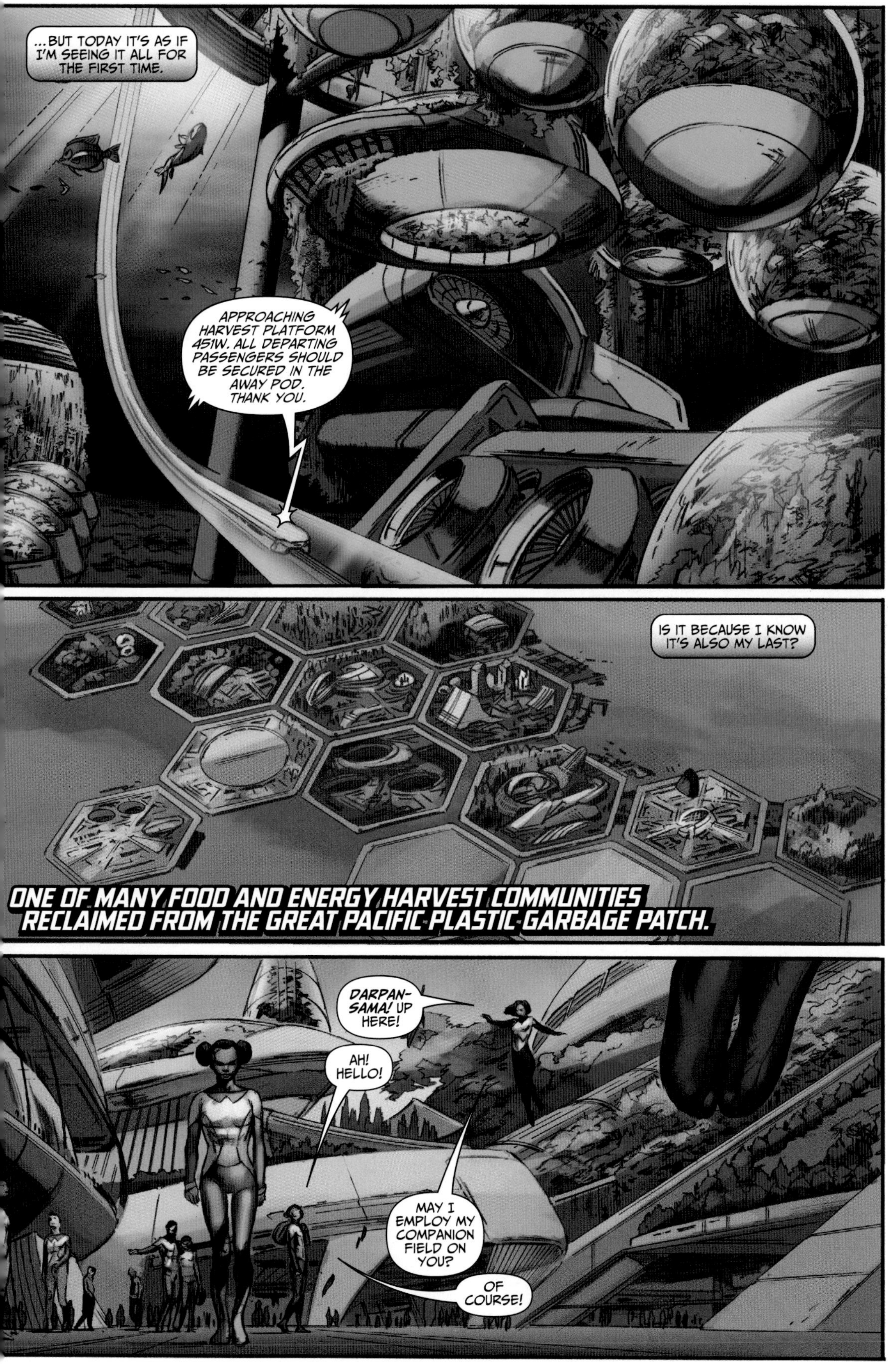

...BUT TODAY IT'S AS IF I'M SEEING IT ALL FOR THE FIRST TIME.
APPROACHING HARVEST PLATFORM 451W. ALL DEPARTING PASSENGERS SHOULD BE SECURED IN THE AWAY POD. THANK YOU.
IS IT BECAUSE I KNOW IT'S ALSO MY LAST?
ONE OF MANY FOOD AND ENERGY HARVEST COMMUNITIES RECLAIMED FROM THE GREAT PACIFIC PLASTIC GARBAGE PATCH.
DARPAN-SAMA! UP HERE!
AH! HELLO!
MAY I EMPLOY MY COMPANION FIELD ON YOU?
OF COURSE!

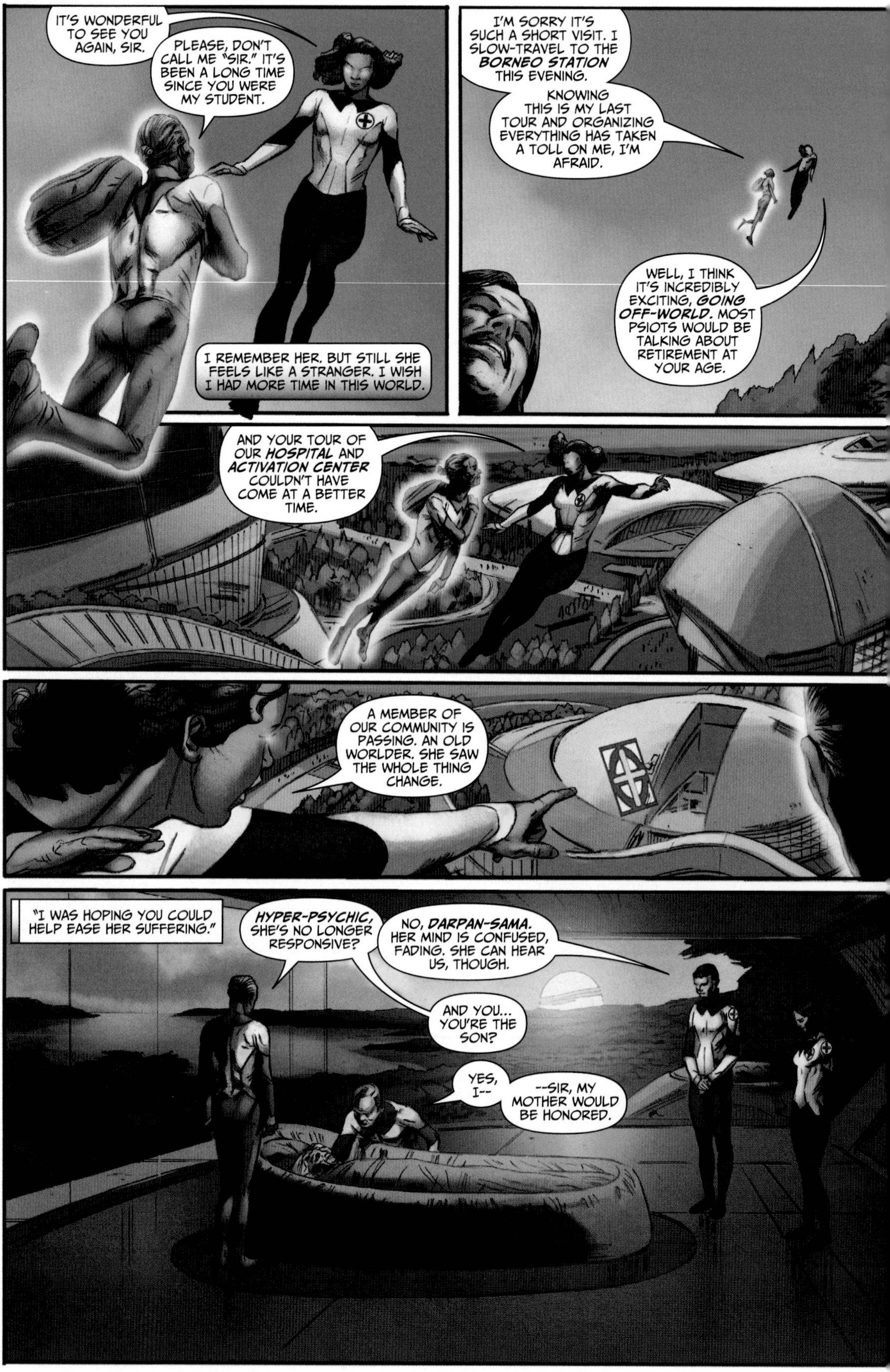

IT'S WONDERFUL TO SEE YOU AGAIN, SIR.
PLEASE, DON'T CALL ME "SIR." IT'S BEEN A LONG TIME SINCE YOU WERE MY STUDENT.
I REMEMBER HER. BUT STILL SHE FEELS LIKE A STRANGER. I WISH I HAD MORE TIME IN THIS WORLD.
I'M SORRY IT'S SUCH A SHORT VISIT. I SLOW-TRAVEL TO THE BORNEO STATION THIS EVENING.
KNOWING THIS IS MY LAST TOUR AND ORGANIZING EVERYTHING HAS TAKEN A TOLL ON ME, I'M AFRAID.
WELL, I THINK IT'S INCREDIBLY EXCITING, GOING OFF-WORLD. MOST PSIOTS WOULD BE TALKING ABOUT RETIREMENT AT YOUR AGE.
AND YOUR TOUR OF OUR HOSPITAL AND ACTIVATION CENTER COULDN'T HAVE COME AT A BETTER TIME.
A MEMBER OF OUR COMMUNITY IS PASSING. AN OLD WORLDER. SHE SAW THE WHOLE THING CHANGE.
"I WAS HOPING YOU COULD HELP EASE HER SUFFERING."
HYPER-PSYCHIC, SHE'S NO LONGER RESPONSIVE?
NO, DARPAN-SAMA. HER MIND IS CONFUSED, FADING. SHE CAN HEAR US, THOUGH.
AND YOU... YOU'RE THE SON?
YES, I--
--SIR, MY MOTHER WOULD BE HONORED.

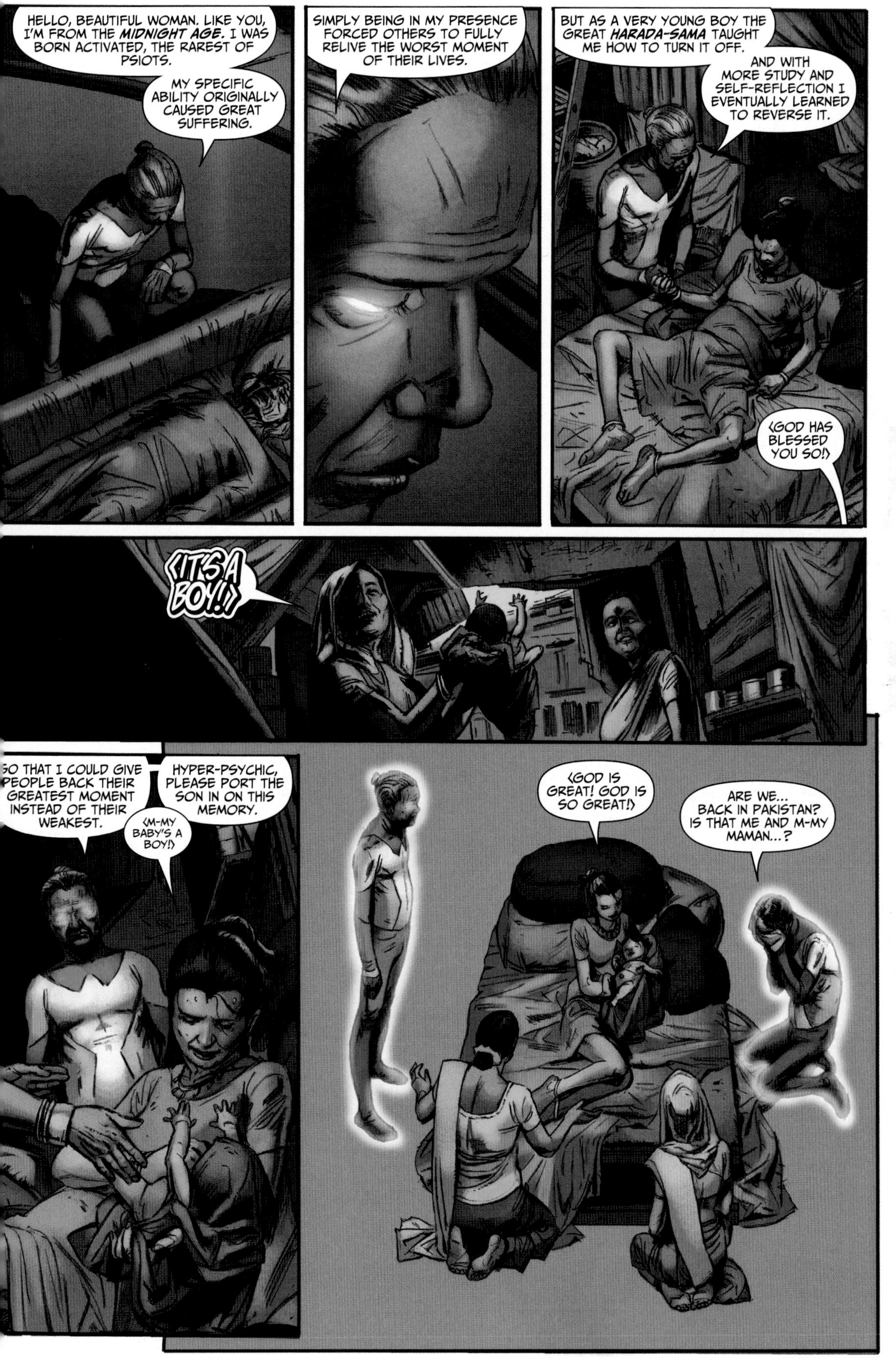
HELLO, BEAUTIFUL WOMAN. LIKE YOU, I'M FROM THE *MIDNIGHT AGE.* I WAS BORN ACTIVATED, THE RAREST OF PSIOTS.
MY SPECIFIC ABILITY ORIGINALLY CAUSED GREAT SUFFERING.
SIMPLY BEING IN MY PRESENCE FORCED OTHERS TO FULLY RELIVE THE WORST MOMENT OF THEIR LIVES.
BUT AS A VERY YOUNG BOY THE GREAT *HARADA-SAMA* TAUGHT ME HOW TO TURN IT OFF.
AND WITH MORE STUDY AND SELF-REFLECTION I EVENTUALLY LEARNED TO REVERSE IT.
‹GOD HAS BLESSED YOU SO!›
‹IT'S A BOY!!›
SO THAT I COULD GIVE PEOPLE BACK THEIR GREATEST MOMENT INSTEAD OF THEIR WEAKEST.
HYPER-PSYCHIC, PLEASE PORT THE SON IN ON THIS MEMORY.
‹M-MY BABY'S A BOY!›
‹GOD IS GREAT! GOD IS SO GREAT!›
ARE WE... BACK IN PAKISTAN? IS THAT ME AND M-MY MAMAN...?

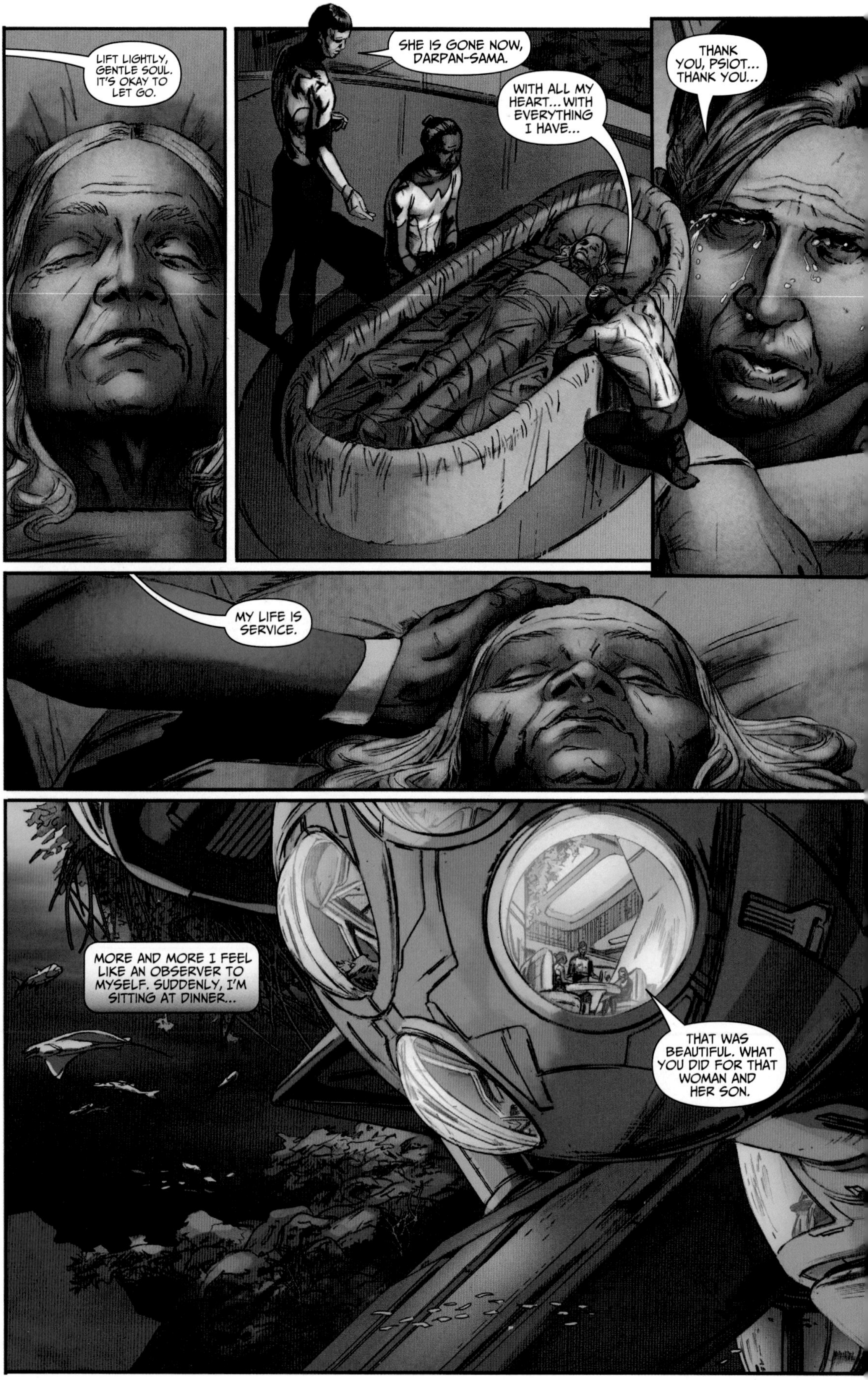

LIFT LIGHTLY, GENTLE SOUL. IT'S OKAY TO LET GO.
SHE IS GONE NOW, DARPAN-SAMA.
WITH ALL MY HEART... WITH EVERYTHING I HAVE...
THANK YOU, PSIOT... THANK YOU...
MY LIFE IS SERVICE.
MORE AND MORE I FEEL LIKE AN OBSERVER TO MYSELF. SUDDENLY, I'M SITTING AT DINNER...
THAT WAS BEAUTIFUL. WHAT YOU DID FOR THAT WOMAN AND HER SON.

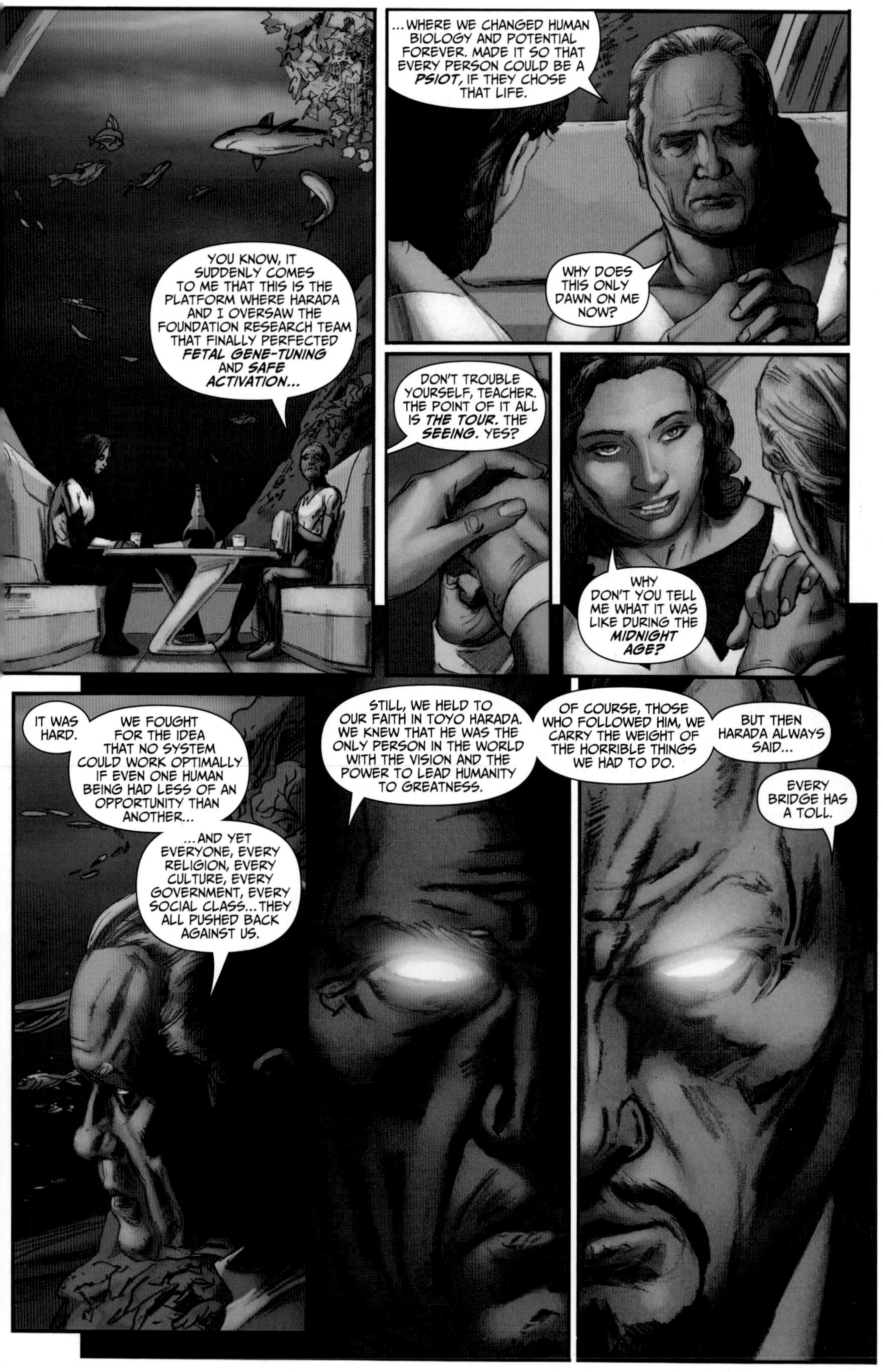
YOU KNOW, IT SUDDENLY COMES TO ME THAT THIS IS THE PLATFORM WHERE HARADA AND I OVERSAW THE FOUNDATION RESEARCH TEAM THAT FINALLY PERFECTED FETAL GENE-TUNING AND SAFE ACTIVATION...
...WHERE WE CHANGED HUMAN BIOLOGY AND POTENTIAL FOREVER. MADE IT SO THAT EVERY PERSON COULD BE A PSIOT, IF THEY CHOSE THAT LIFE.
WHY DOES THIS ONLY DAWN ON ME NOW?
DON'T TROUBLE YOURSELF, TEACHER. THE POINT OF IT ALL IS THE TOUR. THE SEEING. YES?
WHY DON'T YOU TELL ME WHAT IT WAS LIKE DURING THE MIDNIGHT AGE?
IT WAS HARD.
WE FOUGHT FOR THE IDEA THAT NO SYSTEM COULD WORK OPTIMALLY IF EVEN ONE HUMAN BEING HAD LESS OF AN OPPORTUNITY THAN ANOTHER...
...AND YET EVERYONE, EVERY RELIGION, EVERY CULTURE, EVERY GOVERNMENT, EVERY SOCIAL CLASS...THEY ALL PUSHED BACK AGAINST US.
STILL, WE HELD TO OUR FAITH IN TOYO HARADA. WE KNEW THAT HE WAS THE ONLY PERSON IN THE WORLD WITH THE VISION AND THE POWER TO LEAD HUMANITY TO GREATNESS.
OF COURSE, THOSE WHO FOLLOWED HIM, WE CARRY THE WEIGHT OF THE HORRIBLE THINGS WE HAD TO DO.
BUT THEN HARADA ALWAYS SAID...
EVERY BRIDGE HAS A TOLL.

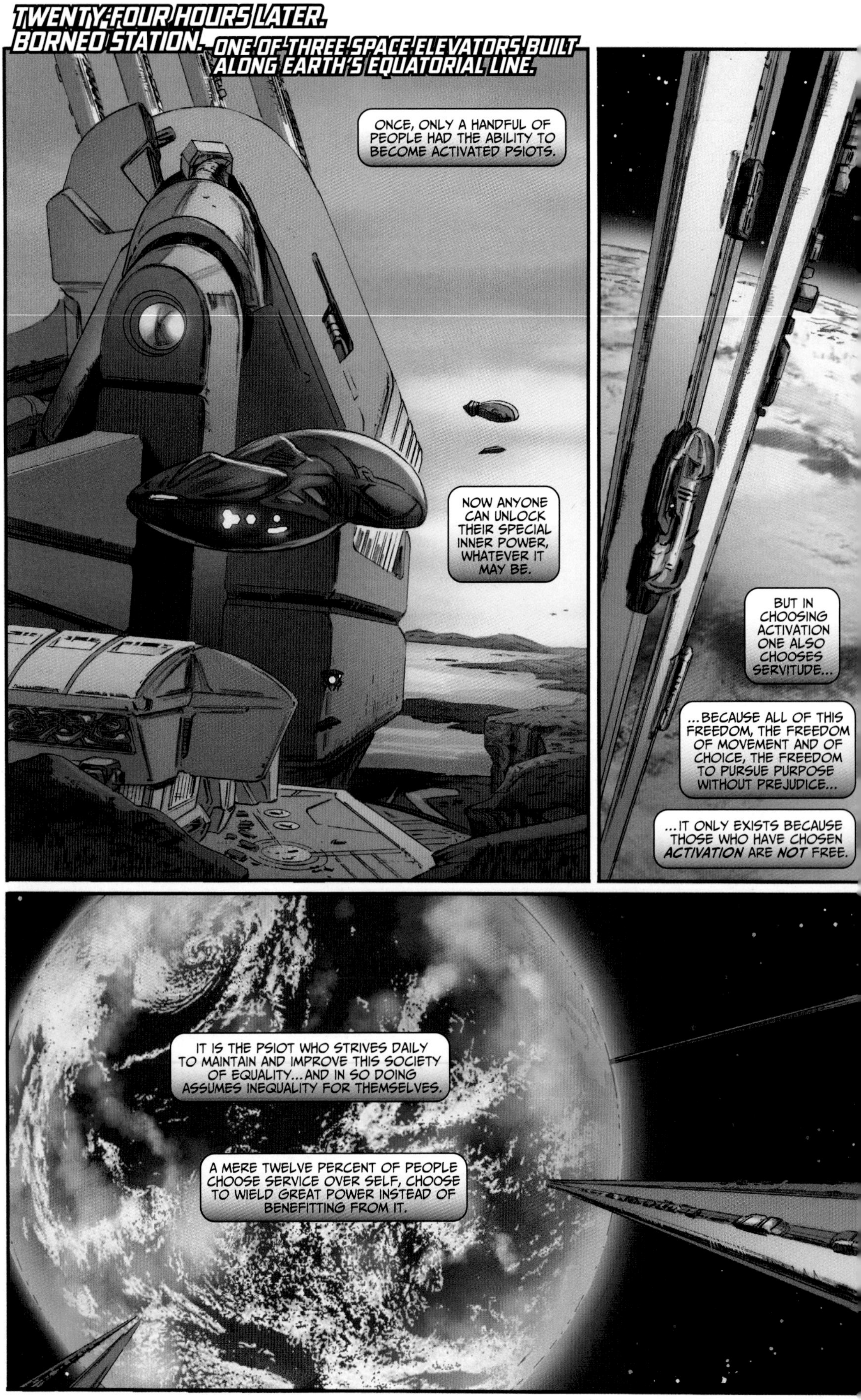
TWENTY-FOUR HOURS LATER. BORNEO STATION.
ONE OF THREE SPACE ELEVATORS BUILT ALONG EARTH'S EQUATORIAL LINE.
ONCE, ONLY A HANDFUL OF PEOPLE HAD THE ABILITY TO BECOME ACTIVATED PSIOTS.
NOW ANYONE CAN UNLOCK THEIR SPECIAL INNER POWER, WHATEVER IT MAY BE.
BUT IN CHOOSING ACTIVATION ONE ALSO CHOOSES SERVITUDE...
...BECAUSE ALL OF THIS FREEDOM, THE FREEDOM OF MOVEMENT AND OF CHOICE, THE FREEDOM TO PURSUE PURPOSE WITHOUT PREJUDICE...
...IT ONLY EXISTS BECAUSE THOSE WHO HAVE CHOSEN ACTIVATION ARE NOT FREE.
IT IS THE PSIOT WHO STRIVES DAILY TO MAINTAIN AND IMPROVE THIS SOCIETY OF EQUALITY...AND IN SO DOING ASSUMES INEQUALITY FOR THEMSELVES.
A MERE TWELVE PERCENT OF PEOPLE CHOOSE SERVICE OVER SELF, CHOOSE TO WIELD GREAT POWER INSTEAD OF BENEFITTING FROM IT.

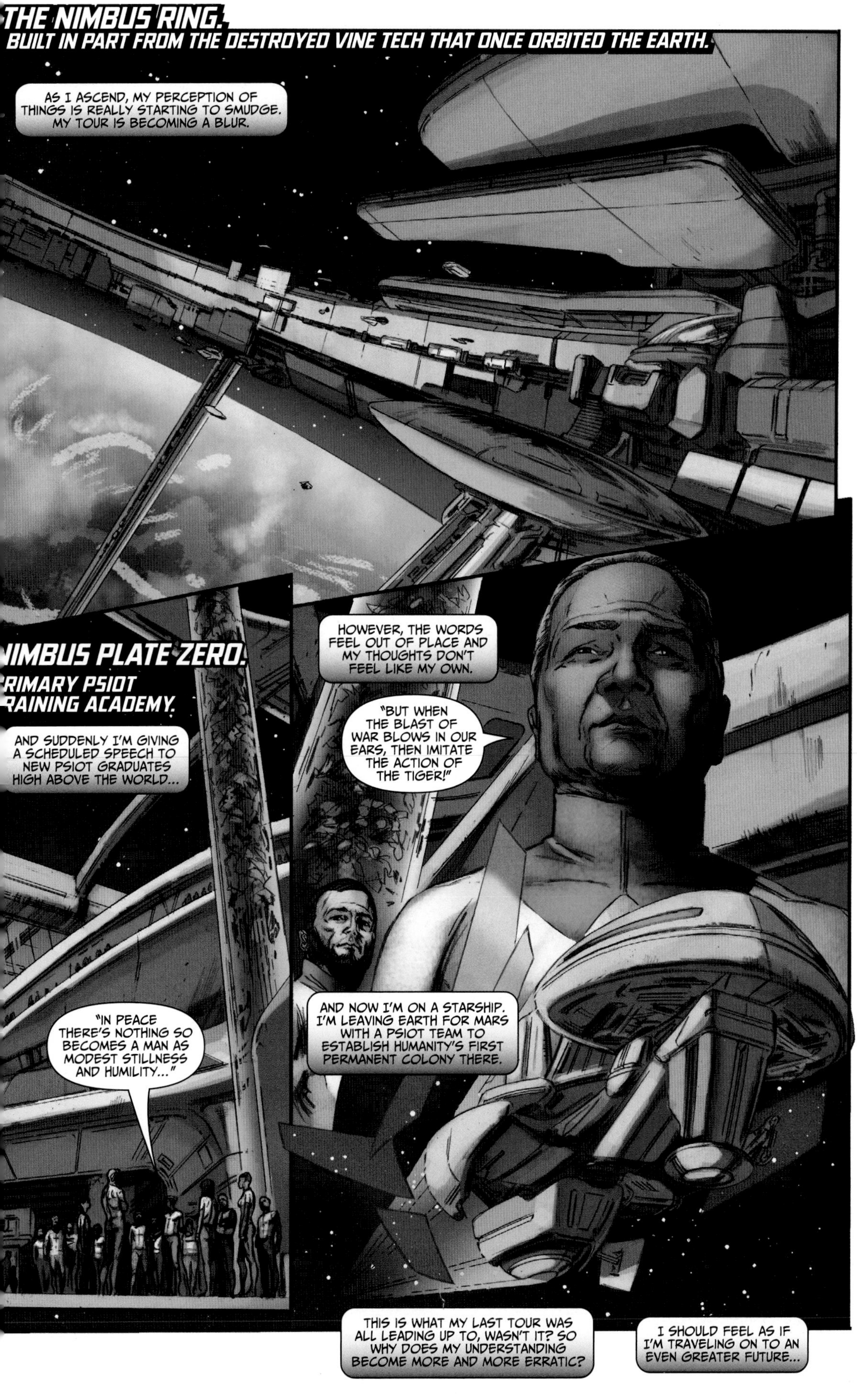
THE NIMBUS RING.
BUILT IN PART FROM THE DESTROYED VINE TECH THAT ONCE ORBITED THE EARTH.
AS I ASCEND, MY PERCEPTION OF THINGS IS REALLY STARTING TO SMUDGE. MY TOUR IS BECOMING A BLUR.
IMBUS PLATE ZERO.
RIMARY PSIOT RAINING ACADEMY.
AND SUDDENLY I'M GIVING A SCHEDULED SPEECH TO NEW PSIOT GRADUATES HIGH ABOVE THE WORLD...
"IN PEACE THERE'S NOTHING SO BECOMES A MAN AS MODEST STILLNESS AND HUMILITY..."
HOWEVER, THE WORDS FEEL OUT OF PLACE AND MY THOUGHTS DON'T FEEL LIKE MY OWN.
"BUT WHEN THE BLAST OF WAR BLOWS IN OUR EARS, THEN IMITATE THE ACTION OF THE TIGER!"
AND NOW I'M ON A STARSHIP. I'M LEAVING EARTH FOR MARS WITH A PSIOT TEAM TO ESTABLISH HUMANITY'S FIRST PERMANENT COLONY THERE.
THIS IS WHAT MY LAST TOUR WAS ALL LEADING UP TO, WASN'T IT? SO WHY DOES MY UNDERSTANDING BECOME MORE AND MORE ERRATIC?
I SHOULD FEEL AS IF I'M TRAVELING ON TO AN EVEN GREATER FUTURE...

...BUT SOMEHOW I FEEL AS IF THE SHIP IS ACTUALLY CARRYING ME BACKWARDS INSTEAD OF FORWARDS. TO AN UNCERTAIN PAST.

I...I THINK...

WHAT'S HAPPENING TO ME? AM I CHANGING?

OR AM I JUST WAKING UP?

...I THINK I WAS THINKING LIKE A REAL GROWN-UP... BUT NOW I FEEL... I--DON'T KNOW... I FEEL FUNNY...

HARBINGER FOUNDATION TROOP TRANSPORT. EN ROUTE TO SECRET LOCATION. NOW.

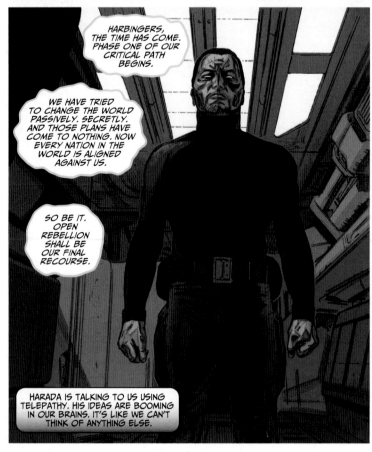

HARBINGERS, THE TIME HAS COME. PHASE ONE OF OUR CRITICAL PATH BEGINS.

WE HAVE TRIED TO CHANGE THE WORLD PASSIVELY. SECRETLY. AND THOSE PLANS HAVE COME TO NOTHING. NOW EVERY NATION IN THE WORLD IS ALIGNED AGAINST US.

SO BE IT. OPEN REBELLION SHALL BE OUR FINAL RECOURSE.

HARADA IS TALKING TO US USING TELEPATHY. HIS IDEAS ARE BOOMING IN OUR BRAINS. IT'S LIKE WE CAN'T THINK OF ANYTHING ELSE.

IT IS TRUE THAT IF YOU STAND WITH ME NOW, YOU MAY DIE IN SERVICE TO THE VISION I'VE JUST PLANTED INSIDE YOUR MINDS.

WE ARE A FEW AGAINST MANY. YET COLLECTIVELY WE WIELD GREATER POWER THAN ANY HAVE EVER SEEN.

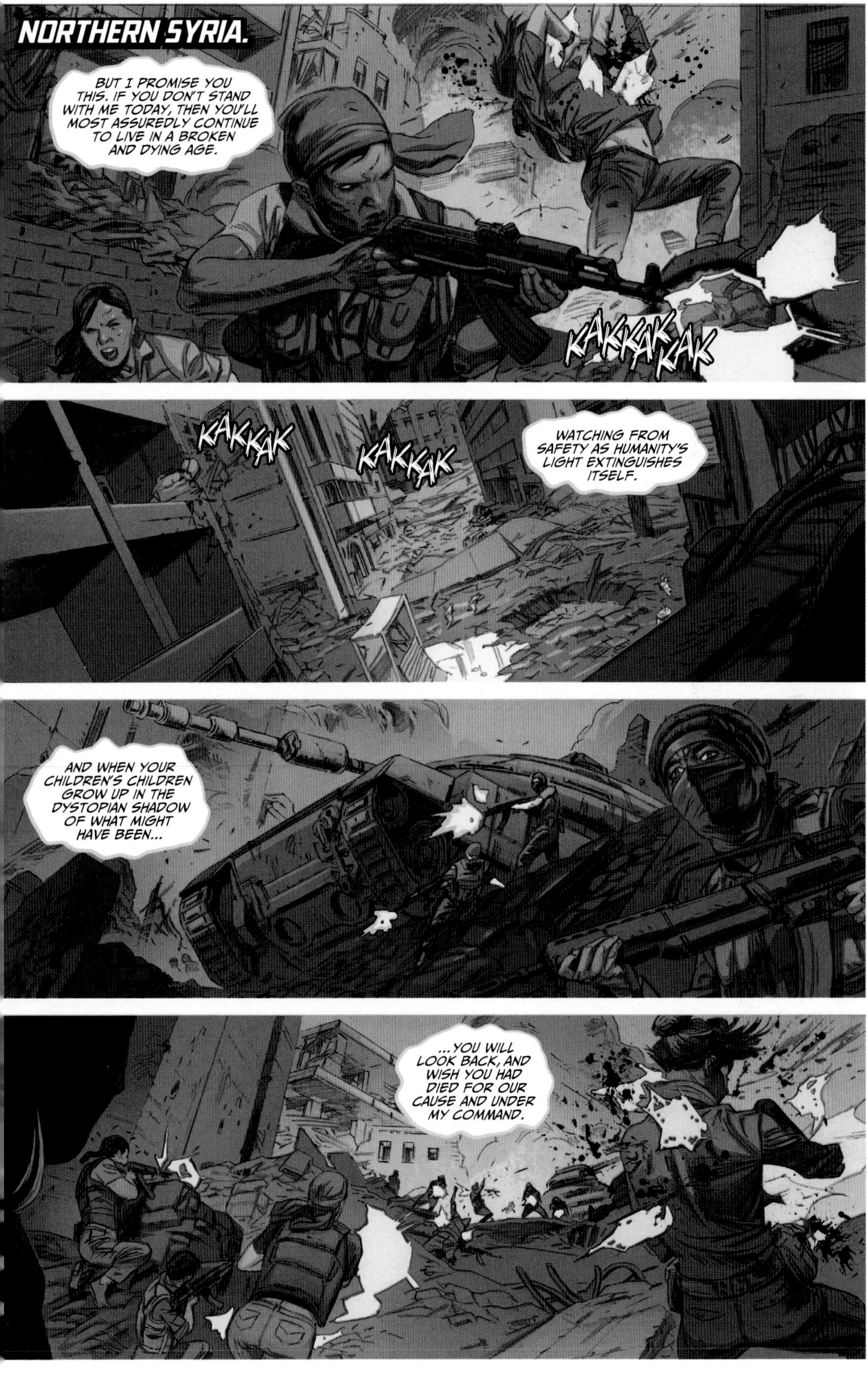
NORTHERN SYRIA.
BUT I PROMISE YOU THIS. IF YOU DON'T STAND WITH ME TODAY, THEN YOU'LL MOST ASSUREDLY CONTINUE TO LIVE IN A BROKEN AND DYING AGE.
KAKKAKKAKKAK
KAKKAK
KAKKAK
WATCHING FROM SAFETY AS HUMANITY'S LIGHT EXTINGUISHES ITSELF.
AND WHEN YOUR CHILDREN'S CHILDREN GROW UP IN THE DYSTOPIAN SHADOW OF WHAT MIGHT HAVE BEEN...
...YOU WILL LOOK BACK, AND WISH YOU HAD DIED FOR OUR CAUSE AND UNDER MY COMMAND.

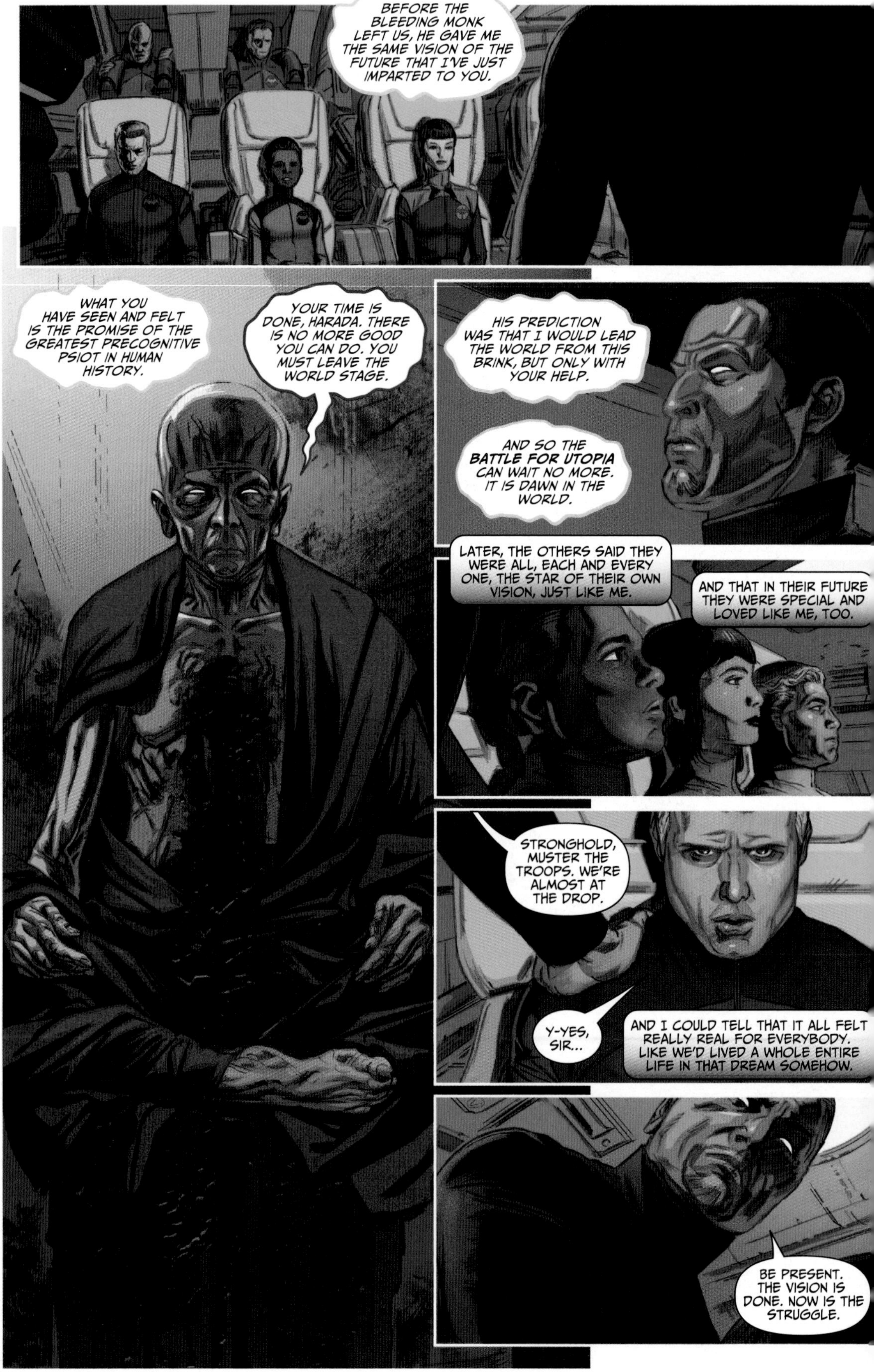

BEFORE THE BLEEDING MONK LEFT US, HE GAVE ME THE SAME VISION OF THE FUTURE THAT I'VE JUST IMPARTED TO YOU.
WHAT YOU HAVE SEEN AND FELT IS THE PROMISE OF THE GREATEST PRECOGNITIVE PSIOT IN HUMAN HISTORY.
YOUR TIME IS DONE, HARADA. THERE IS NO MORE GOOD YOU CAN DO. YOU MUST LEAVE THE WORLD STAGE.
HIS PREDICTION WAS THAT I WOULD LEAD THE WORLD FROM THIS BRINK, BUT ONLY WITH YOUR HELP.
AND SO THE BATTLE FOR UTOPIA CAN WAIT NO MORE. IT IS DAWN IN THE WORLD.
LATER, THE OTHERS SAID THEY WERE ALL, EACH AND EVERY ONE, THE STAR OF THEIR OWN VISION, JUST LIKE ME.
AND THAT IN THEIR FUTURE THEY WERE SPECIAL AND LOVED LIKE ME, TOO.
STRONGHOLD, MUSTER THE TROOPS. WE'RE ALMOST AT THE DROP.
Y-YES, SIR...
AND I COULD TELL THAT IT ALL FELT REALLY REAL FOR EVERYBODY. LIKE WE'D LIVED A WHOLE ENTIRE LIFE IN THAT DREAM SOMEHOW.
BE PRESENT. THE VISION IS DONE. NOW IS THE STRUGGLE.

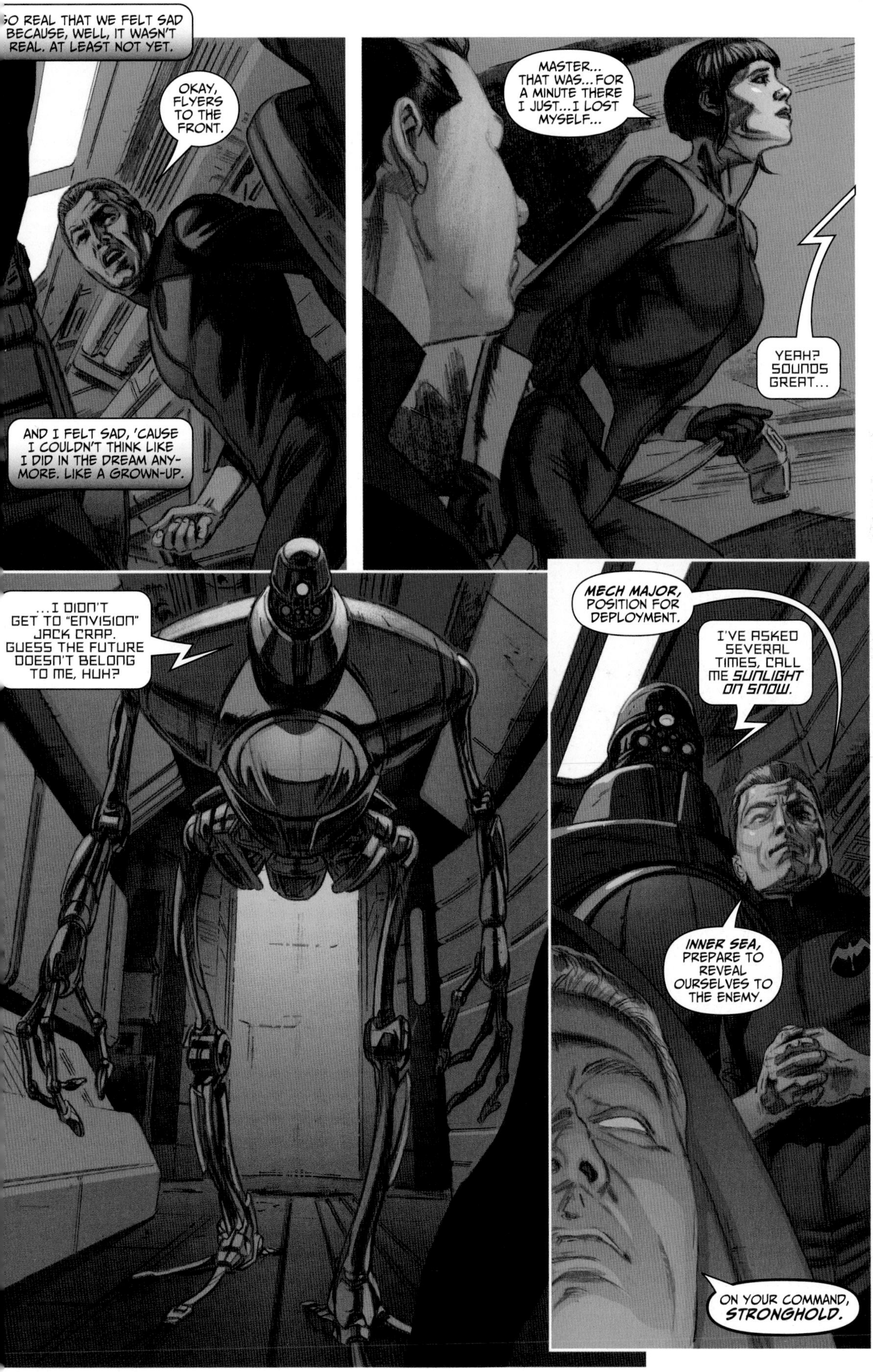

SO REAL THAT WE FELT SAD BECAUSE, WELL, IT WASN'T REAL. AT LEAST NOT YET.
OKAY, FLYERS TO THE FRONT.
AND I FELT SAD, 'CAUSE I COULDN'T THINK LIKE I DID IN THE DREAM ANY-MORE. LIKE A GROWN-UP.
MASTER... THAT WAS...FOR A MINUTE THERE I JUST...I LOST MYSELF...
YEAH? SOUNDS GREAT...
...I DIDN'T GET TO "ENVISION" JACK CRAP. GUESS THE FUTURE DOESN'T BELONG TO ME, HUH?
MECH MAJOR, POSITION FOR DEPLOYMENT.
I'VE ASKED SEVERAL TIMES, CALL ME SUNLIGHT ON SNOW.
INNER SEA, PREPARE TO REVEAL OURSELVES TO THE ENEMY.
ON YOUR COMMAND, STRONGHOLD.

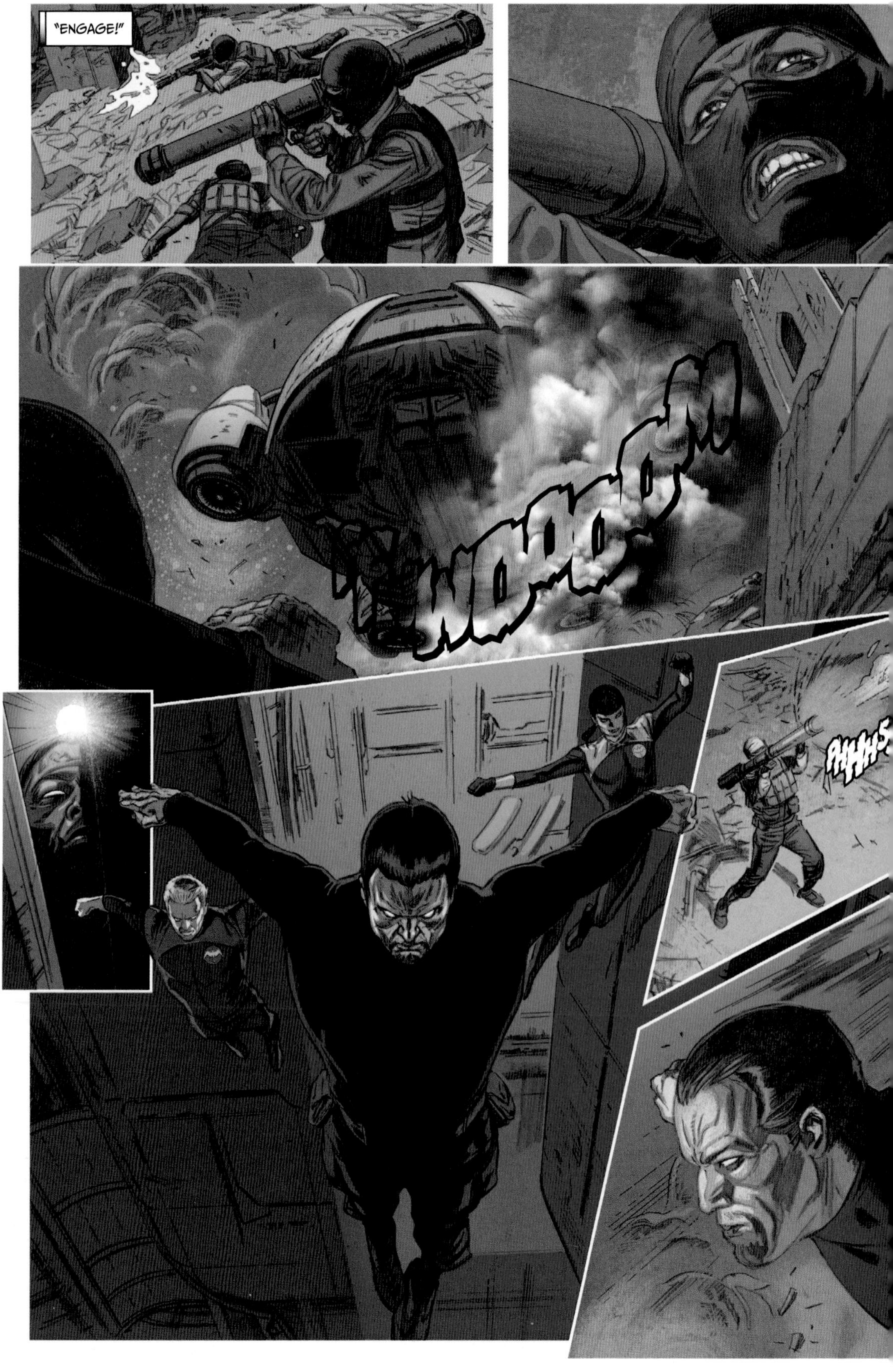
"ENGAGE!"
PHHHS

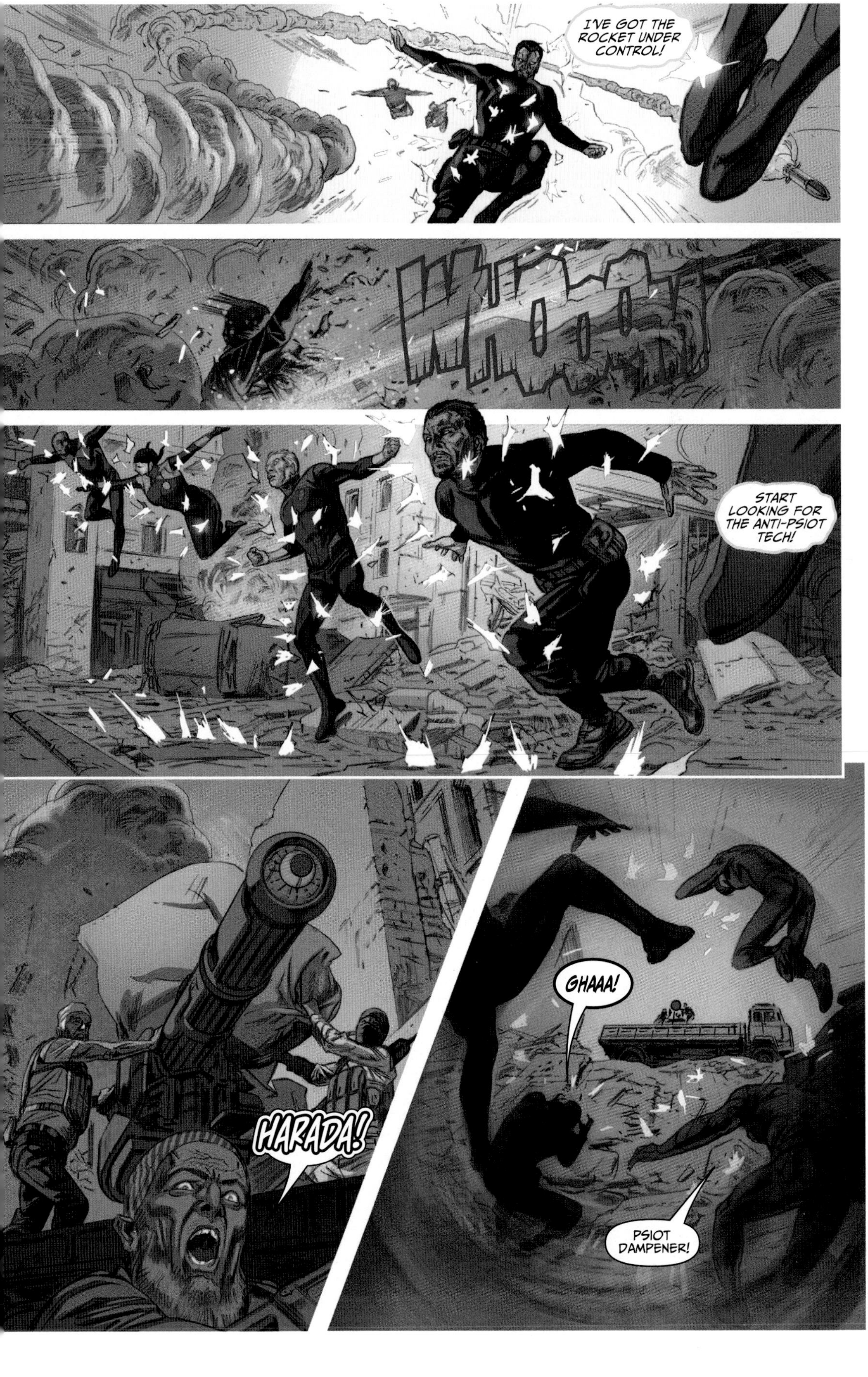

I'VE GOT THE ROCKET UNDER CONTROL!
START LOOKING FOR THE ANTI-PSIOT TECH!
HARADA!
GHAAA!
PSIOT DAMPENER!

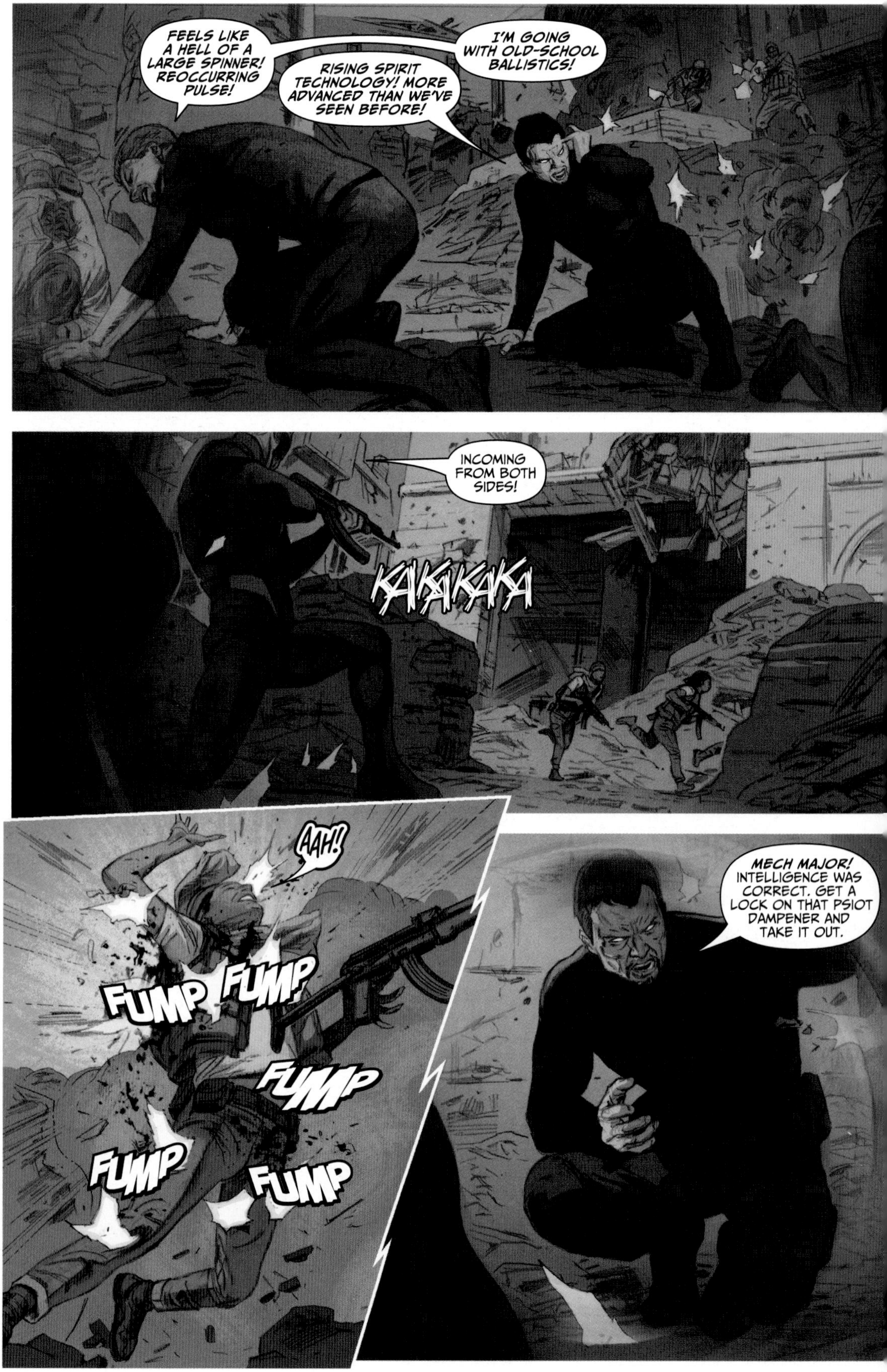
FEELS LIKE A HELL OF A LARGE SPINNER! REOCCURRING PULSE!
I'M GOING WITH OLD-SCHOOL BALLISTICS!
RISING SPIRIT TECHNOLOGY! MORE ADVANCED THAN WE'VE SEEN BEFORE!
INCOMING FROM BOTH SIDES!
KAKAKAKA
AAH!
FUMP FUMP
FUMP
FUMP
FUMP
MECH MAJOR! INTELLIGENCE WAS CORRECT. GET A LOCK ON THAT PSIOT DAMPENER AND TAKE IT OUT.

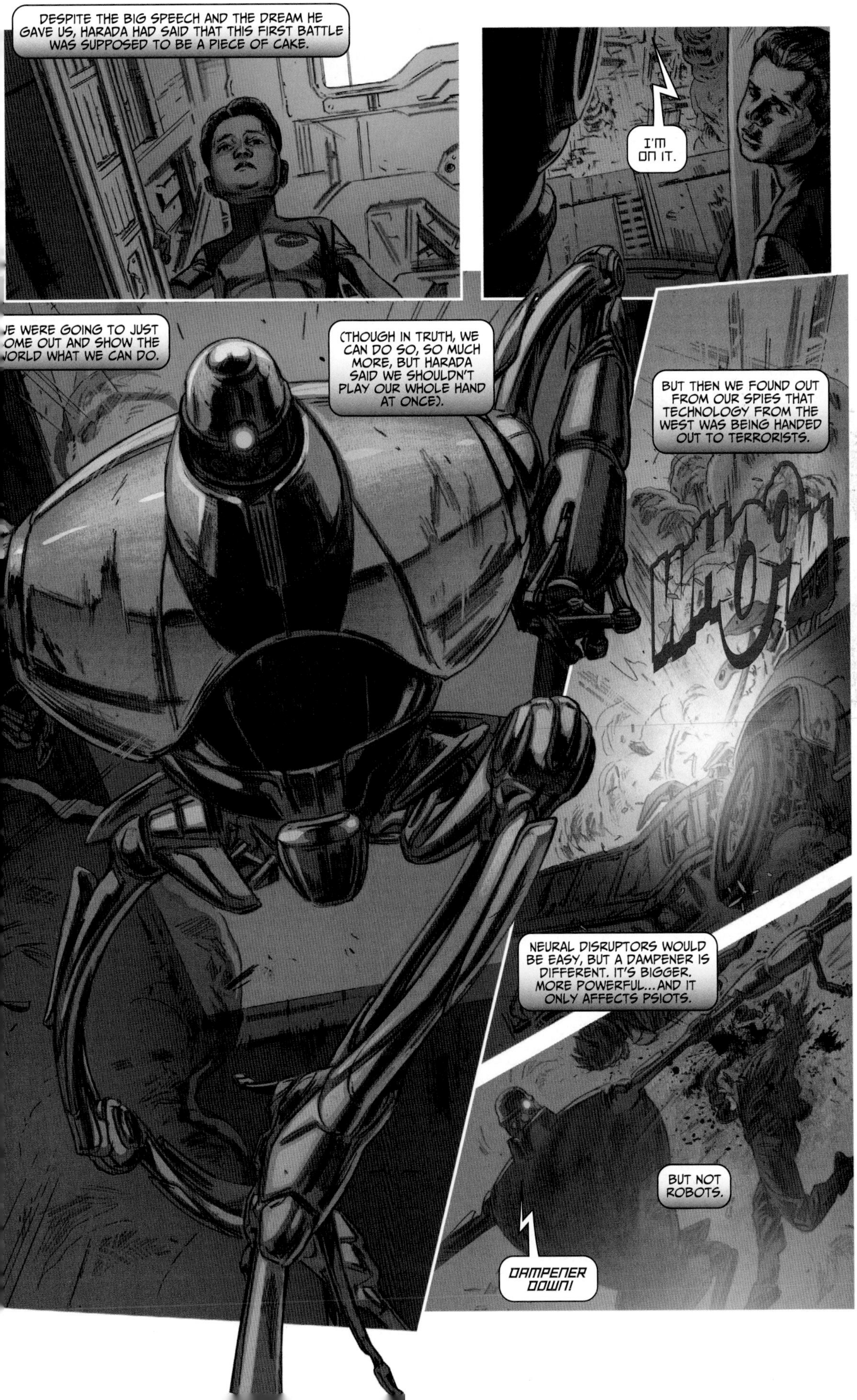
DESPITE THE BIG SPEECH AND THE DREAM HE GAVE US, HARADA HAD SAID THAT THIS FIRST BATTLE WAS SUPPOSED TO BE A PIECE OF CAKE.
I'M ON IT.
WE WERE GOING TO JUST COME OUT AND SHOW THE WORLD WHAT WE CAN DO.
(THOUGH IN TRUTH, WE CAN DO SO, SO MUCH MORE, BUT HARADA SAID WE SHOULDN'T PLAY OUR WHOLE HAND AT ONCE).
BUT THEN WE FOUND OUT FROM OUR SPIES THAT TECHNOLOGY FROM THE WEST WAS BEING HANDED OUT TO TERRORISTS.
NEURAL DISRUPTORS WOULD BE EASY, BUT A DAMPENER IS DIFFERENT. IT'S BIGGER. MORE POWERFUL... AND IT ONLY AFFECTS PSIOTS.
BUT NOT ROBOTS.
DAMPENER DOWN!

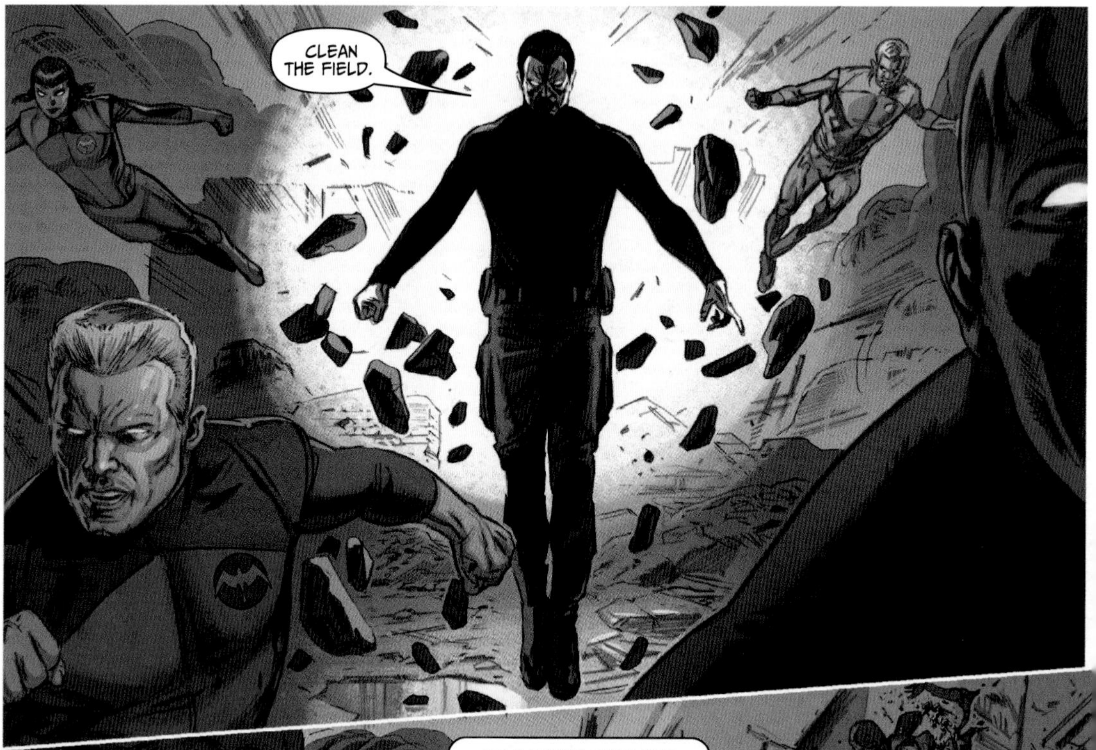
CLEAN THE FIELD.

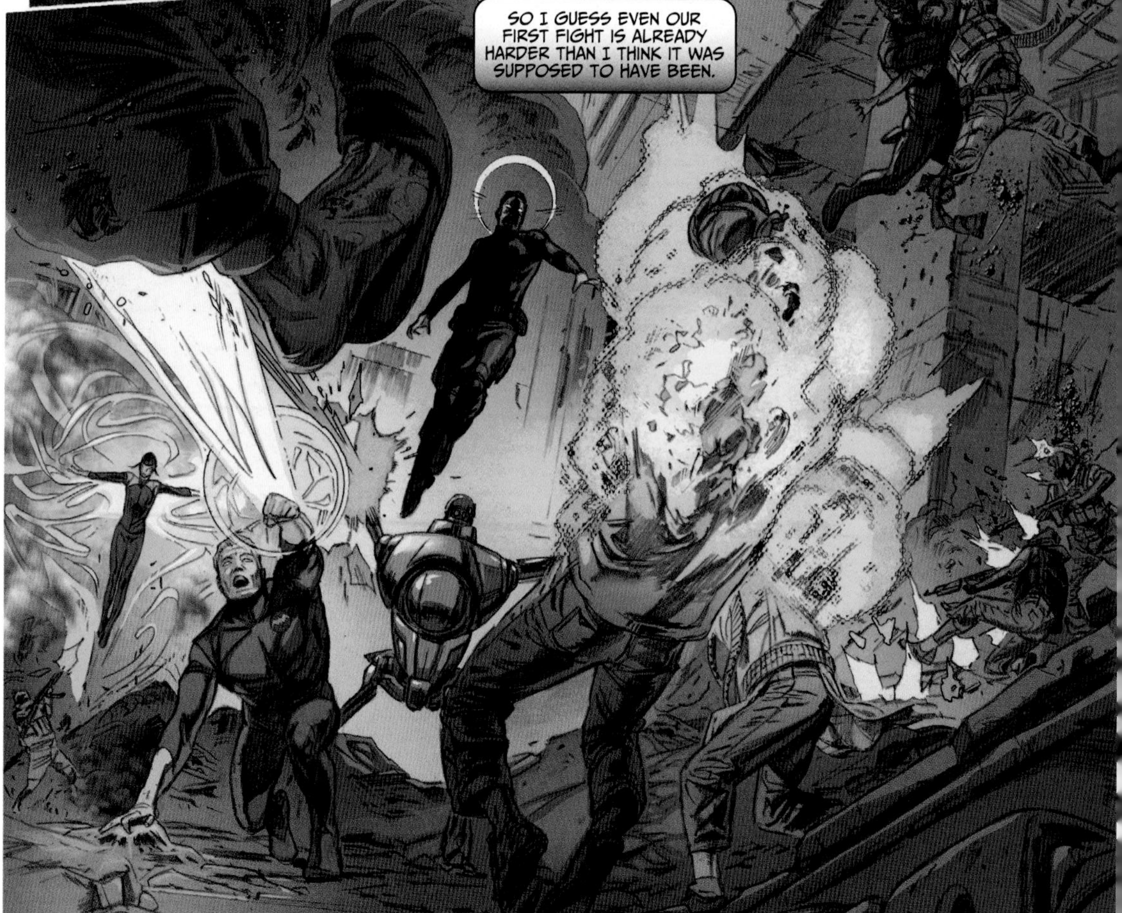
SO I GUESS EVEN OUR FIRST FIGHT IS ALREADY HARDER THAN I THINK IT WAS SUPPOSED TO HAVE BEEN.

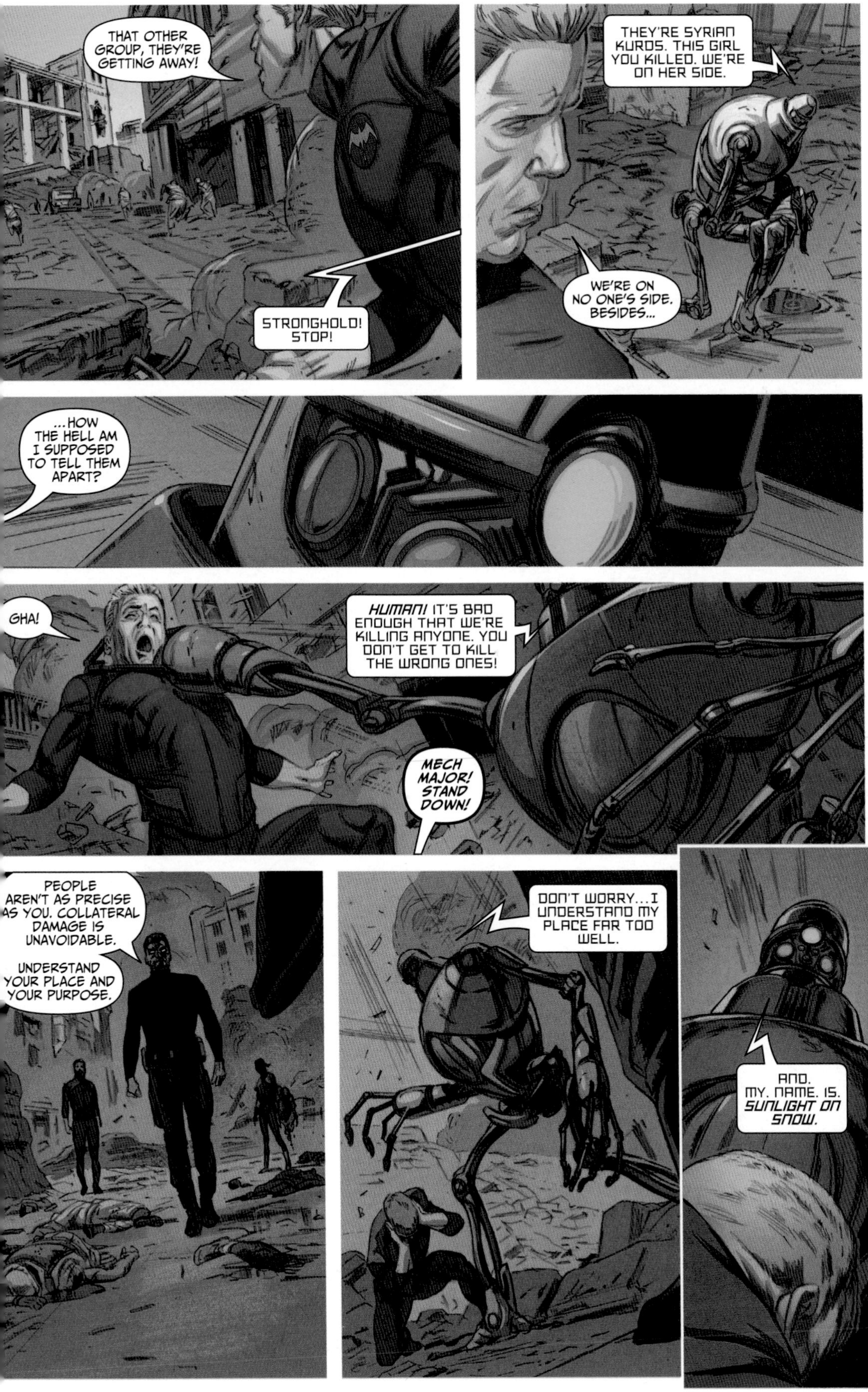
THAT OTHER GROUP, THEY'RE GETTING AWAY!
STRONGHOLD! STOP!
THEY'RE SYRIAN KURDS. THIS GIRL YOU KILLED. WE'RE ON HER SIDE.
WE'RE ON NO ONE'S SIDE. BESIDES...
...HOW THE HELL AM I SUPPOSED TO TELL THEM APART?
GHA!
HUMAN! IT'S BAD ENOUGH THAT WE'RE KILLING ANYONE. YOU DON'T GET TO KILL THE WRONG ONES!
MECH MAJOR! STAND DOWN!
PEOPLE AREN'T AS PRECISE AS YOU. COLLATERAL DAMAGE IS UNAVOIDABLE.
UNDERSTAND YOUR PLACE AND YOUR PURPOSE.
DON'T WORRY... I UNDERSTAND MY PLACE FAR TOO WELL.
AND. MY. NAME. IS. SUNLIGHT ON SNOW.

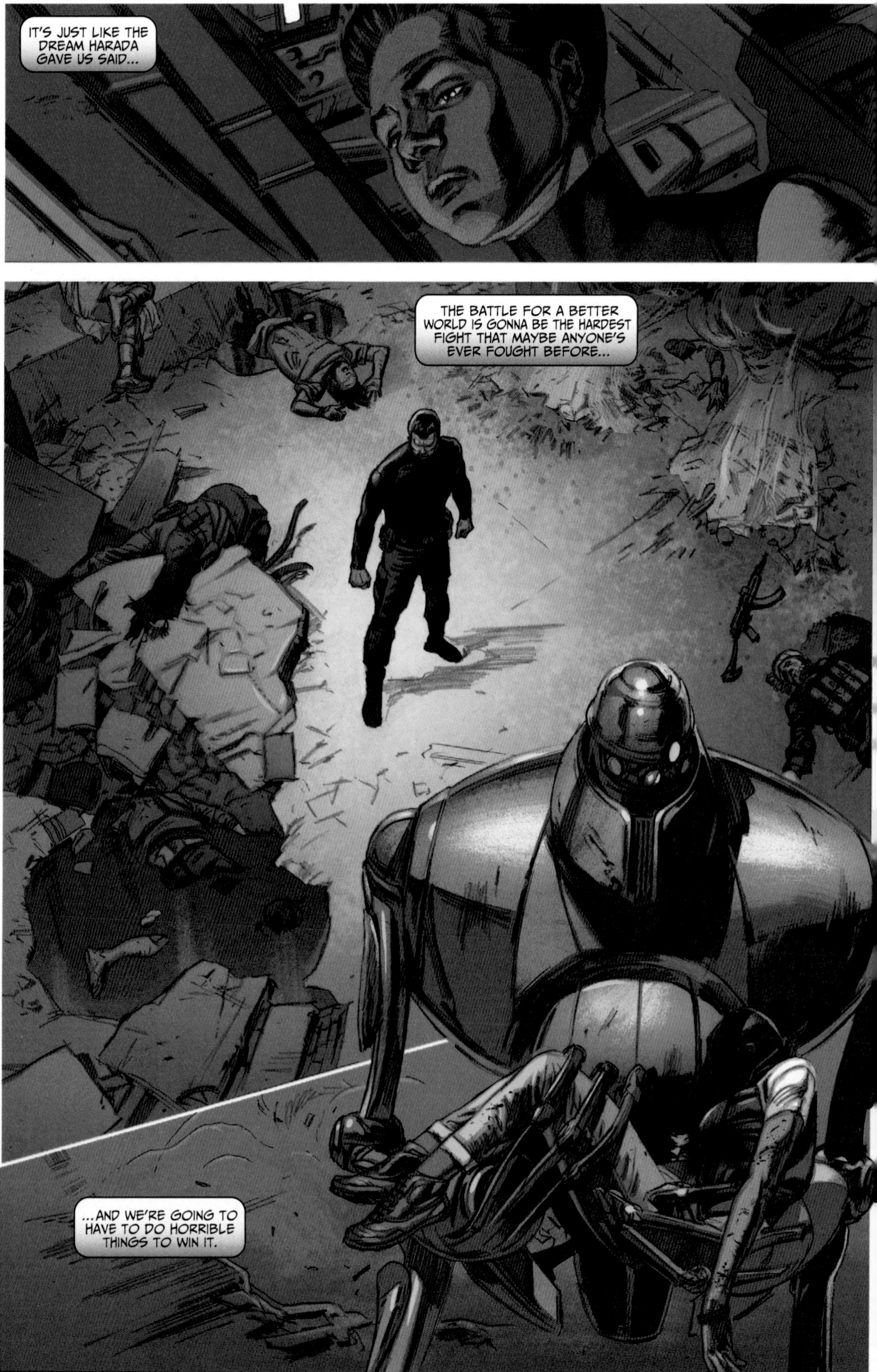
IT'S JUST LIKE THE DREAM HARADA GAVE US SAID...
THE BATTLE FOR A BETTER WORLD IS GONNA BE THE HARDEST FIGHT THAT MAYBE ANYONE'S EVER FOUGHT BEFORE...
...AND WE'RE GOING TO HAVE TO DO HORRIBLE THINGS TO WIN IT.

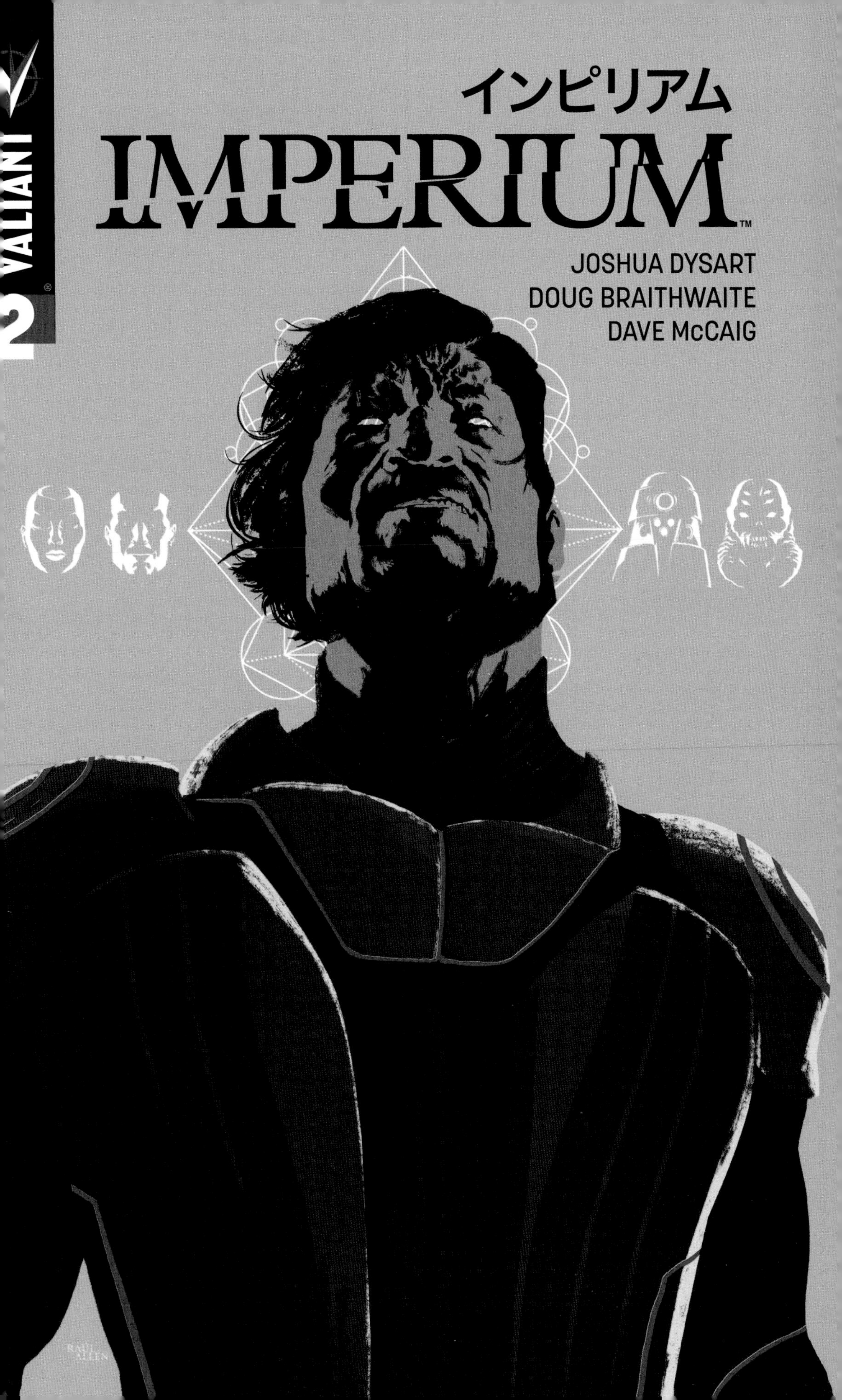
VALIANT
2
インピリアム
IMPERIUM™
JOSHUA DYSART
DOUG BRAITHWAITE
DAVE McCAIG

インビジブム

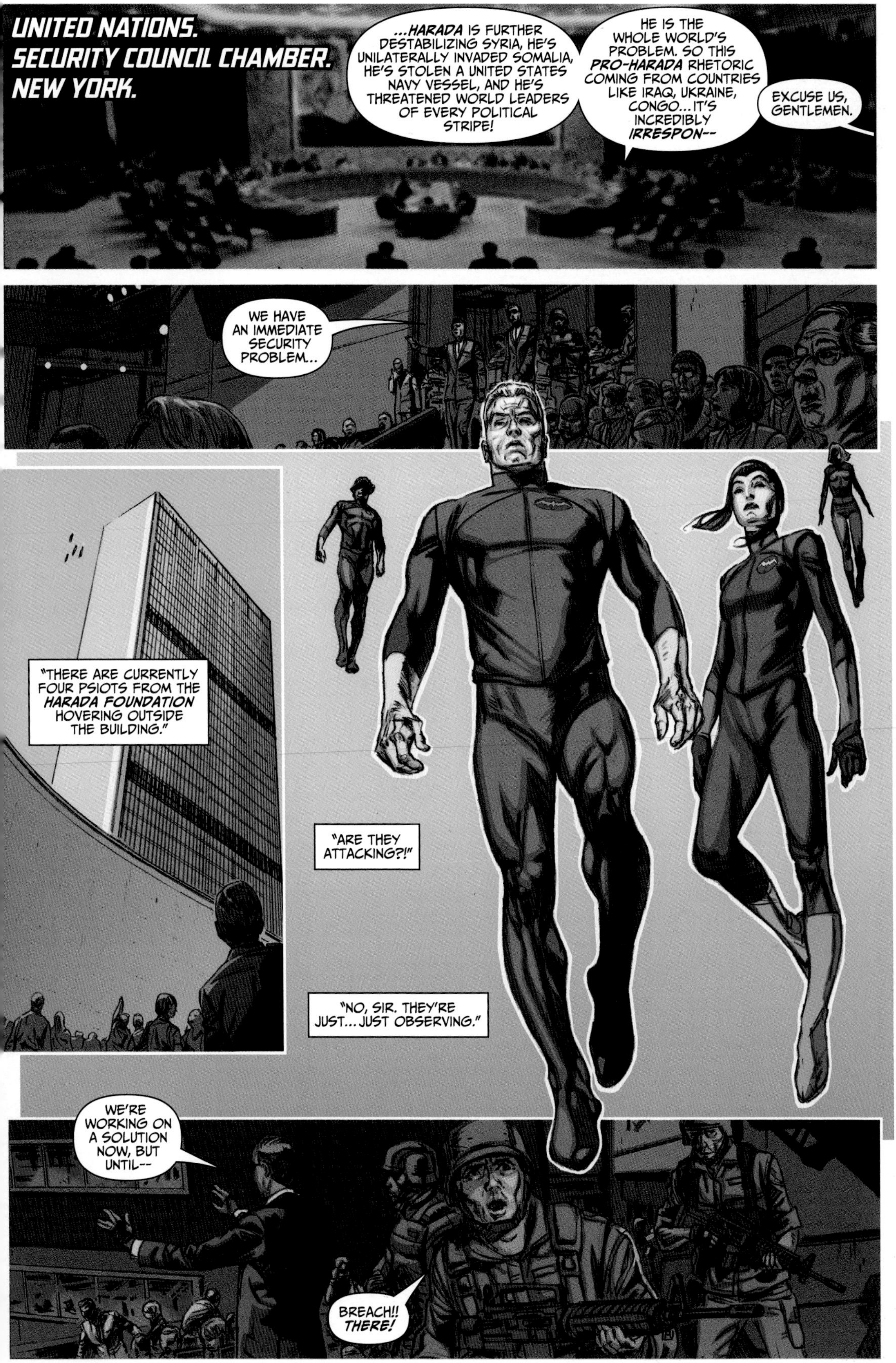
UNITED NATIONS. SECURITY COUNCIL CHAMBER. NEW YORK.
...HARADA IS FURTHER DESTABILIZING SYRIA, HE'S UNILATERALLY INVADED SOMALIA, HE'S STOLEN A UNITED STATES NAVY VESSEL, AND HE'S THREATENED WORLD LEADERS OF EVERY POLITICAL STRIPE!
HE IS THE WHOLE WORLD'S PROBLEM. SO THIS PRO-HARADA RHETORIC COMING FROM COUNTRIES LIKE IRAQ, UKRAINE, CONGO...IT'S INCREDIBLY IRRESPON--
EXCUSE US, GENTLEMEN.
WE HAVE AN IMMEDIATE SECURITY PROBLEM...
"THERE ARE CURRENTLY FOUR PSIOTS FROM THE HARADA FOUNDATION HOVERING OUTSIDE THE BUILDING."
"ARE THEY ATTACKING?!"
"NO, SIR. THEY'RE JUST... JUST OBSERVING."
WE'RE WORKING ON A SOLUTION NOW, BUT UNTIL--
BREACH!! THERE!

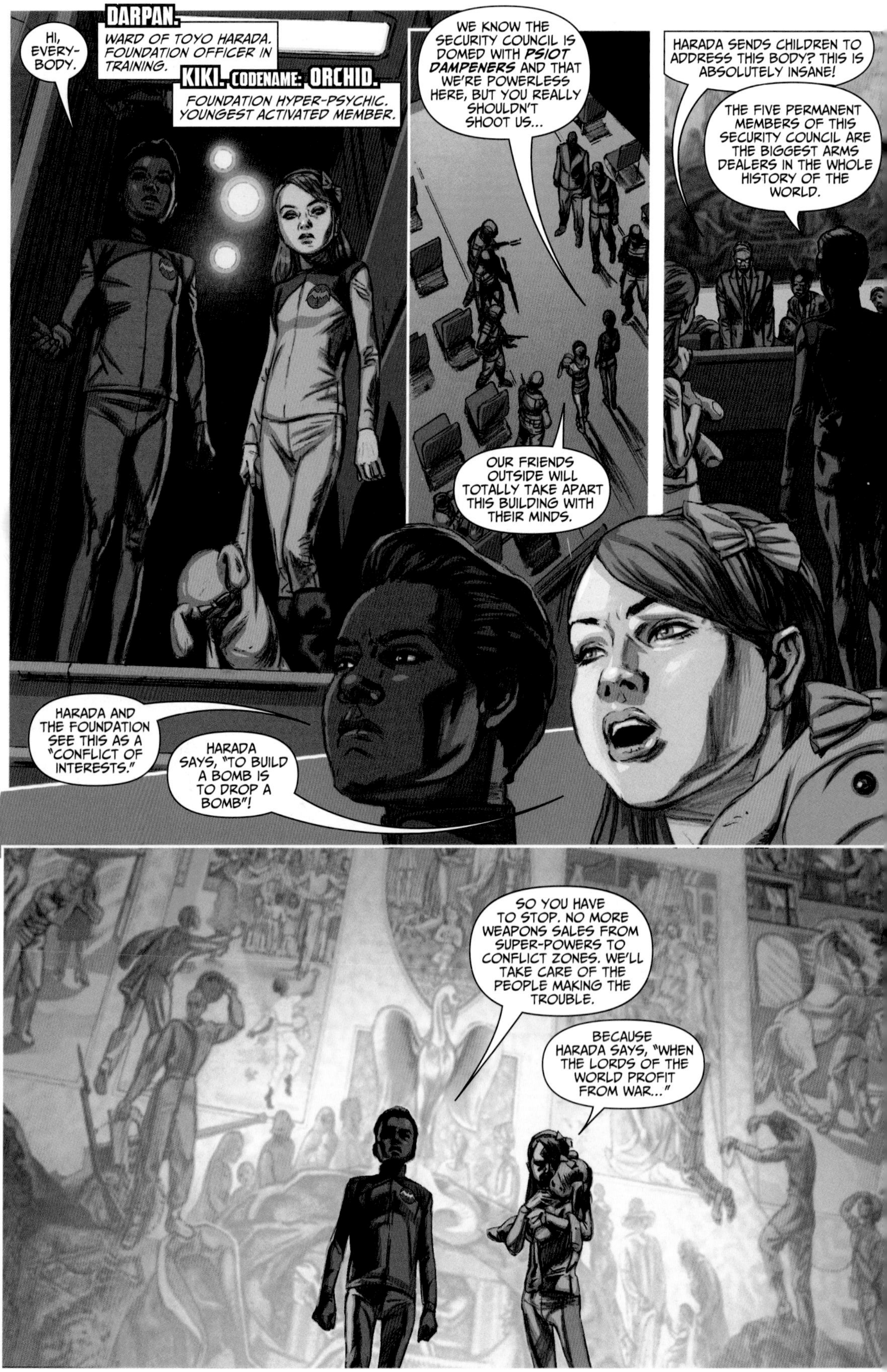
HI, EVERY-BODY.
DARPAN.
WARD OF TOYO HARADA. FOUNDATION OFFICER IN TRAINING.
KIKI. CODENAME: ORCHID.
FOUNDATION HYPER-PSYCHIC. YOUNGEST ACTIVATED MEMBER.
WE KNOW THE SECURITY COUNCIL IS DOMED WITH PSIOT DAMPENERS AND THAT WE'RE POWERLESS HERE, BUT YOU REALLY SHOULDN'T SHOOT US...
OUR FRIENDS OUTSIDE WILL TOTALLY TAKE APART THIS BUILDING WITH THEIR MINDS.
HARADA SENDS CHILDREN TO ADDRESS THIS BODY? THIS IS ABSOLUTELY INSANE!
THE FIVE PERMANENT MEMBERS OF THIS SECURITY COUNCIL ARE THE BIGGEST ARMS DEALERS IN THE WHOLE HISTORY OF THE WORLD.
HARADA AND THE FOUNDATION SEE THIS AS A "CONFLICT OF INTERESTS."
HARADA SAYS, "TO BUILD A BOMB IS TO DROP A BOMB"!
SO YOU HAVE TO STOP. NO MORE WEAPONS SALES FROM SUPER-POWERS TO CONFLICT ZONES. WE'LL TAKE CARE OF THE PEOPLE MAKING THE TROUBLE.
BECAUSE HARADA SAYS, "WHEN THE LORDS OF THE WORLD PROFIT FROM WAR..."

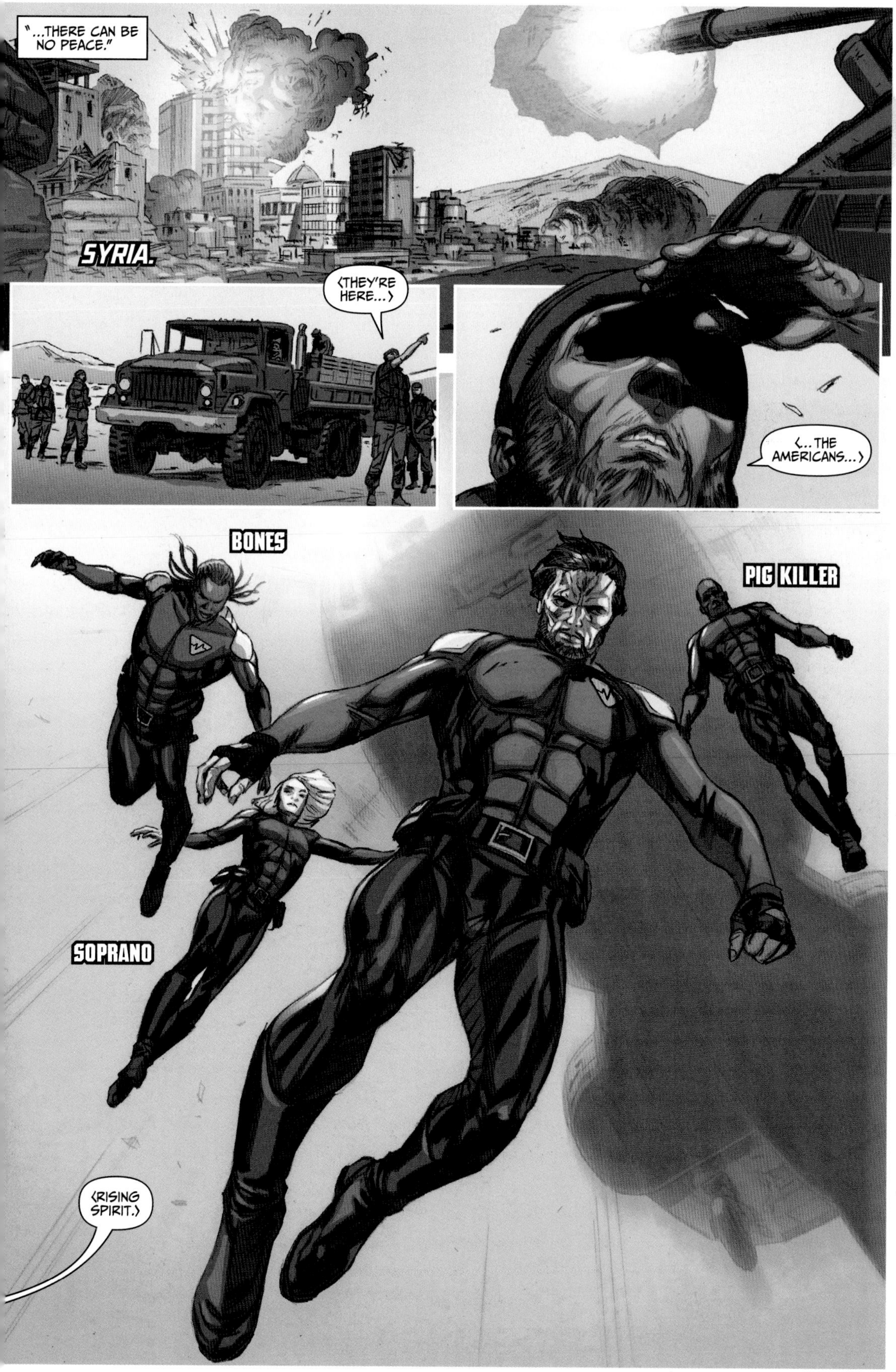
"...THERE CAN BE NO PEACE."
SYRIA.
‹THEY'RE HERE...›
‹...THE AMERICANS...›
BONES
PIG KILLER
SOPRANO
‹RISING SPIRIT.›

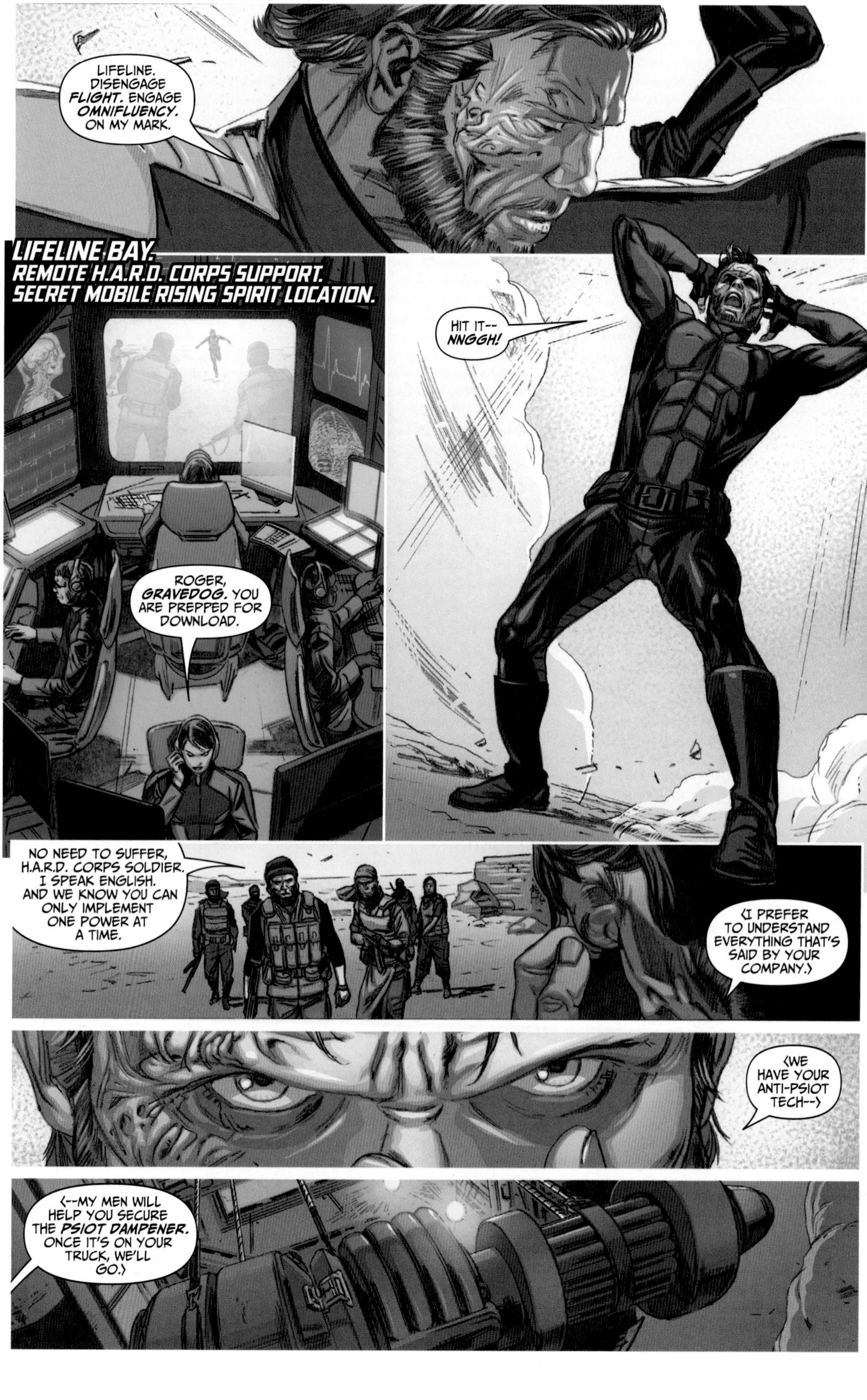
LIFELINE. DISENGAGE FLIGHT. ENGAGE OMNIFLUENCY. ON MY MARK.
LIFELINE BAY. REMOTE H.A.R.D. CORPS SUPPORT. SECRET MOBILE RISING SPIRIT LOCATION.
ROGER, GRAVEDOG. YOU ARE PREPPED FOR DOWNLOAD.
HIT IT-- NNGGH!
NO NEED TO SUFFER, H.A.R.D. CORPS SOLDIER. I SPEAK ENGLISH. AND WE KNOW YOU CAN ONLY IMPLEMENT ONE POWER AT A TIME.
⟨I PREFER TO UNDERSTAND EVERYTHING THAT'S SAID BY YOUR COMPANY.⟩
⟨WE HAVE YOUR ANTI-PSIOT TECH--⟩
⟨--MY MEN WILL HELP YOU SECURE THE PSIOT DAMPENER. ONCE IT'S ON YOUR TRUCK, WE'LL GO.⟩

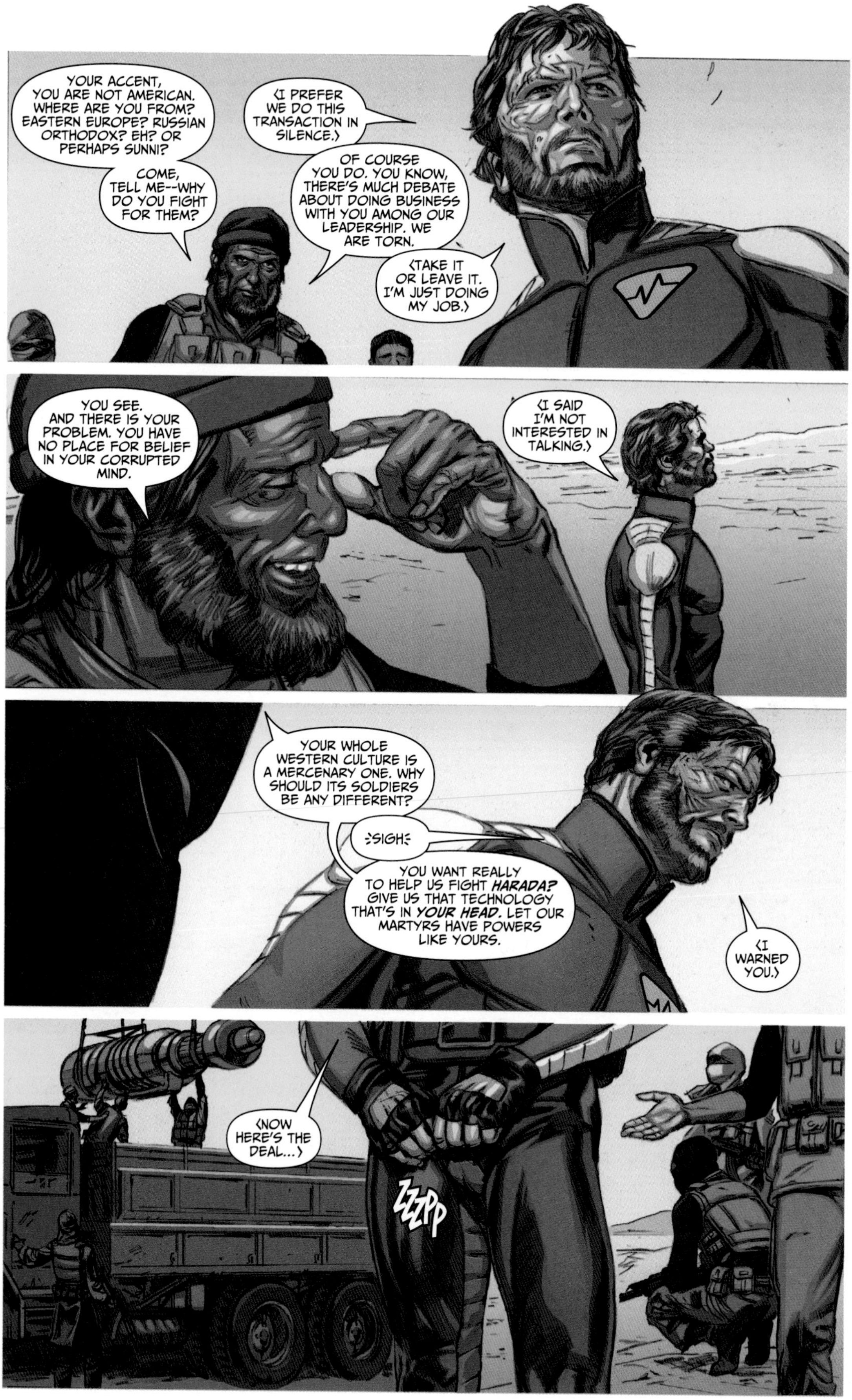
YOUR ACCENT, YOU ARE NOT AMERICAN. WHERE ARE YOU FROM? EASTERN EUROPE? RUSSIAN ORTHODOX? EH? OR PERHAPS SUNNI?
COME, TELL ME--WHY DO YOU FIGHT FOR THEM?
‹I PREFER WE DO THIS TRANSACTION IN SILENCE.›
OF COURSE YOU DO. YOU KNOW, THERE'S MUCH DEBATE ABOUT DOING BUSINESS WITH YOU AMONG OUR LEADERSHIP. WE ARE TORN.
‹TAKE IT OR LEAVE IT. I'M JUST DOING MY JOB.›
YOU SEE. AND THERE IS YOUR PROBLEM. YOU HAVE NO PLACE FOR BELIEF IN YOUR CORRUPTED MIND.
‹I SAID I'M NOT INTERESTED IN TALKING.›
YOUR WHOLE WESTERN CULTURE IS A MERCENARY ONE. WHY SHOULD ITS SOLDIERS BE ANY DIFFERENT?
SIGH
YOU WANT REALLY TO HELP US FIGHT *HARADA?* GIVE US THAT TECHNOLOGY THAT'S IN *YOUR HEAD.* LET OUR MARTYRS HAVE POWERS LIKE YOURS.
‹I WARNED YOU.›
‹NOW HERE'S THE DEAL...›
ZZZPP

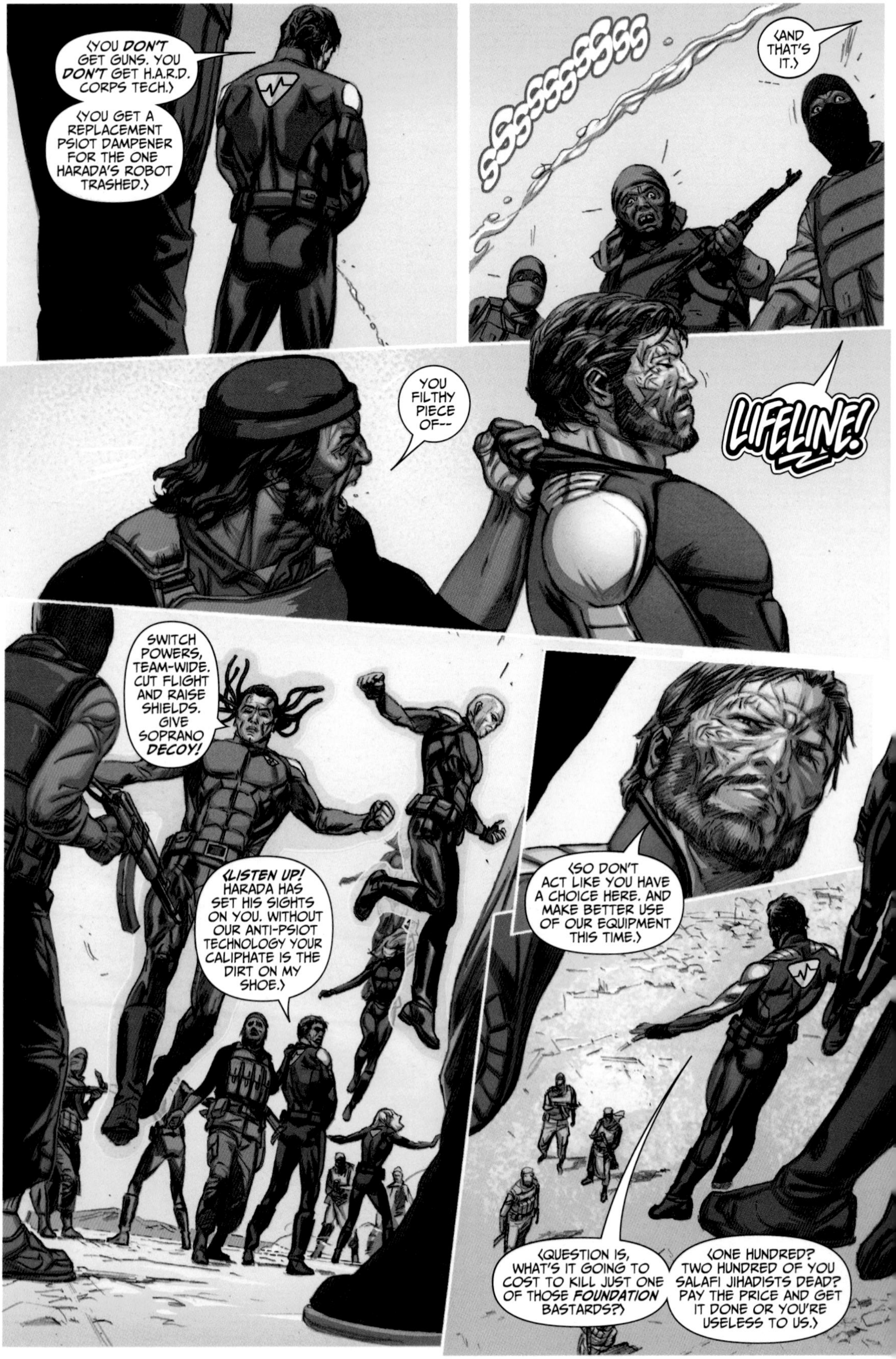
‹YOU DON'T GET GUNS. YOU DON'T GET H.A.R.D. CORPS TECH.›
‹YOU GET A REPLACEMENT PSIOT DAMPENER FOR THE ONE HARADA'S ROBOT TRASHED.›
SSSSSSSSSS
‹AND THAT'S IT.›
YOU FILTHY PIECE OF--
LIFELINE!
SWITCH POWERS, TEAM-WIDE. CUT FLIGHT AND RAISE SHIELDS. GIVE SOPRANO DECOY!
‹LISTEN UP! HARADA HAS SET HIS SIGHTS ON YOU. WITHOUT OUR ANTI-PSIOT TECHNOLOGY YOUR CALIPHATE IS THE DIRT ON MY SHOE.›
‹SO DON'T ACT LIKE YOU HAVE A CHOICE HERE. AND MAKE BETTER USE OF OUR EQUIPMENT THIS TIME.›
‹QUESTION IS, WHAT'S IT GOING TO COST TO KILL JUST ONE OF THOSE FOUNDATION BASTARDS?›
‹ONE HUNDRED? TWO HUNDRED OF YOU SALAFI JIHADISTS DEAD? PAY THE PRICE AND GET IT DONE OR YOU'RE USELESS TO US.›

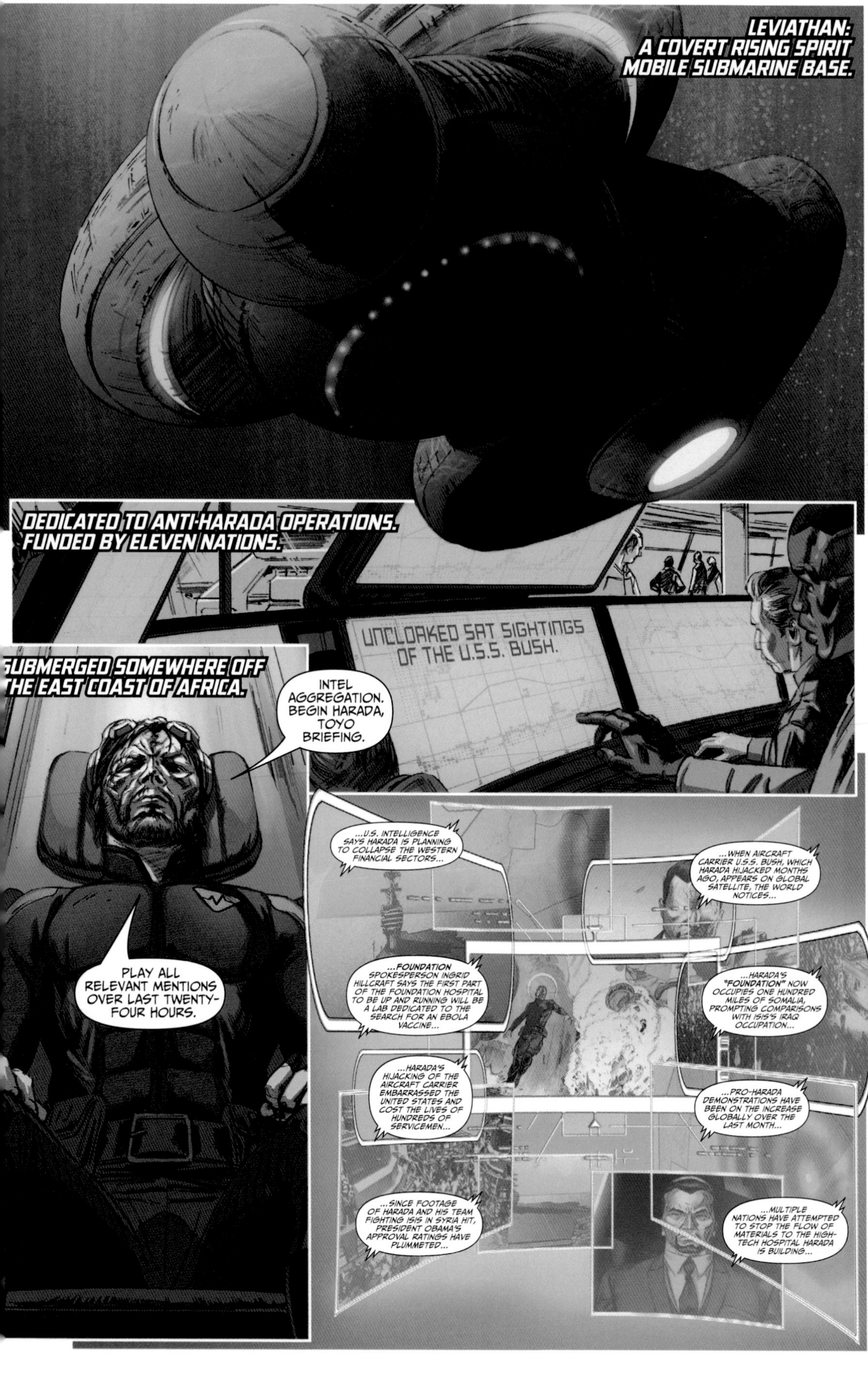
LEVIATHAN: A COVERT RISING SPIRIT MOBILE SUBMARINE BASE.
DEDICATED TO ANTI-HARADA OPERATIONS. FUNDED BY ELEVEN NATIONS.
UNCLOAKED SAT SIGHTINGS OF THE U.S.S. BUSH.
SUBMERGED SOMEWHERE OFF THE EAST COAST OF AFRICA.
INTEL AGGREGATION. BEGIN HARADA, TOYO BRIEFING.
PLAY ALL RELEVANT MENTIONS OVER LAST TWENTY-FOUR HOURS.
...U.S. INTELLIGENCE SAYS HARADA IS PLANNING TO COLLAPSE THE WESTERN FINANCIAL SECTORS...
...WHEN AIRCRAFT CARRIER U.S.S. BUSH, WHICH HARADA HIJACKED MONTHS AGO, APPEARS ON GLOBAL SATELLITE, THE WORLD NOTICES...
...FOUNDATION SPOKESPERSON INGRID HILLCRAFT SAYS THE FIRST PART OF THE FOUNDATION HOSPITAL TO BE UP AND RUNNING WILL BE A LAB DEDICATED TO THE SEARCH FOR AN EBOLA VACCINE...
...HARADA'S "FOUNDATION" NOW OCCUPIES ONE HUNDRED MILES OF SOMALIA, PROMPTING COMPARISONS WITH ISIS'S IRAQ OCCUPATION...
...HARADA'S HIJACKING OF THE AIRCRAFT CARRIER EMBARRASSED THE UNITED STATES AND COST THE LIVES OF HUNDREDS OF SERVICEMEN...
...PRO-HARADA DEMONSTRATIONS HAVE BEEN ON THE INCREASE GLOBALLY OVER THE LAST MONTH...
...SINCE FOOTAGE OF HARADA AND HIS TEAM FIGHTING ISIS IN SYRIA HIT, PRESIDENT OBAMA'S APPROVAL RATINGS HAVE PLUMMETED...
...MULTIPLE NATIONS HAVE ATTEMPTED TO STOP THE FLOW OF MATERIALS TO THE HIGH-TECH HOSPITAL HARADA IS BUILDING...

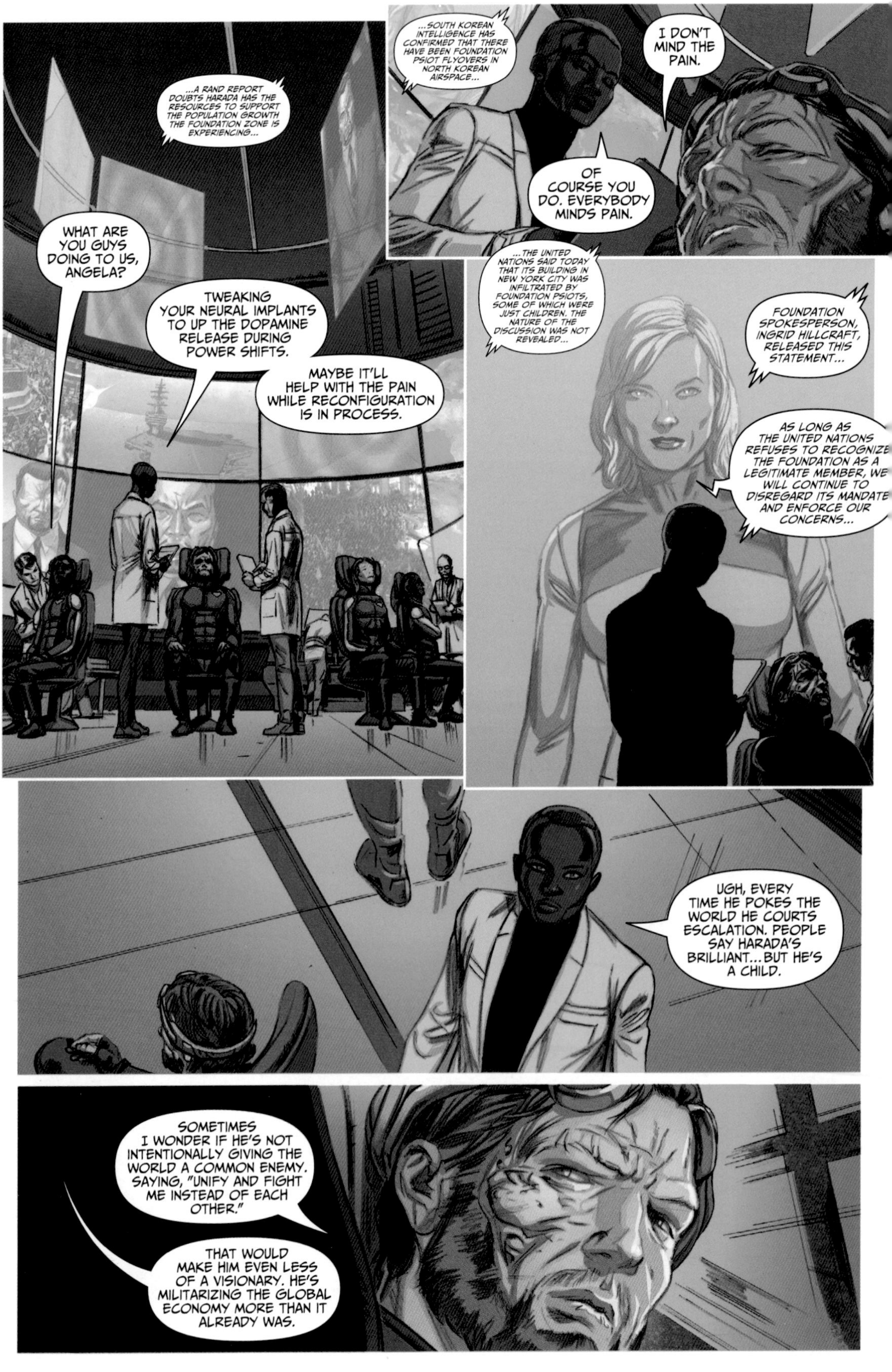
...A RAND REPORT DOUBTS HARADA HAS THE RESOURCES TO SUPPORT THE POPULATION GROWTH THE FOUNDATION ZONE IS EXPERIENCING...
WHAT ARE YOU GUYS DOING TO US, ANGELA?
TWEAKING YOUR NEURAL IMPLANTS TO UP THE DOPAMINE RELEASE DURING POWER SHIFTS.
MAYBE IT'LL HELP WITH THE PAIN WHILE RECONFIGURATION IS IN PROCESS.
...SOUTH KOREAN INTELLIGENCE HAS CONFIRMED THAT THERE HAVE BEEN FOUNDATION PSIOT FLYOVERS IN NORTH KOREAN AIRSPACE...
I DON'T MIND THE PAIN.
OF COURSE YOU DO. EVERYBODY MINDS PAIN.
...THE UNITED NATIONS SAID TODAY THAT ITS BUILDING IN NEW YORK CITY WAS INFILTRATED BY FOUNDATION PSIOTS, SOME OF WHICH WERE JUST CHILDREN. THE NATURE OF THE DISCUSSION WAS NOT REVEALED...
FOUNDATION SPOKESPERSON, INGRID HILLCRAFT, RELEASED THIS STATEMENT...
AS LONG AS THE UNITED NATIONS REFUSES TO RECOGNIZE THE FOUNDATION AS A LEGITIMATE MEMBER, WE WILL CONTINUE TO DISREGARD ITS MANDATE AND ENFORCE OUR CONCERNS...
UGH, EVERY TIME HE POKES THE WORLD HE COURTS ESCALATION. PEOPLE SAY HARADA'S BRILLIANT... BUT HE'S A CHILD.
SOMETIMES I WONDER IF HE'S NOT INTENTIONALLY GIVING THE WORLD A COMMON ENEMY. SAYING, "UNIFY AND FIGHT ME INSTEAD OF EACH OTHER."
THAT WOULD MAKE HIM EVEN LESS OF A VISIONARY. HE'S MILITARIZING THE GLOBAL ECONOMY MORE THAN IT ALREADY WAS.

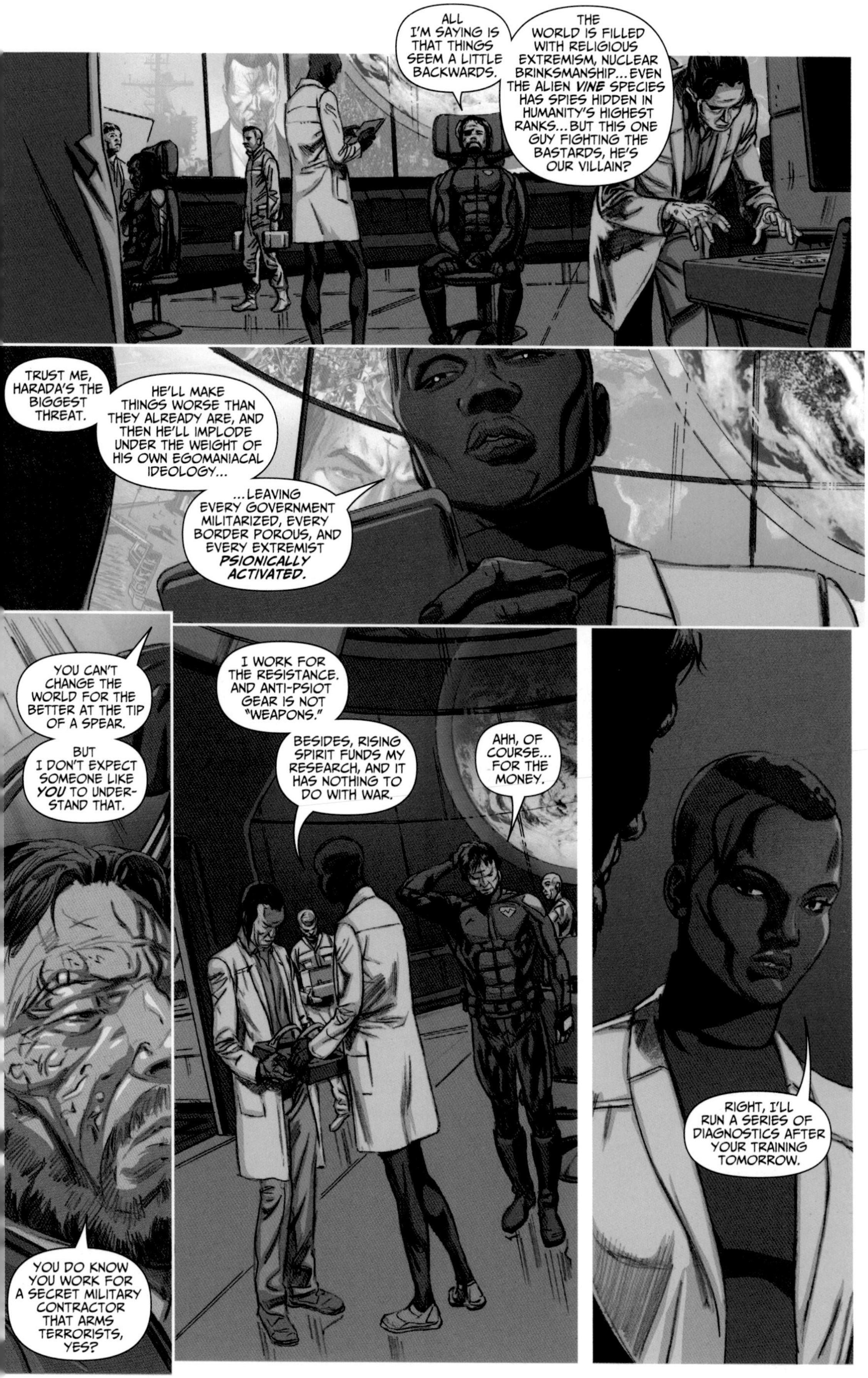
ALL I'M SAYING IS THAT THINGS SEEM A LITTLE BACKWARDS.
THE WORLD IS FILLED WITH RELIGIOUS EXTREMISM, NUCLEAR BRINKSMANSHIP... EVEN THE ALIEN VINE SPECIES HAS SPIES HIDDEN IN HUMANITY'S HIGHEST RANKS... BUT THIS ONE GUY FIGHTING THE BASTARDS, HE'S OUR VILLAIN?
TRUST ME, HARADA'S THE BIGGEST THREAT.
HE'LL MAKE THINGS WORSE THAN THEY ALREADY ARE, AND THEN HE'LL IMPLODE UNDER THE WEIGHT OF HIS OWN EGOMANIACAL IDEOLOGY...
...LEAVING EVERY GOVERNMENT MILITARIZED, EVERY BORDER POROUS, AND EVERY EXTREMIST PSIONICALLY ACTIVATED.
YOU CAN'T CHANGE THE WORLD FOR THE BETTER AT THE TIP OF A SPEAR.
BUT I DON'T EXPECT SOMEONE LIKE YOU TO UNDER-STAND THAT.
YOU DO KNOW YOU WORK FOR A SECRET MILITARY CONTRACTOR THAT ARMS TERRORISTS, YES?
I WORK FOR THE RESISTANCE. AND ANTI-PSIOT GEAR IS NOT "WEAPONS."
BESIDES, RISING SPIRIT FUNDS MY RESEARCH, AND IT HAS NOTHING TO DO WITH WAR.
AHH, OF COURSE... FOR THE MONEY.
RIGHT, I'LL RUN A SERIES OF DIAGNOSTICS AFTER YOUR TRAINING TOMORROW.

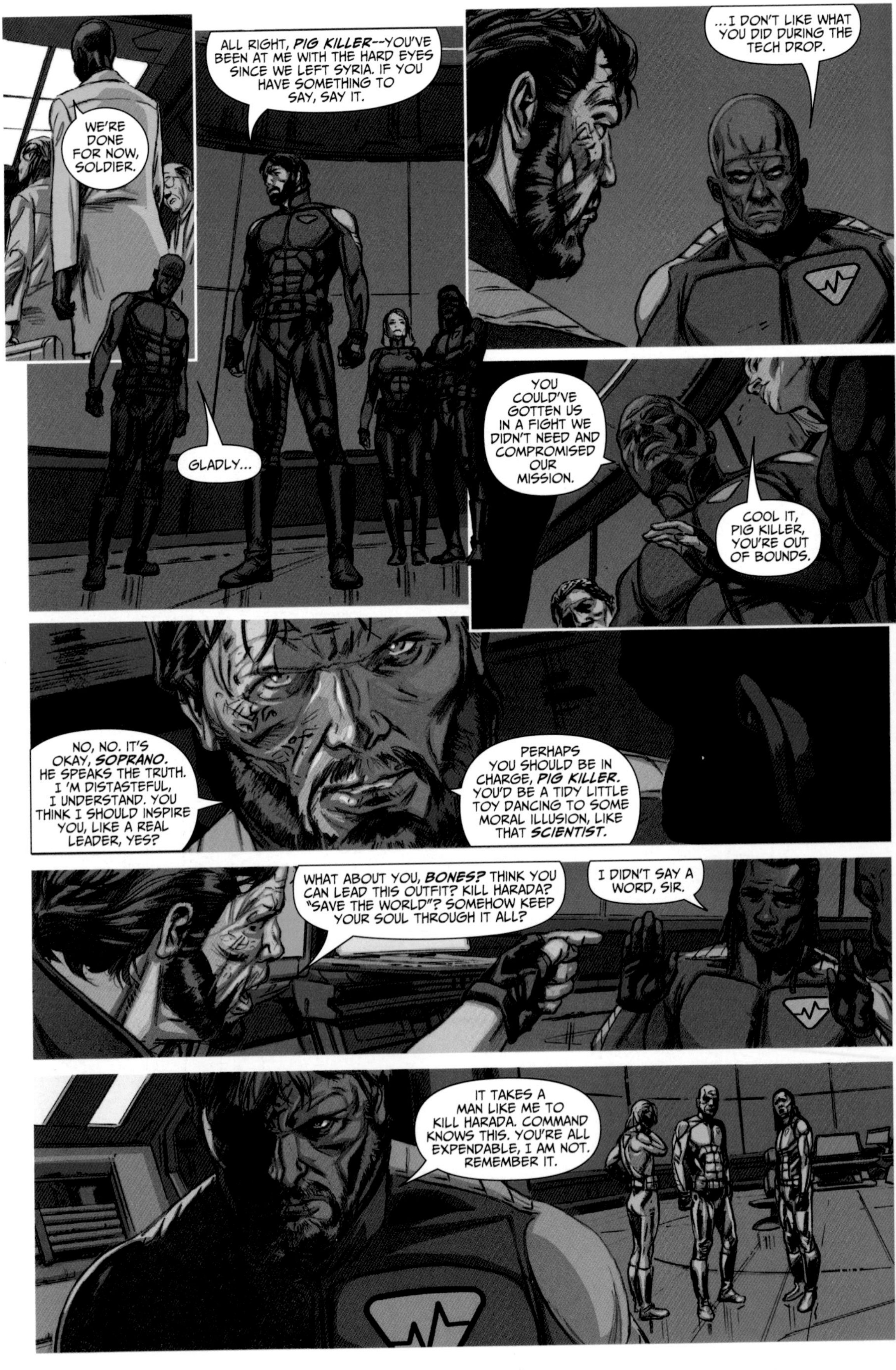
WE'RE DONE FOR NOW, SOLDIER.
ALL RIGHT, PIG KILLER--YOU'VE BEEN AT ME WITH THE HARD EYES SINCE WE LEFT SYRIA. IF YOU HAVE SOMETHING TO SAY, SAY IT.
GLADLY...
...I DON'T LIKE WHAT YOU DID DURING THE TECH DROP.
YOU COULD'VE GOTTEN US IN A FIGHT WE DIDN'T NEED AND COMPROMISED OUR MISSION.
COOL IT, PIG KILLER, YOU'RE OUT OF BOUNDS.
NO, NO. IT'S OKAY, SOPRANO. HE SPEAKS THE TRUTH. I'M DISTASTEFUL, I UNDERSTAND. YOU THINK I SHOULD INSPIRE YOU, LIKE A REAL LEADER, YES?
PERHAPS YOU SHOULD BE IN CHARGE, PIG KILLER. YOU'D BE A TIDY LITTLE TOY DANCING TO SOME MORAL ILLUSION, LIKE THAT SCIENTIST.
WHAT ABOUT YOU, BONES? THINK YOU CAN LEAD THIS OUTFIT? KILL HARADA? "SAVE THE WORLD"? SOMEHOW KEEP YOUR SOUL THROUGH IT ALL?
I DIDN'T SAY A WORD, SIR.
IT TAKES A MAN LIKE ME TO KILL HARADA. COMMAND KNOWS THIS. YOU'RE ALL EXPENDABLE, I AM NOT. REMEMBER IT.

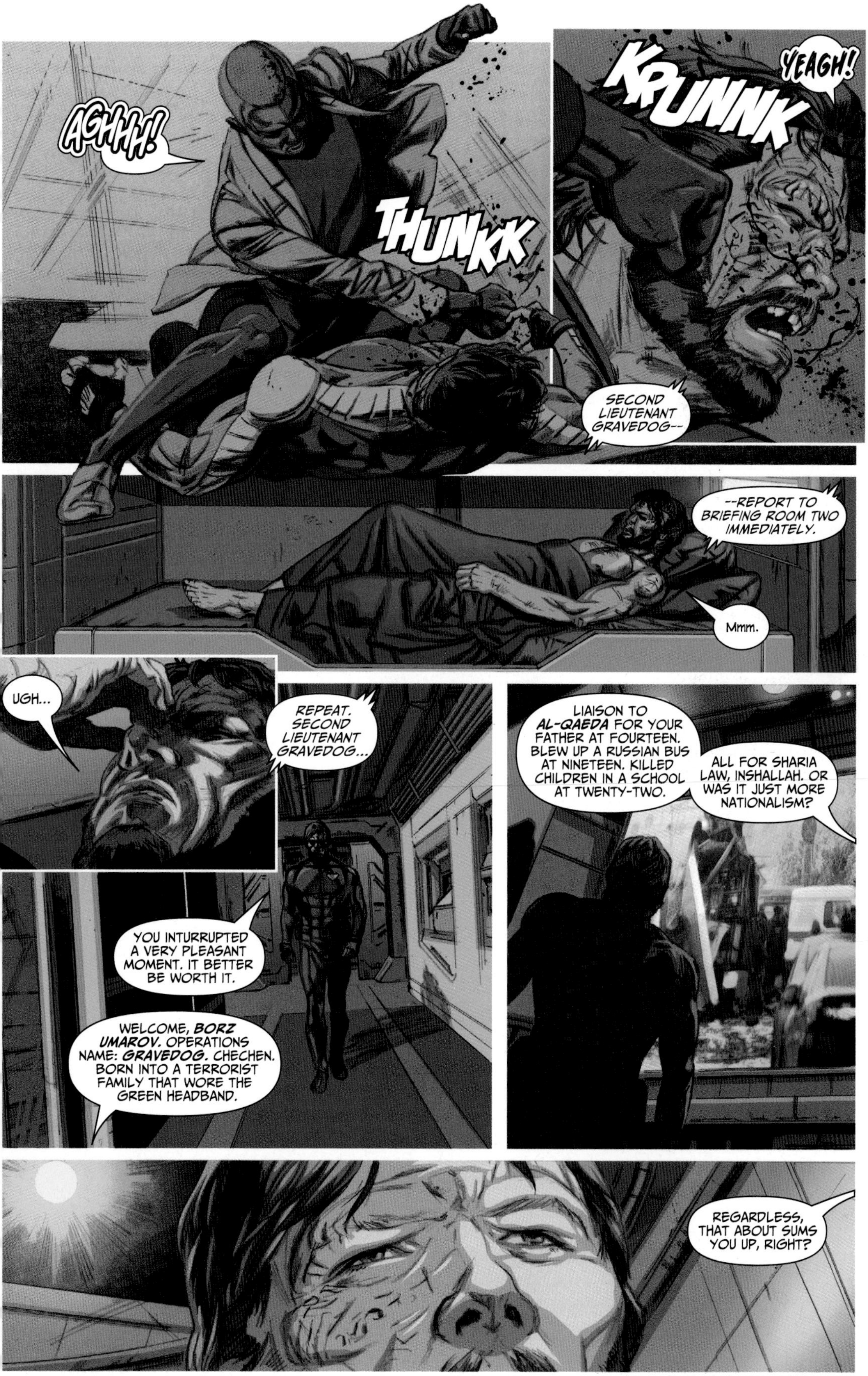

AGHHH!
THUNKK
KRUNNNK
YEAGH!
SECOND LIEUTENANT GRAVEDOG--
--REPORT TO BRIEFING ROOM TWO IMMEDIATELY.
Mmm.
UGH...
REPEAT. SECOND LIEUTENANT GRAVEDOG...
YOU INTURRUPTED A VERY PLEASANT MOMENT. IT BETTER BE WORTH IT.
WELCOME, BORZ UMAROV. OPERATIONS NAME: GRAVEDOG. CHECHEN. BORN INTO A TERRORIST FAMILY THAT WORE THE GREEN HEADBAND.
LIAISON TO AL-QAEDA FOR YOUR FATHER AT FOURTEEN. BLEW UP A RUSSIAN BUS AT NINETEEN. KILLED CHILDREN IN A SCHOOL AT TWENTY-TWO.
ALL FOR SHARIA LAW, INSHALLAH. OR WAS IT JUST MORE NATIONALISM?
REGARDLESS, THAT ABOUT SUMS YOU UP, RIGHT?

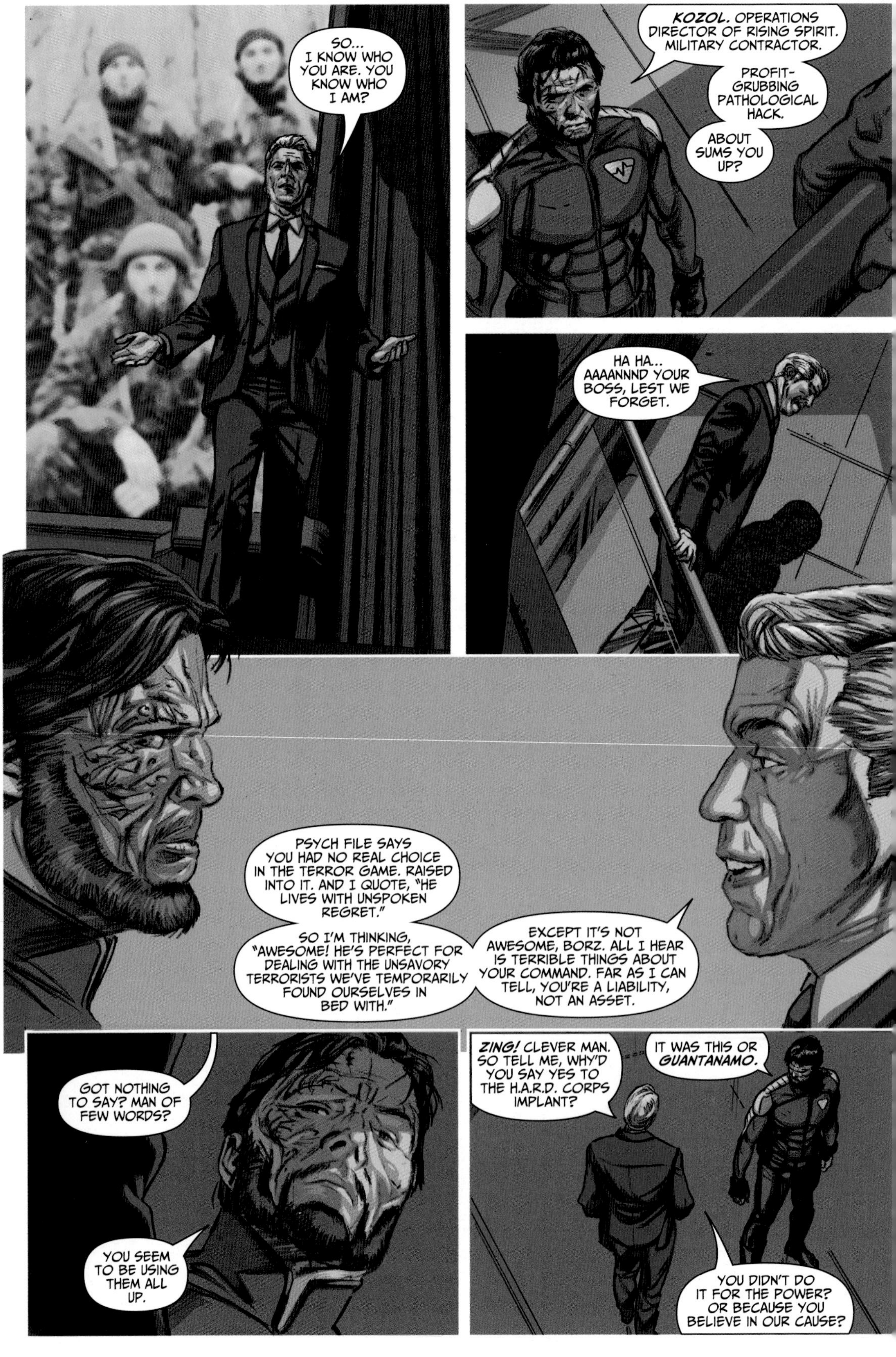
SO... I KNOW WHO YOU ARE. YOU KNOW WHO I AM?
KOZOL. OPERATIONS DIRECTOR OF RISING SPIRIT. MILITARY CONTRACTOR.
PROFIT-GRUBBING PATHOLOGICAL HACK.
ABOUT SUMS YOU UP?
HA HA... AAAANNND YOUR BOSS, LEST WE FORGET.
PSYCH FILE SAYS YOU HAD NO REAL CHOICE IN THE TERROR GAME. RAISED INTO IT. AND I QUOTE, "HE LIVES WITH UNSPOKEN REGRET."
SO I'M THINKING, "AWESOME! HE'S PERFECT FOR DEALING WITH THE UNSAVORY TERRORISTS WE'VE TEMPORARILY FOUND OURSELVES IN BED WITH."
EXCEPT IT'S NOT AWESOME, BORZ. ALL I HEAR IS TERRIBLE THINGS ABOUT YOUR COMMAND. FAR AS I CAN TELL, YOU'RE A LIABILITY, NOT AN ASSET.
GOT NOTHING TO SAY? MAN OF FEW WORDS?
YOU SEEM TO BE USING THEM ALL UP.
ZING! CLEVER MAN. SO TELL ME, WHY'D YOU SAY YES TO THE H.A.R.D. CORPS IMPLANT?
IT WAS THIS OR *GUANTANAMO.*
YOU DIDN'T DO IT FOR THE POWER? OR BECAUSE YOU BELIEVE IN OUR CAUSE?

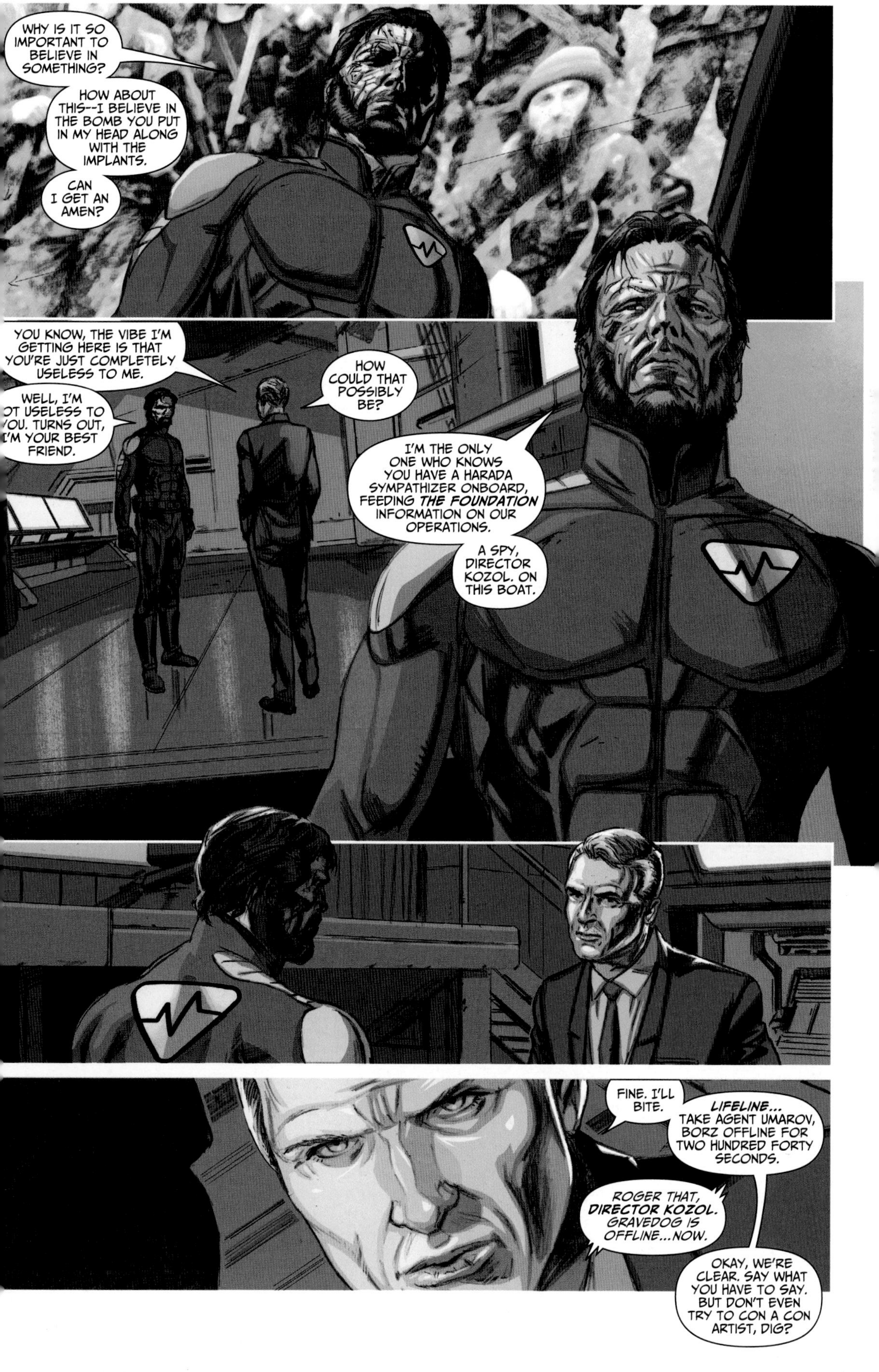
WHY IS IT SO IMPORTANT TO BELIEVE IN SOMETHING?
HOW ABOUT THIS--I BELIEVE IN THE BOMB YOU PUT IN MY HEAD ALONG WITH THE IMPLANTS.
CAN I GET AN AMEN?
YOU KNOW, THE VIBE I'M GETTING HERE IS THAT YOU'RE JUST COMPLETELY USELESS TO ME.
WELL, I'M OT USELESS TO YOU. TURNS OUT, I'M YOUR BEST FRIEND.
HOW COULD THAT POSSIBLY BE?
I'M THE ONLY ONE WHO KNOWS YOU HAVE A HARADA SYMPATHIZER ONBOARD, FEEDING *THE FOUNDATION* INFORMATION ON OUR OPERATIONS.
A SPY, DIRECTOR KOZOL. ON THIS BOAT.
FINE. I'LL BITE.
LIFELINE... TAKE AGENT UMAROV, BORZ OFFLINE FOR TWO HUNDRED FORTY SECONDS.
*ROGER THAT, **DIRECTOR KOZOL.** GRAVEDOG IS OFFLINE...NOW.*
OKAY, WE'RE CLEAR. SAY WHAT YOU HAVE TO SAY. BUT DON'T EVEN TRY TO CON A CON ARTIST, DIG?

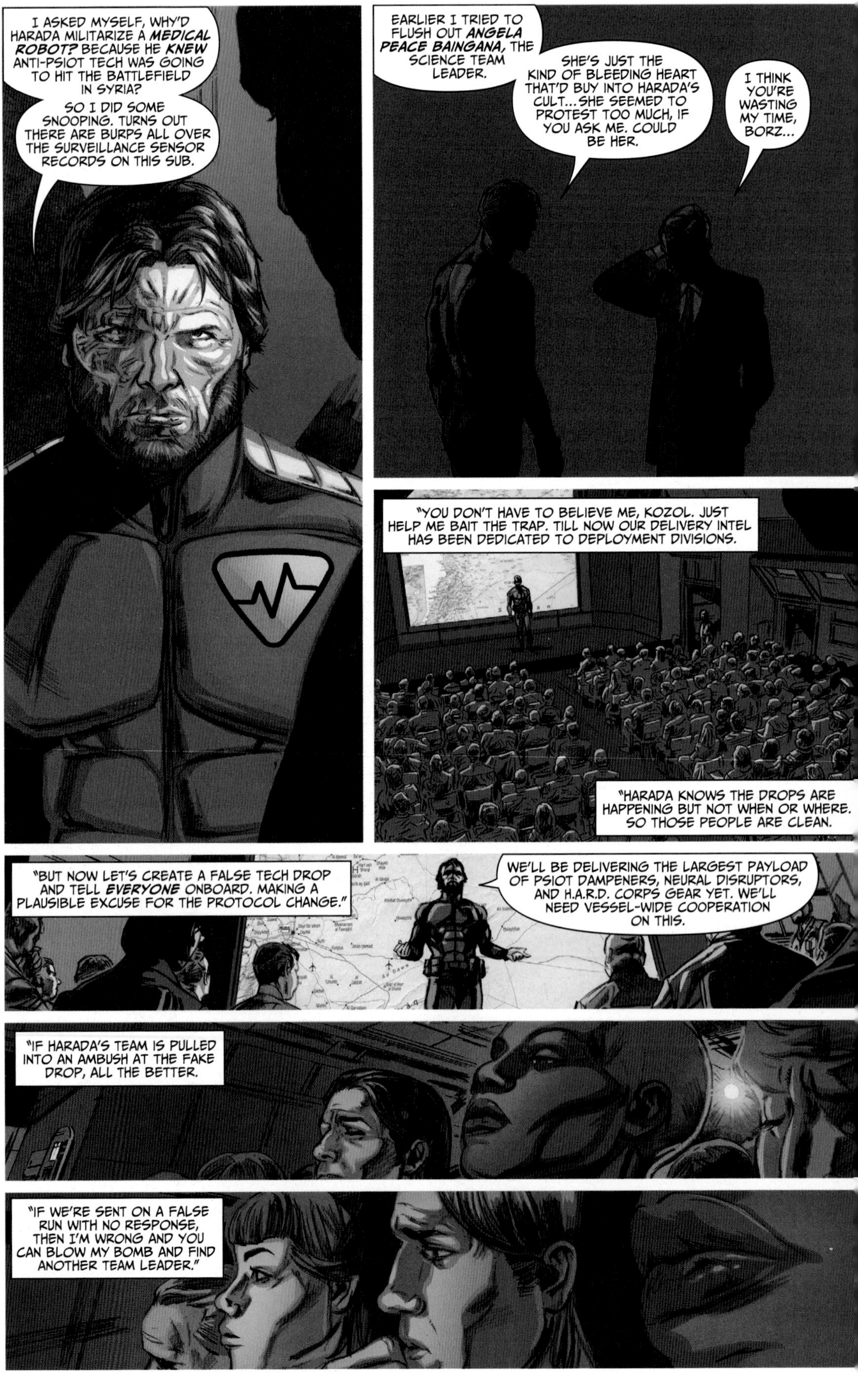
I ASKED MYSELF, WHY'D HARADA MILITARIZE A MEDICAL ROBOT? BECAUSE HE KNEW ANTI-PSIOT TECH WAS GOING TO HIT THE BATTLEFIELD IN SYRIA?
SO I DID SOME SNOOPING. TURNS OUT THERE ARE BURPS ALL OVER THE SURVEILLANCE SENSOR RECORDS ON THIS SUB.
EARLIER I TRIED TO FLUSH OUT ANGELA PEACE BAINGANA, THE SCIENCE TEAM LEADER.
SHE'S JUST THE KIND OF BLEEDING HEART THAT'D BUY INTO HARADA'S CULT... SHE SEEMED TO PROTEST TOO MUCH, IF YOU ASK ME. COULD BE HER.
I THINK YOU'RE WASTING MY TIME, BORZ...
"YOU DON'T HAVE TO BELIEVE ME, KOZOL. JUST HELP ME BAIT THE TRAP. TILL NOW OUR DELIVERY INTEL HAS BEEN DEDICATED TO DEPLOYMENT DIVISIONS.
"HARADA KNOWS THE DROPS ARE HAPPENING BUT NOT WHEN OR WHERE. SO THOSE PEOPLE ARE CLEAN.
"BUT NOW LET'S CREATE A FALSE TECH DROP AND TELL EVERYONE ONBOARD. MAKING A PLAUSIBLE EXCUSE FOR THE PROTOCOL CHANGE."
WE'LL BE DELIVERING THE LARGEST PAYLOAD OF PSIOT DAMPENERS, NEURAL DISRUPTORS, AND H.A.R.D. CORPS GEAR YET. WE'LL NEED VESSEL-WIDE COOPERATION ON THIS.
"IF HARADA'S TEAM IS PULLED INTO AN AMBUSH AT THE FAKE DROP, ALL THE BETTER.
"IF WE'RE SENT ON A FALSE RUN WITH NO RESPONSE, THEN I'M WRONG AND YOU CAN BLOW MY BOMB AND FIND ANOTHER TEAM LEADER."

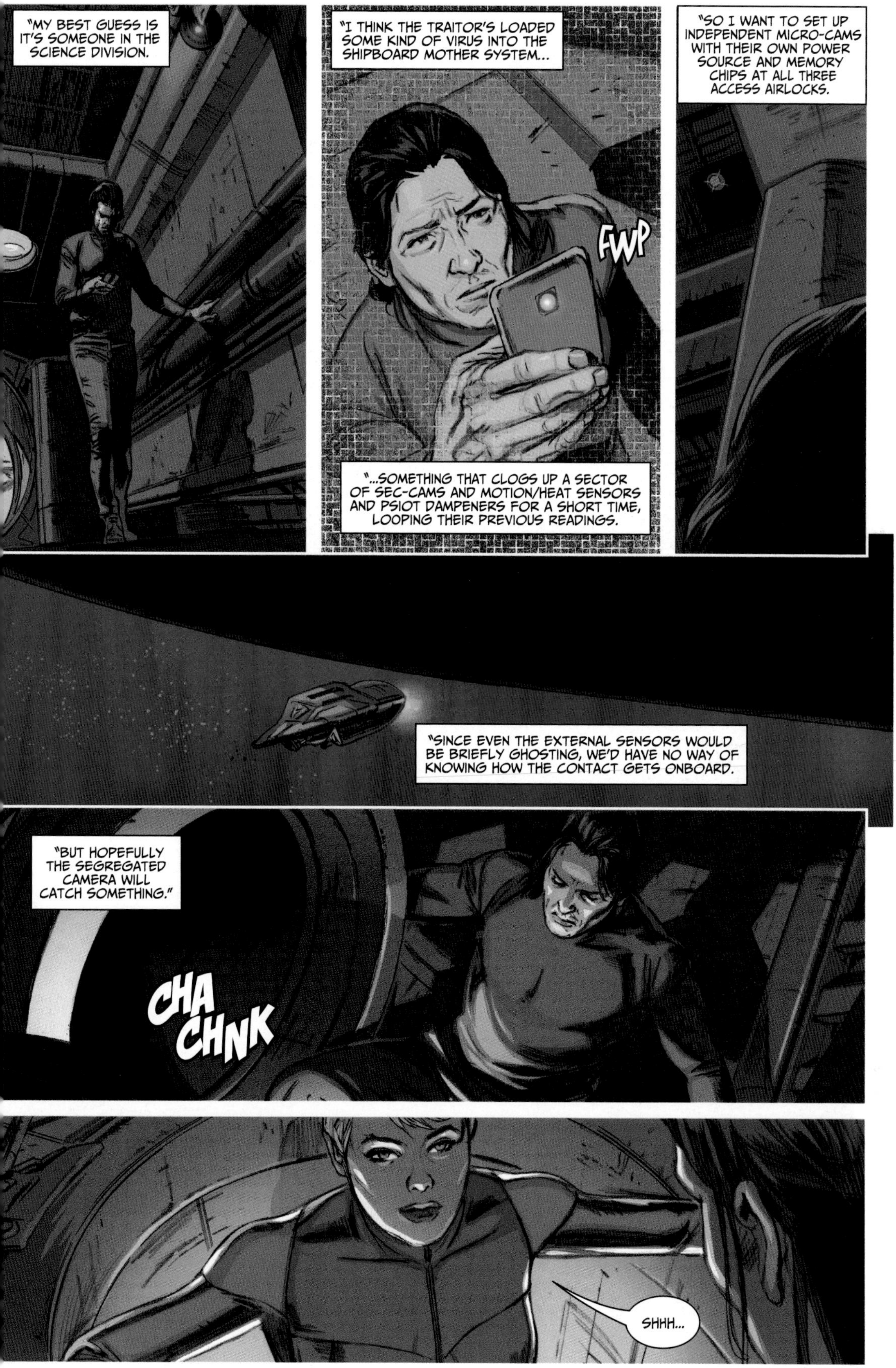
"MY BEST GUESS IS IT'S SOMEONE IN THE SCIENCE DIVISION.
"I THINK THE TRAITOR'S LOADED SOME KIND OF VIRUS INTO THE SHIPBOARD MOTHER SYSTEM...
FWP
"...SOMETHING THAT CLOGS UP A SECTOR OF SEC-CAMS AND MOTION/HEAT SENSORS AND PSIOT DAMPENERS FOR A SHORT TIME, LOOPING THEIR PREVIOUS READINGS.
"SO I WANT TO SET UP INDEPENDENT MICRO-CAMS WITH THEIR OWN POWER SOURCE AND MEMORY CHIPS AT ALL THREE ACCESS AIRLOCKS.
"SINCE EVEN THE EXTERNAL SENSORS WOULD BE BRIEFLY GHOSTING, WE'D HAVE NO WAY OF KNOWING HOW THE CONTACT GETS ONBOARD.
"BUT HOPEFULLY THE SEGREGATED CAMERA WILL CATCH SOMETHING."
CHA CHNK
SHHH...

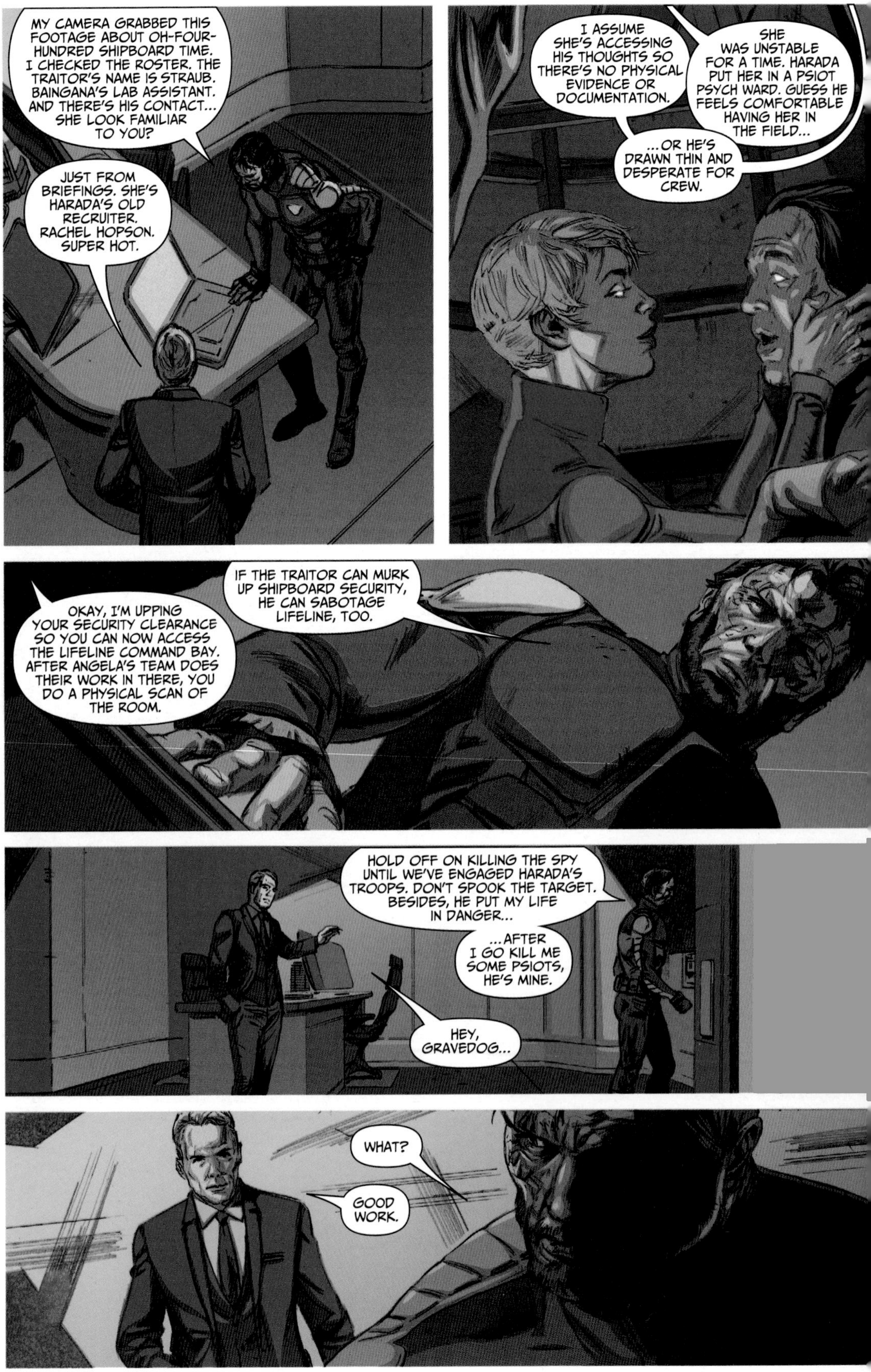
MY CAMERA GRABBED THIS FOOTAGE ABOUT OH-FOUR-HUNDRED SHIPBOARD TIME. I CHECKED THE ROSTER. THE TRAITOR'S NAME IS STRAUB. BAINGANA'S LAB ASSISTANT. AND THERE'S HIS CONTACT... SHE LOOK FAMILIAR TO YOU?
JUST FROM BRIEFINGS. SHE'S HARADA'S OLD RECRUITER. RACHEL HOPSON. SUPER HOT.
I ASSUME SHE'S ACCESSING HIS THOUGHTS SO THERE'S NO PHYSICAL EVIDENCE OR DOCUMENTATION.
SHE WAS UNSTABLE FOR A TIME. HARADA PUT HER IN A PSIOT PSYCH WARD. GUESS HE FEELS COMFORTABLE HAVING HER IN THE FIELD...
...OR HE'S DRAWN THIN AND DESPERATE FOR CREW.
OKAY, I'M UPPING YOUR SECURITY CLEARANCE SO YOU CAN NOW ACCESS THE LIFELINE COMMAND BAY. AFTER ANGELA'S TEAM DOES THEIR WORK IN THERE, YOU DO A PHYSICAL SCAN OF THE ROOM.
IF THE TRAITOR CAN MURK UP SHIPBOARD SECURITY, HE CAN SABOTAGE LIFELINE, TOO.
HOLD OFF ON KILLING THE SPY UNTIL WE'VE ENGAGED HARADA'S TROOPS. DON'T SPOOK THE TARGET. BESIDES, HE PUT MY LIFE IN DANGER...
...AFTER I GO KILL ME SOME PSIOTS, HE'S MINE.
HEY, GRAVEDOG...
WHAT?
GOOD WORK.

"I MADE AN EXCELLENT DECISION WHEN I PUT YOU IN CHARGE OF THIS UNIT."

WHMP WHMP WHM

〈RISING SPIRIT CHOPPER APPROACHING.〉

HMP WHMP WHMP

FWWOOOOM

〈FOUNDATION TRANSPORT UNCLOAKING!! PULL BACK!〉

KAKKAK

KAK

OFFOFFOFFOFFOFFOFFOFFOFF

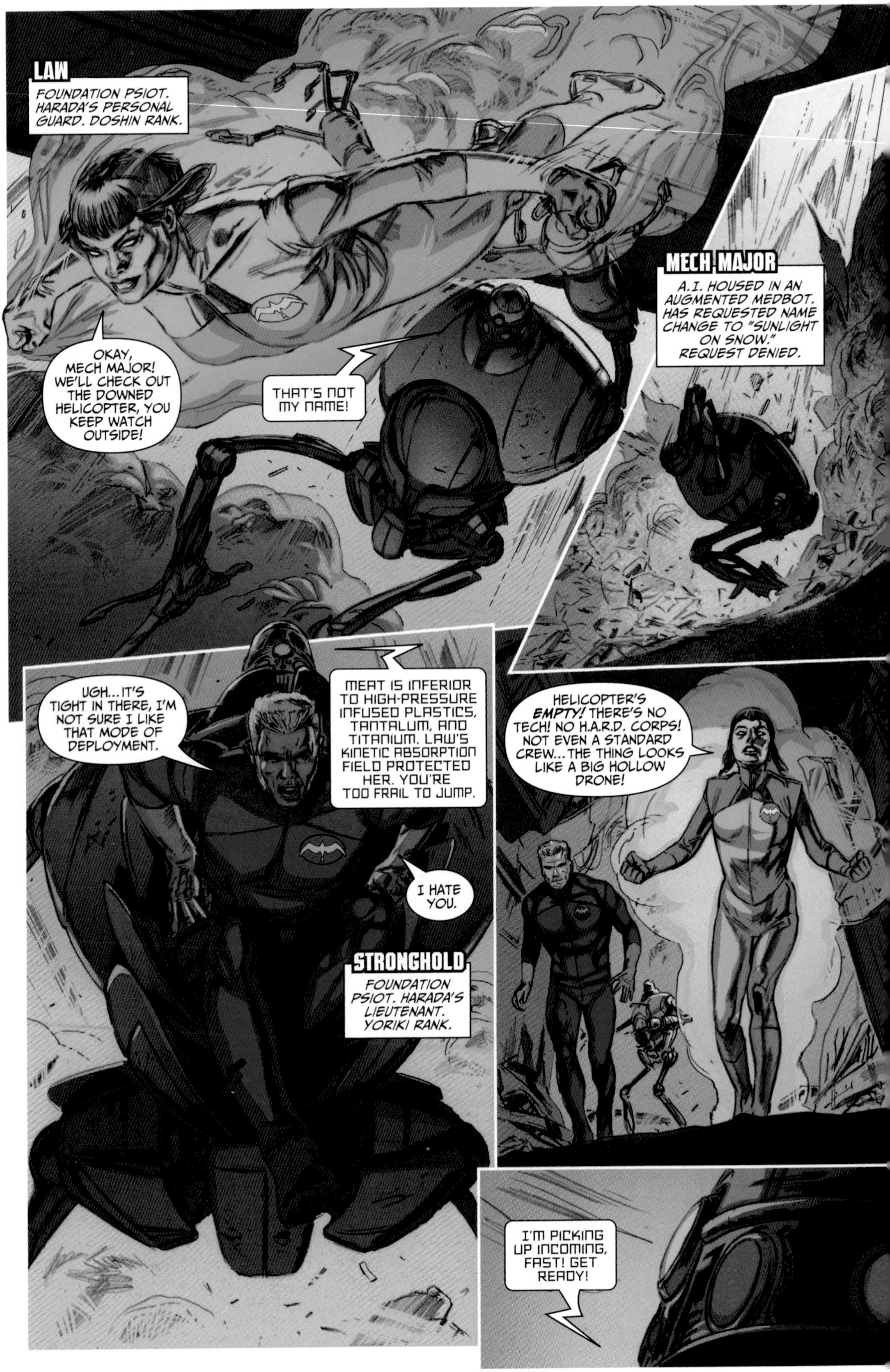

LAW
FOUNDATION PSIOT. HARADA'S PERSONAL GUARD. DOSHIN RANK.
OKAY, MECH MAJOR! WE'LL CHECK OUT THE DOWNED HELICOPTER, YOU KEEP WATCH OUTSIDE!
THAT'S NOT MY NAME!
MECH MAJOR
A.I. HOUSED IN AN AUGMENTED MEDBOT. HAS REQUESTED NAME CHANGE TO "SUNLIGHT ON SNOW." REQUEST DENIED.
UGH...IT'S TIGHT IN THERE, I'M NOT SURE I LIKE THAT MODE OF DEPLOYMENT.
MEAT IS INFERIOR TO HIGH-PRESSURE INFUSED PLASTICS, TANTALUM, AND TITANIUM. LAW'S KINETIC ABSORPTION FIELD PROTECTED HER. YOU'RE TOO FRAIL TO JUMP.
I HATE YOU.
STRONGHOLD
FOUNDATION PSIOT. HARADA'S LIEUTENANT. YORIKI RANK.
HELICOPTER'S EMPTY! THERE'S NO TECH! NO H.A.R.D. CORPS! NOT EVEN A STANDARD CREW...THE THING LOOKS LIKE A BIG HOLLOW DRONE!
I'M PICKING UP INCOMING, FAST! GET READY!

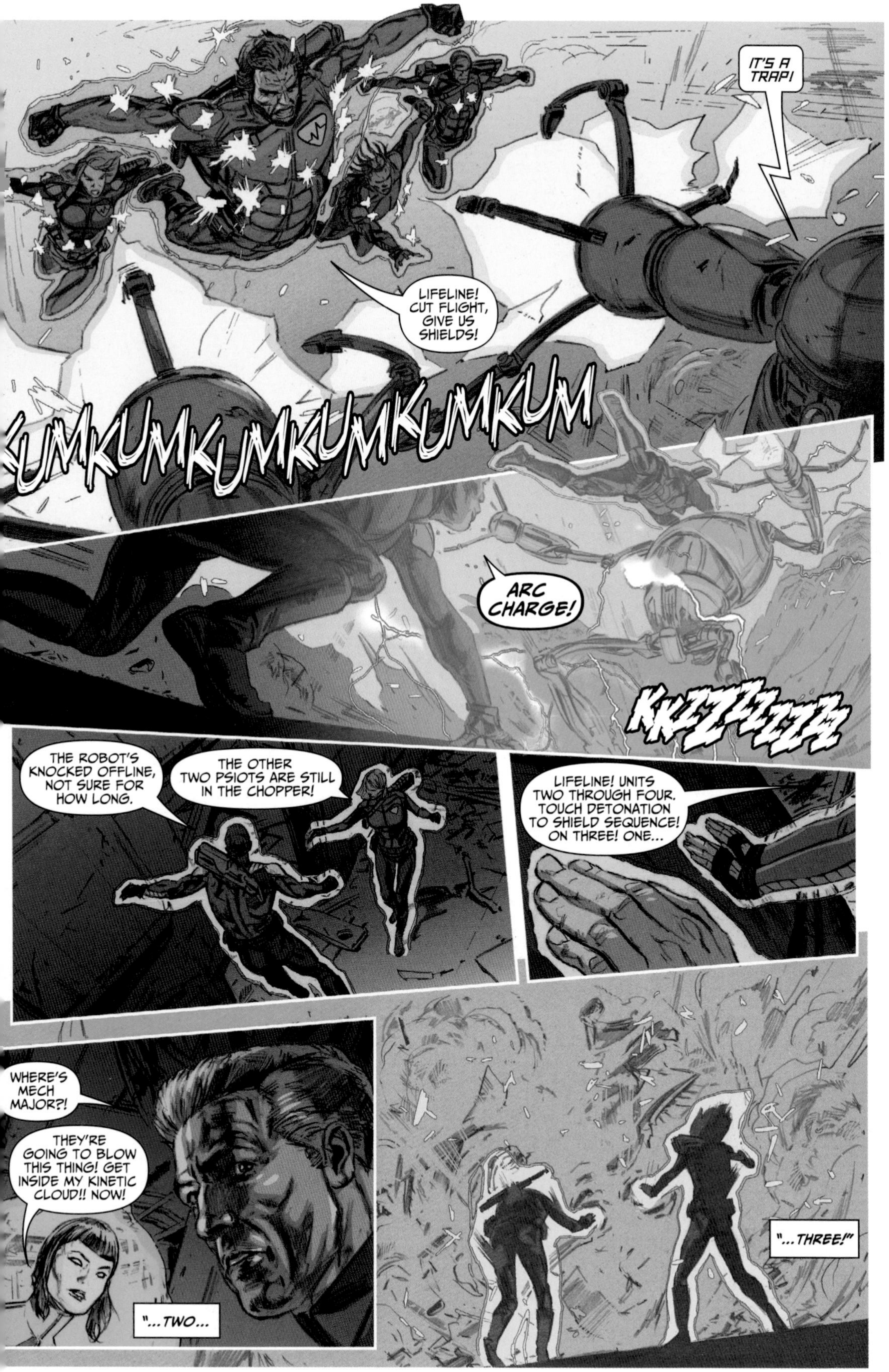
IT'S A TRAP!
LIFELINE! CUT FLIGHT, GIVE US SHIELDS!
KUMKUMKUMKUMKUMKUM
ARC CHARGE!
KKZZZZZZZ
THE ROBOT'S KNOCKED OFFLINE, NOT SURE FOR HOW LONG.
THE OTHER TWO PSIOTS ARE STILL IN THE CHOPPER!
LIFELINE! UNITS TWO THROUGH FOUR. TOUCH DETONATION TO SHIELD SEQUENCE! ON THREE! ONE...
WHERE'S MECH MAJOR?!
THEY'RE GOING TO BLOW THIS THING! GET INSIDE MY KINETIC CLOUD!! NOW!
"...TWO...
"...THREE!"

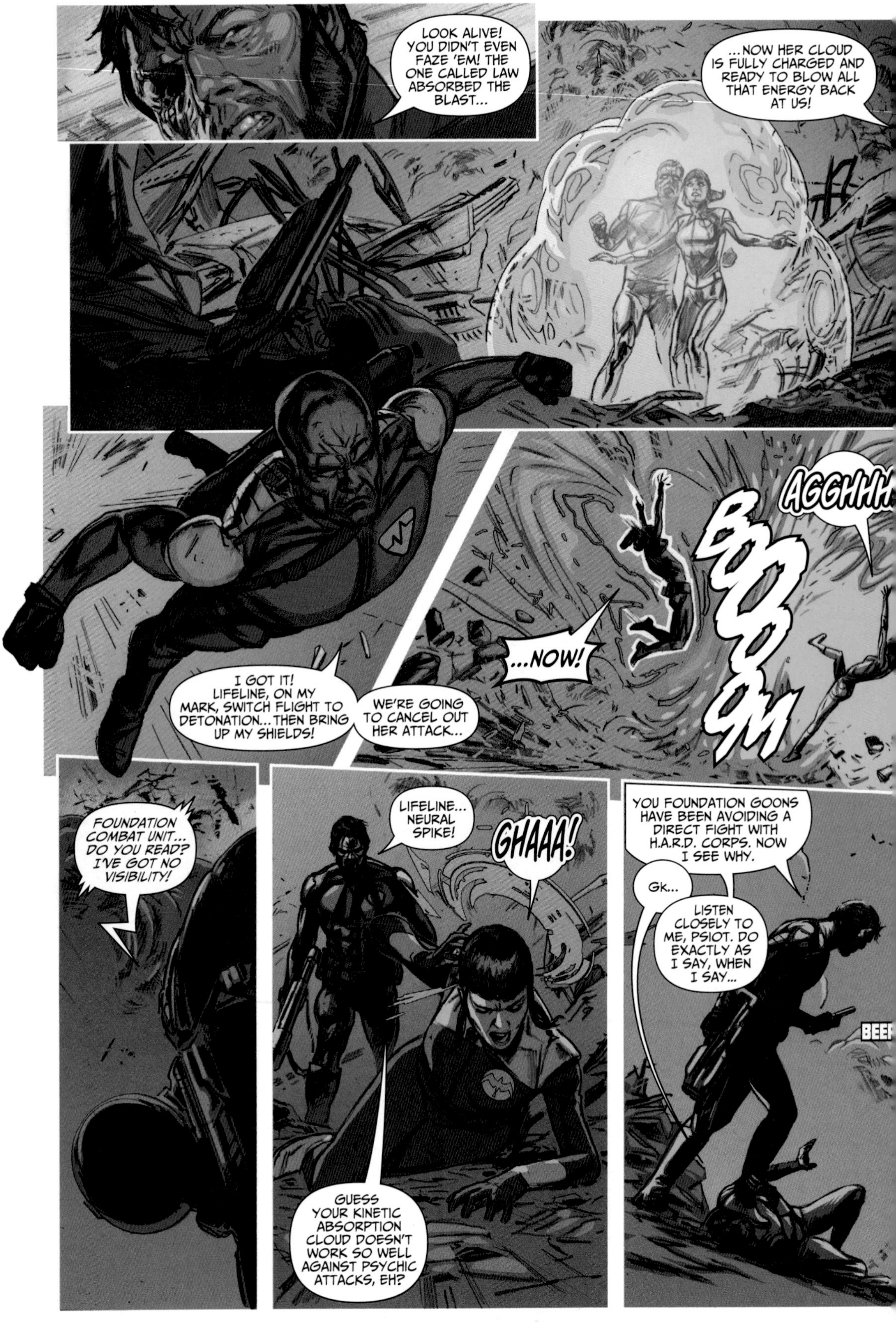

LOOK ALIVE! YOU DIDN'T EVEN FAZE 'EM! THE ONE CALLED LAW ABSORBED THE BLAST...
...NOW HER CLOUD IS FULLY CHARGED AND READY TO BLOW ALL THAT ENERGY BACK AT US!
I GOT IT! LIFELINE, ON MY MARK, SWITCH FLIGHT TO DETONATION...THEN BRING UP MY SHIELDS!
WE'RE GOING TO CANCEL OUT HER ATTACK...
...NOW!
BOOOOM
AGGHHH
FOUNDATION COMBAT UNIT... DO YOU READ? I'VE GOT NO VISIBILITY!
LIFELINE... NEURAL SPIKE!
GHAAA!
GUESS YOUR KINETIC ABSORPTION CLOUD DOESN'T WORK SO WELL AGAINST PSYCHIC ATTACKS, EH?
YOU FOUNDATION GOONS HAVE BEEN AVOIDING A DIRECT FIGHT WITH H.A.R.D. CORPS. NOW I SEE WHY.
Gk...
LISTEN CLOSELY TO ME, PSIOT. DO EXACTLY AS I SAY, WHEN I SAY...

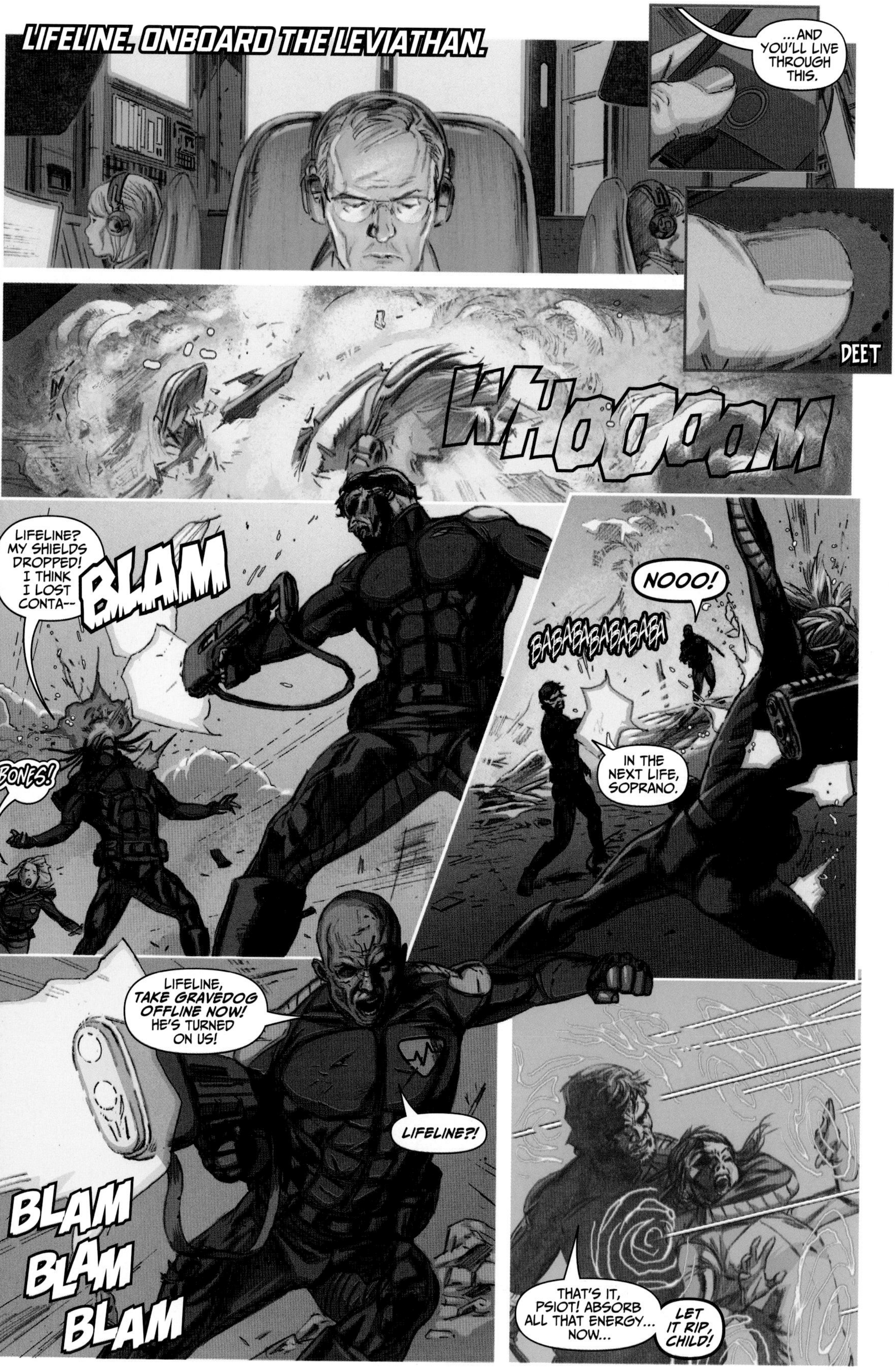
LIFELINE. ONBOARD THE LEVIATHAN.
...AND YOU'LL LIVE THROUGH THIS.
DEET
WHOOOOOM
LIFELINE? MY SHIELDS DROPPED! I THINK I LOST CONTA--
BLAM
BONES!
NOOO!
BABABABABABABA
IN THE NEXT LIFE, SOPRANO.
LIFELINE, TAKE GRAVEDOG OFFLINE NOW! HE'S TURNED ON US!
LIFELINE?!
BLAM
BLAM
BLAM
THAT'S IT, PSIOT! ABSORB ALL THAT ENERGY... NOW...
LET IT RIP, CHILD!

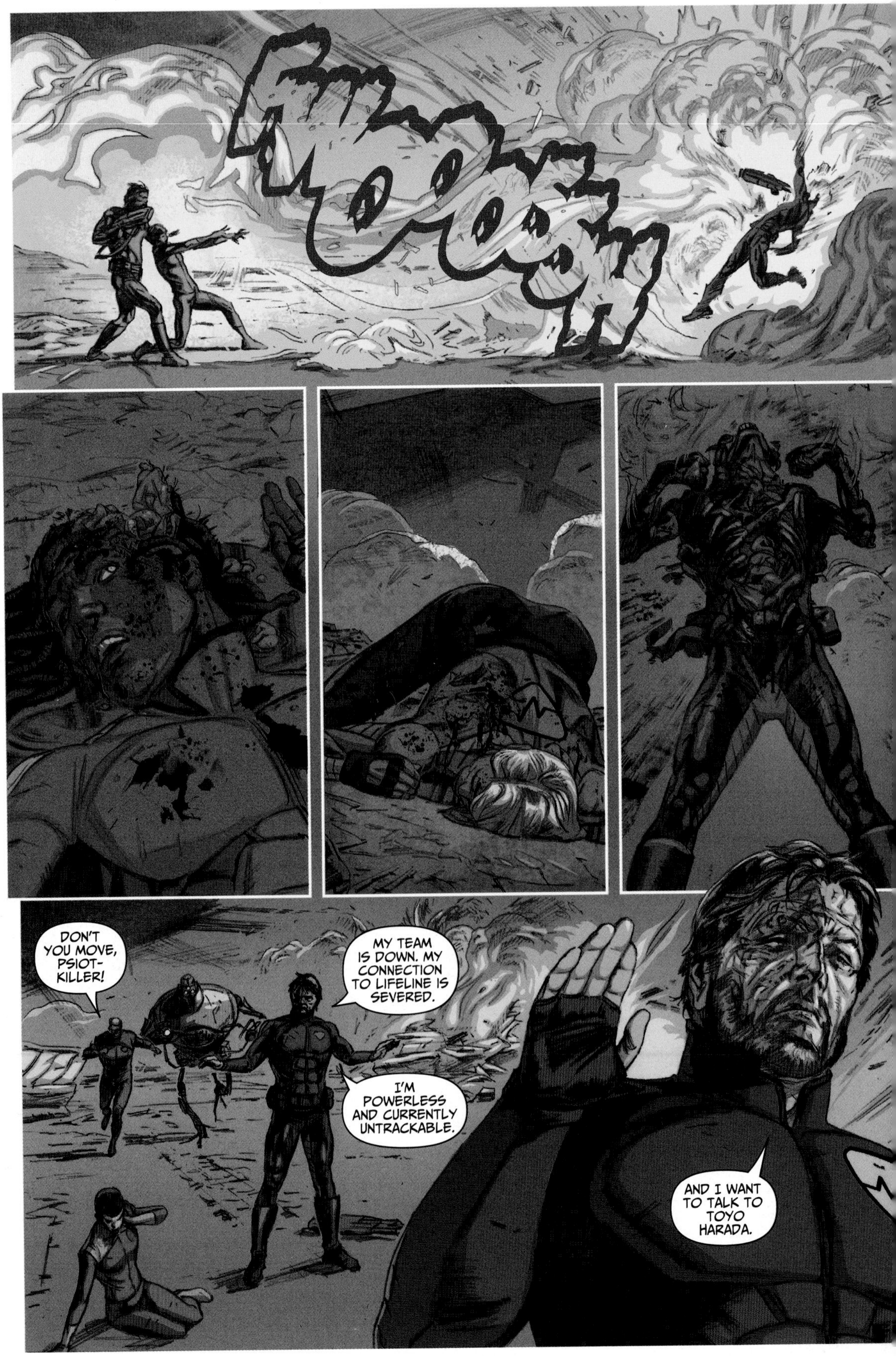
DON'T YOU MOVE, PSIOT-KILLER!
MY TEAM IS DOWN. MY CONNECTION TO LIFELINE IS SEVERED.
I'M POWERLESS AND CURRENTLY UNTRACKABLE.
AND I WANT TO TALK TO TOYO HARADA.

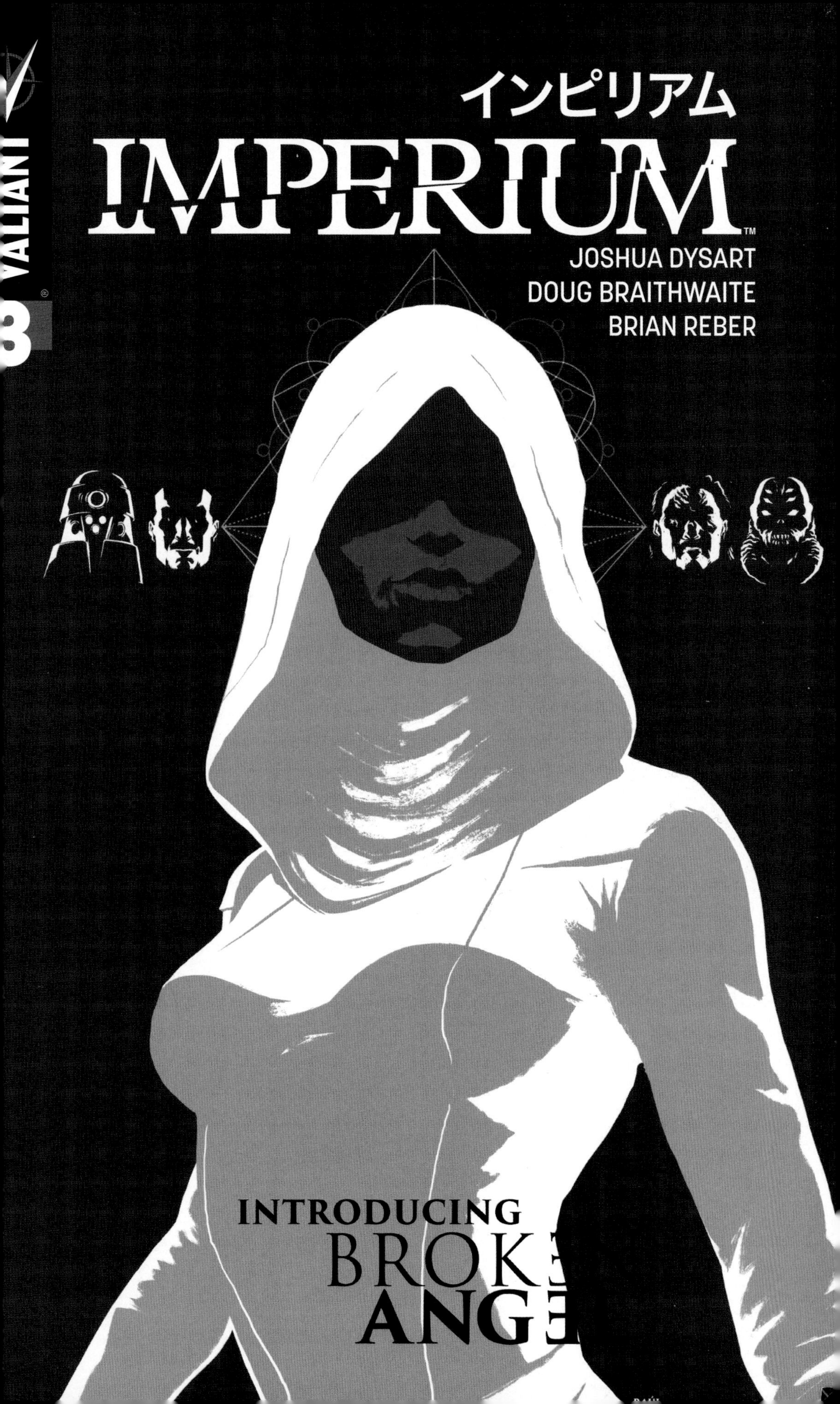
VALIANT
3
インピリアム
IMPERIUM™
JOSHUA DYSART
DOUG BRAITHWAITE
BRIAN REBER
INTRODUCING
BROK
ANG

インピリアム

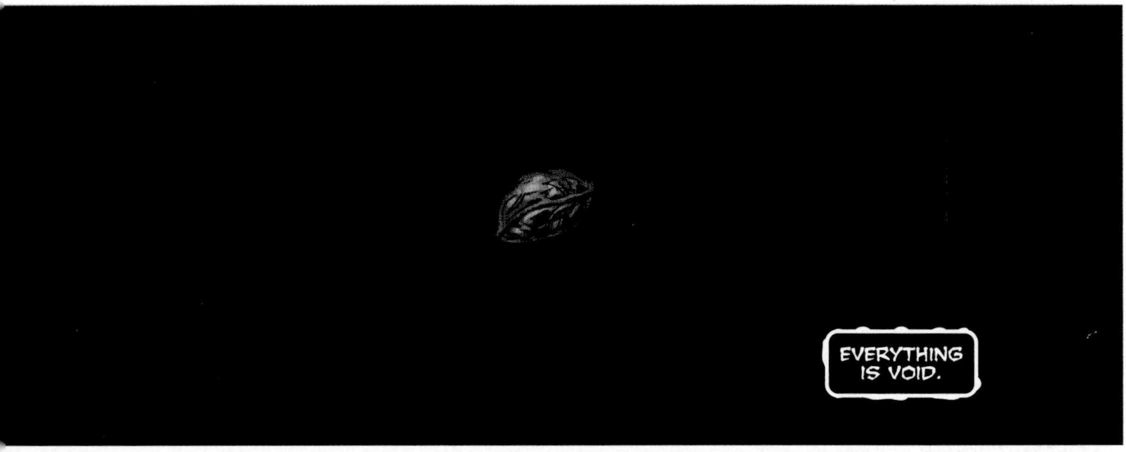
EVERYTHING IS VOID.

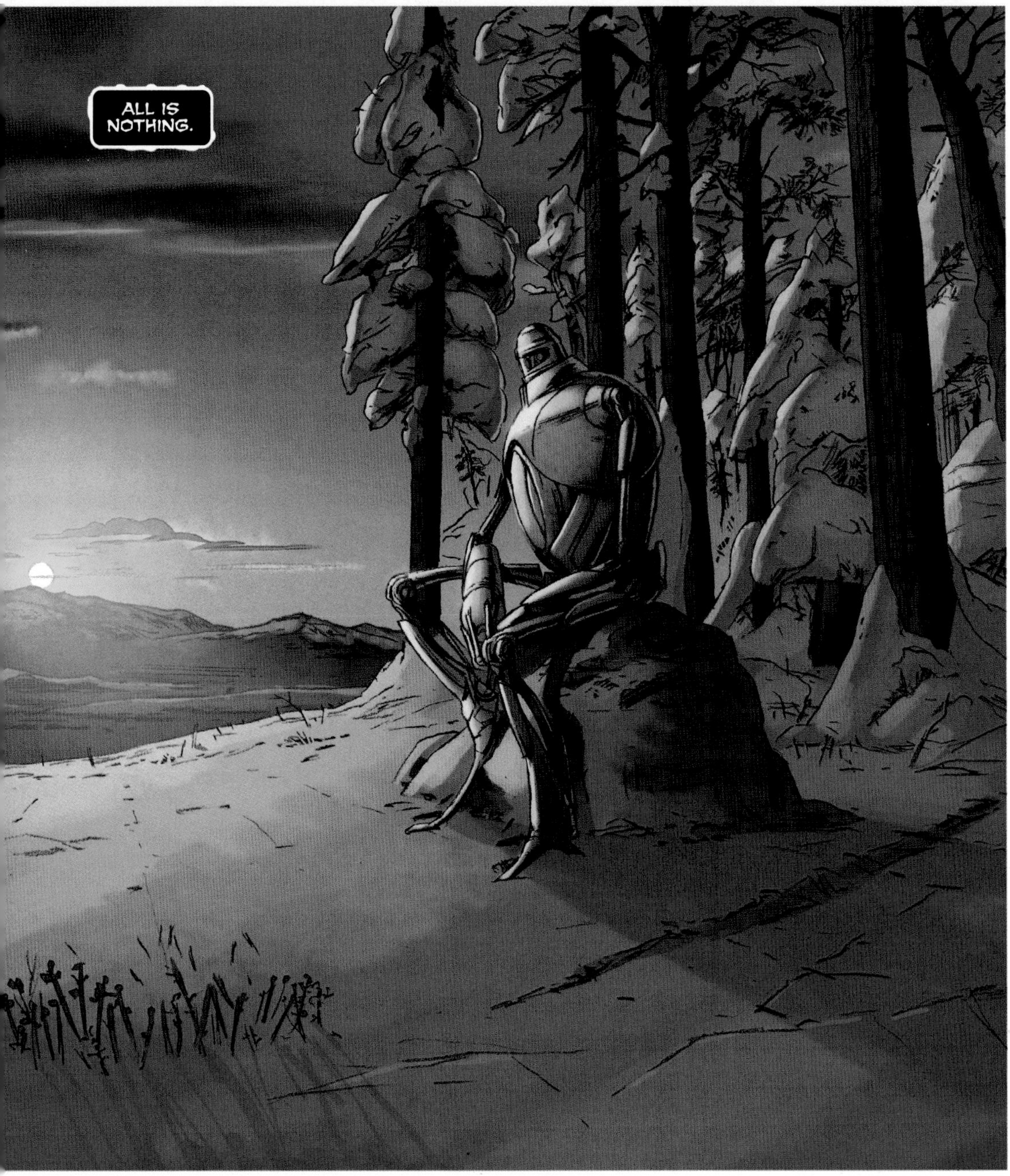
ALL IS NOTHING.

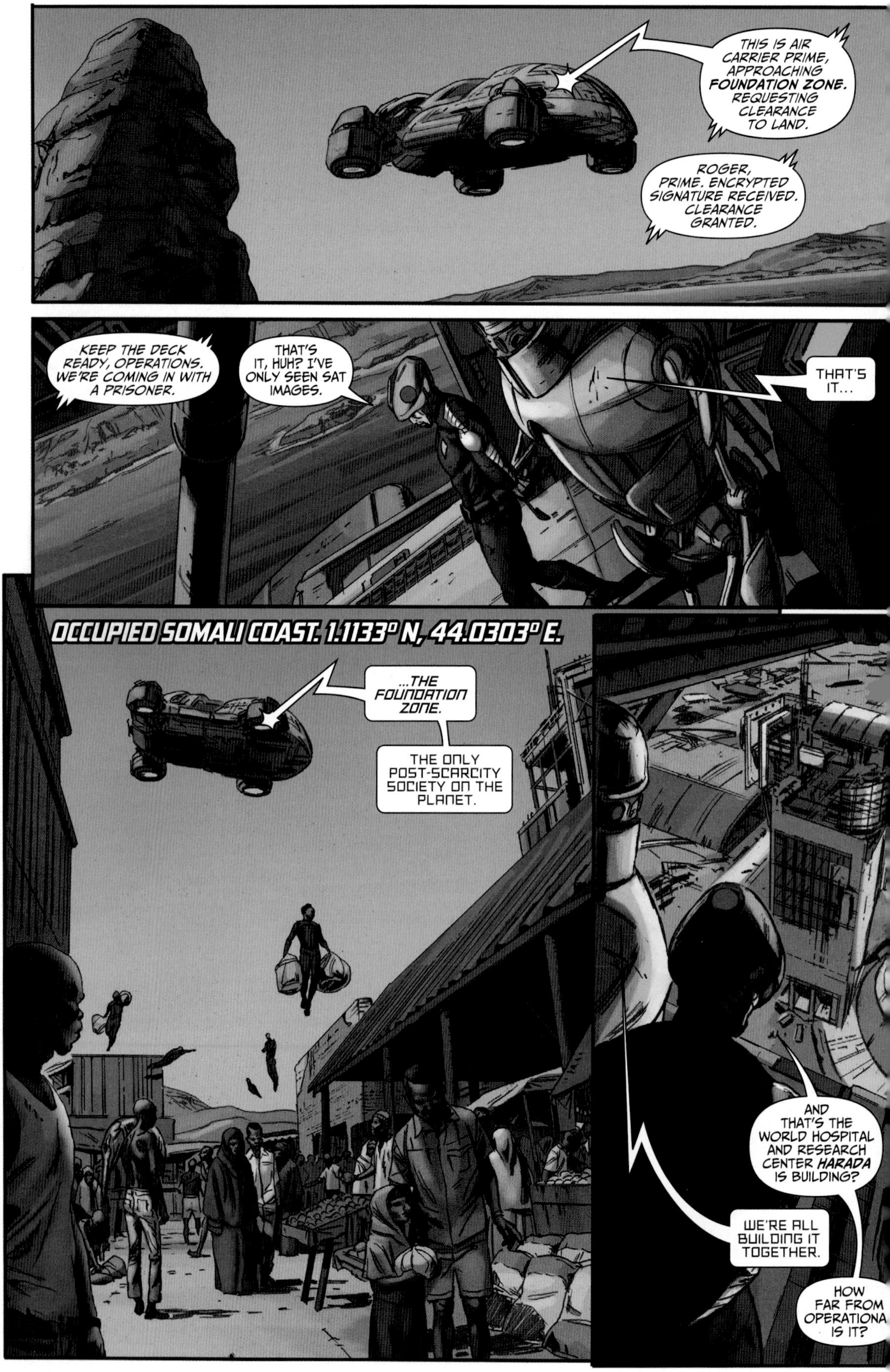

THIS IS AIR CARRIER PRIME, APPROACHING FOUNDATION ZONE. REQUESTING CLEARANCE TO LAND.
ROGER, PRIME. ENCRYPTED SIGNATURE RECEIVED. CLEARANCE GRANTED.
KEEP THE DECK READY, OPERATIONS. WE'RE COMING IN WITH A PRISONER.
THAT'S IT, HUH? I'VE ONLY SEEN SAT IMAGES.
THAT'S IT...
OCCUPIED SOMALI COAST. 1.1133° N, 44.0303° E.
...THE FOUNDATION ZONE.
THE ONLY POST-SCARCITY SOCIETY ON THE PLANET.
AND THAT'S THE WORLD HOSPITAL AND RESEARCH CENTER HARADA IS BUILDING?
WE'RE ALL BUILDING IT TOGETHER.
HOW FAR FROM OPERATIONA IS IT?

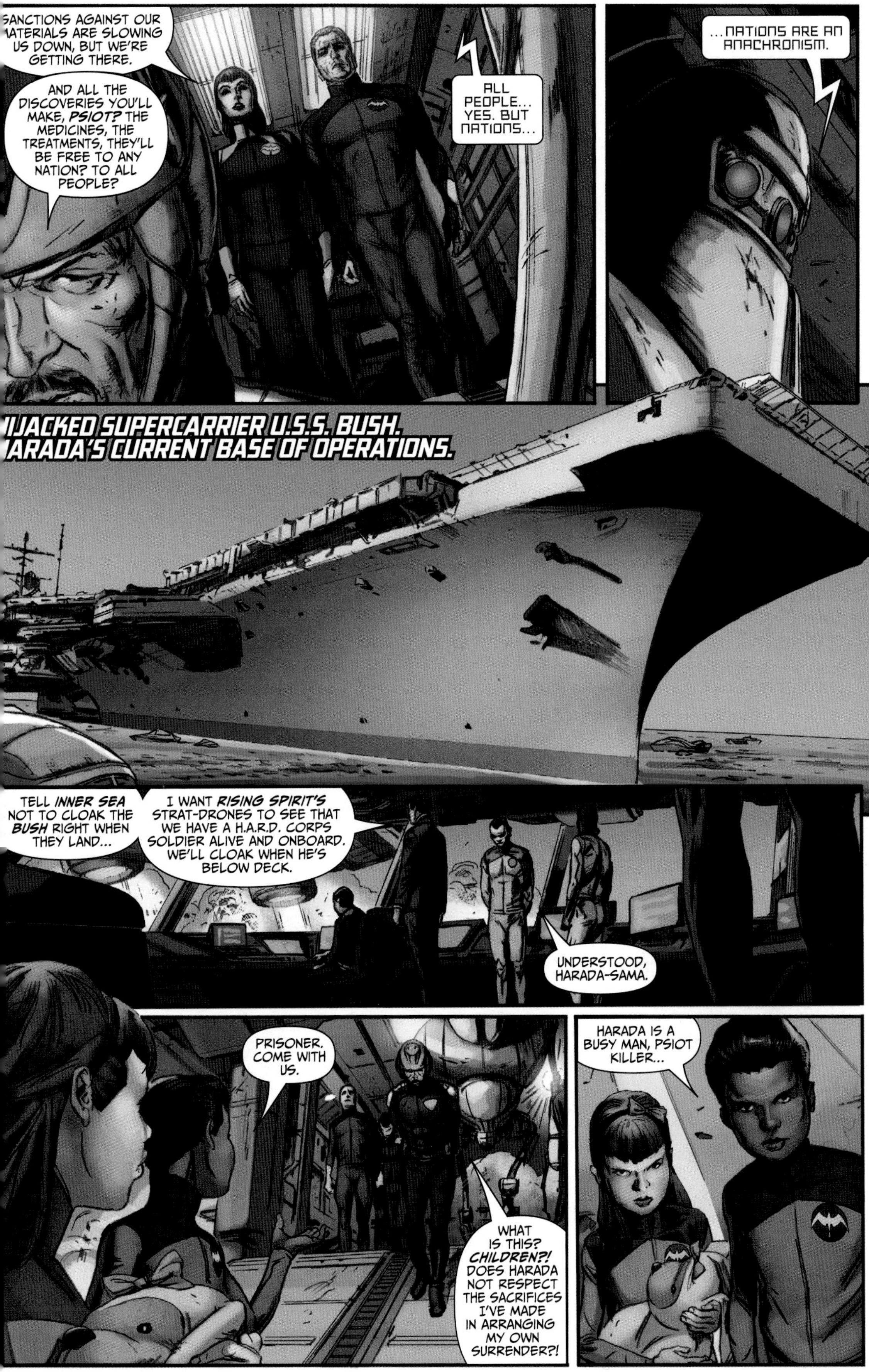
SANCTIONS AGAINST OUR MATERIALS ARE SLOWING US DOWN, BUT WE'RE GETTING THERE.
AND ALL THE DISCOVERIES YOU'LL MAKE, PSIOT? THE MEDICINES, THE TREATMENTS, THEY'LL BE FREE TO ANY NATION? TO ALL PEOPLE?
ALL PEOPLE... YES. BUT NATIONS...
...NATIONS ARE AN ANACHRONISM.
IJACKED SUPERCARRIER U.S.S. BUSH.
ARADA'S CURRENT BASE OF OPERATIONS.
TELL INNER SEA NOT TO CLOAK THE BUSH RIGHT WHEN THEY LAND...
I WANT RISING SPIRIT'S STRAT-DRONES TO SEE THAT WE HAVE A H.A.R.D. CORPS SOLDIER ALIVE AND ONBOARD. WE'LL CLOAK WHEN HE'S BELOW DECK.
UNDERSTOOD, HARADA-SAMA.
PRISONER. COME WITH US.
WHAT IS THIS? CHILDREN?! DOES HARADA NOT RESPECT THE SACRIFICES I'VE MADE IN ARRANGING MY OWN SURRENDER?!
HARADA IS A BUSY MAN, PSIOT KILLER...

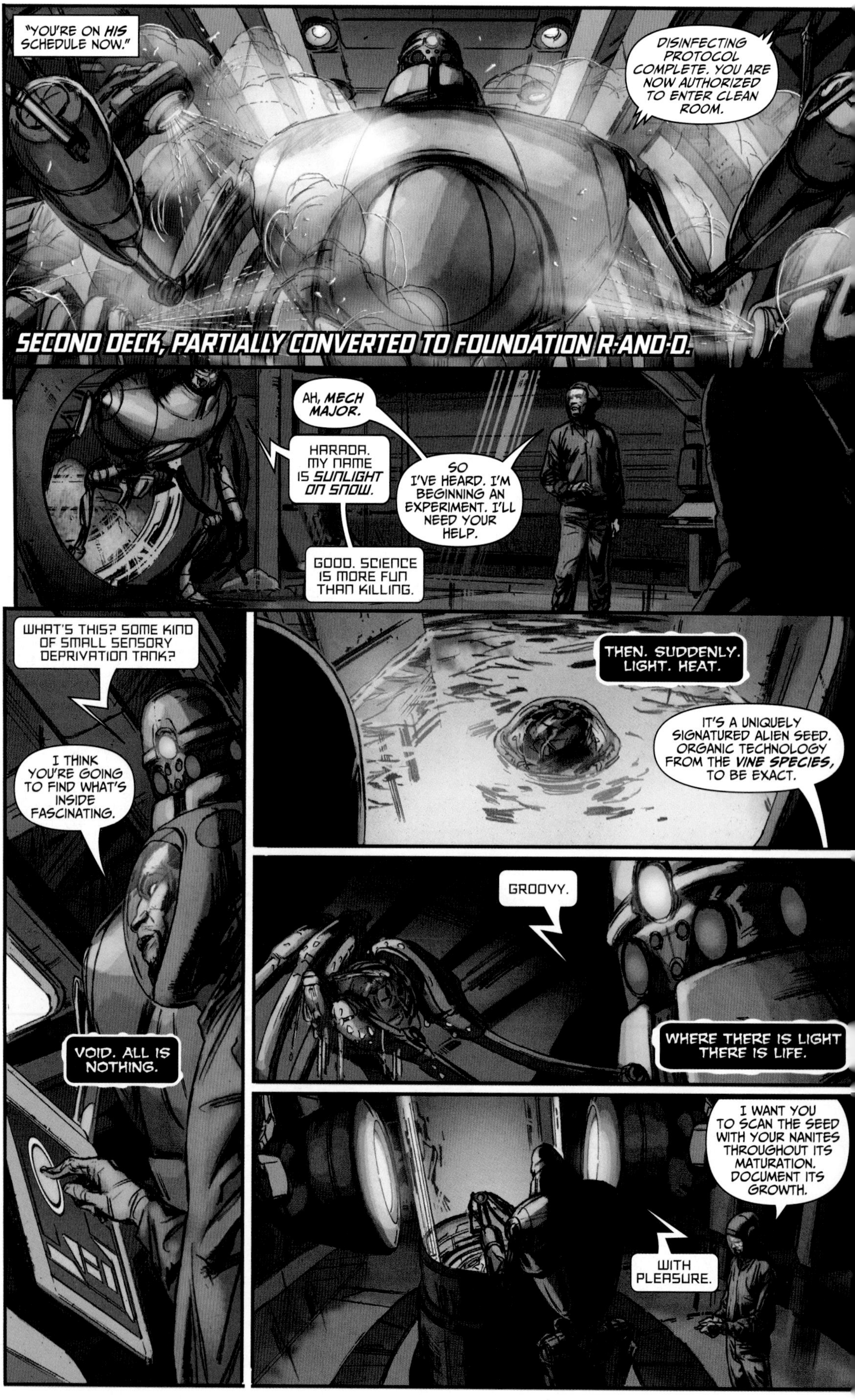

"YOU'RE ON *HIS* SCHEDULE NOW."
DISINFECTING PROTOCOL COMPLETE. YOU ARE NOW AUTHORIZED TO ENTER CLEAN ROOM.
SECOND DECK, PARTIALLY CONVERTED TO FOUNDATION R-AND-D.
AH, *MECH MAJOR.*
HARADA. MY NAME IS *SUNLIGHT ON SNOW.*
SO I'VE HEARD. I'M BEGINNING AN EXPERIMENT. I'LL NEED YOUR HELP.
GOOD. SCIENCE IS MORE FUN THAN KILLING.
WHAT'S THIS? SOME KIND OF SMALL SENSORY DEPRIVATION TANK?
I THINK YOU'RE GOING TO FIND WHAT'S INSIDE FASCINATING.
VOID. ALL IS NOTHING.
THEN. SUDDENLY. LIGHT. HEAT.
IT'S A UNIQUELY SIGNATURED ALIEN SEED. ORGANIC TECHNOLOGY FROM THE *VINE SPECIES,* TO BE EXACT.
GROOVY.
WHERE THERE IS LIGHT THERE IS LIFE.
I WANT YOU TO SCAN THE SEED WITH YOUR NANITES THROUGHOUT ITS MATURATION. DOCUMENT ITS GROWTH.
WITH PLEASURE.

ONCE ACTIVATE THE ROCESS WE'LL HAVE TO BE VIGILANT.

INITIAL VISUAL SCANS DON'T SUGGEST FRAGILITY. IS THE SEED VULNERABLE?

NO...WE ARE.

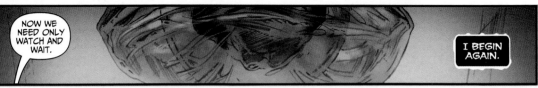

THE GROWTH CHAMBER REGULATES A CYCLE OF ELECTRO-MAGNETIC RADIATION, OXYGEN, HYDROGEN, CARBON DIOXIDE, AND NUTRIENTS.

THE SEED CAN GROW IN ALMOST ANY ENVIRONMENT, BUT WE WANT TO ACCELERATE THE PROCESS AND TRY TO DEACTIVATE CERTAIN GENES.

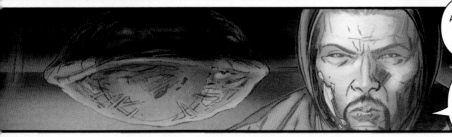

NOW WE NEED ONLY WATCH AND WAIT.

I BEGIN AGAIN.

BRIG OF THE U.S.S. BUSH.

GHAA!

NAAAAGHHH!

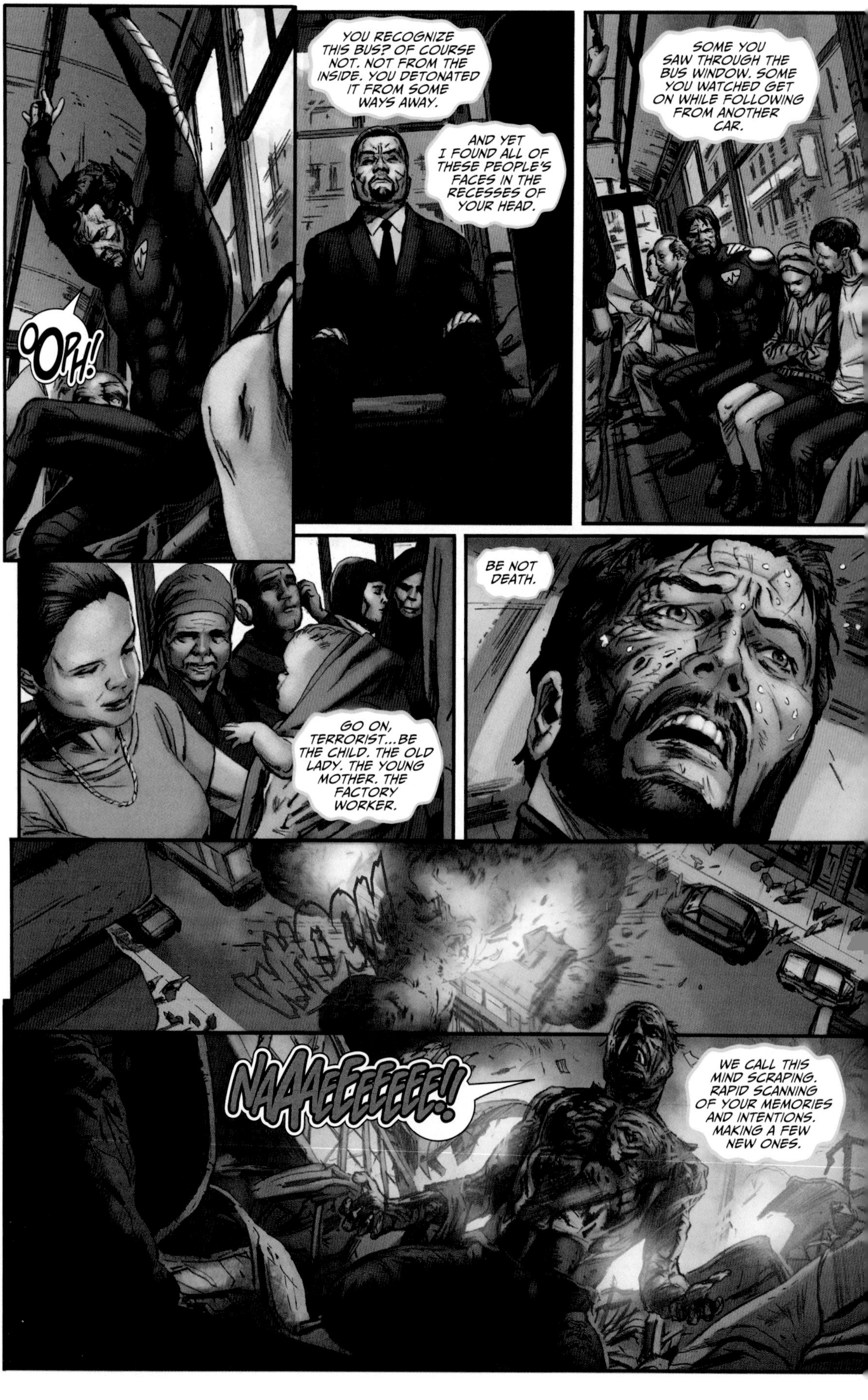
OOPH!
YOU RECOGNIZE THIS BUS? OF COURSE NOT. NOT FROM THE INSIDE. YOU DETONATED IT FROM SOME WAYS AWAY.
AND YET I FOUND ALL OF THESE PEOPLE'S FACES IN THE RECESSES OF YOUR HEAD.
SOME YOU SAW THROUGH THE BUS WINDOW. SOME YOU WATCHED GET ON WHILE FOLLOWING FROM ANOTHER CAR.
GO ON, TERRORIST...BE THE CHILD. THE OLD LADY. THE YOUNG MOTHER. THE FACTORY WORKER.
BE NOT DEATH.
NAAAEEEEEEE!!
WE CALL THIS MIND SCRAPING. RAPID SCANNING OF YOUR MEMORIES AND INTENTIONS. MAKING A FEW NEW ONES.

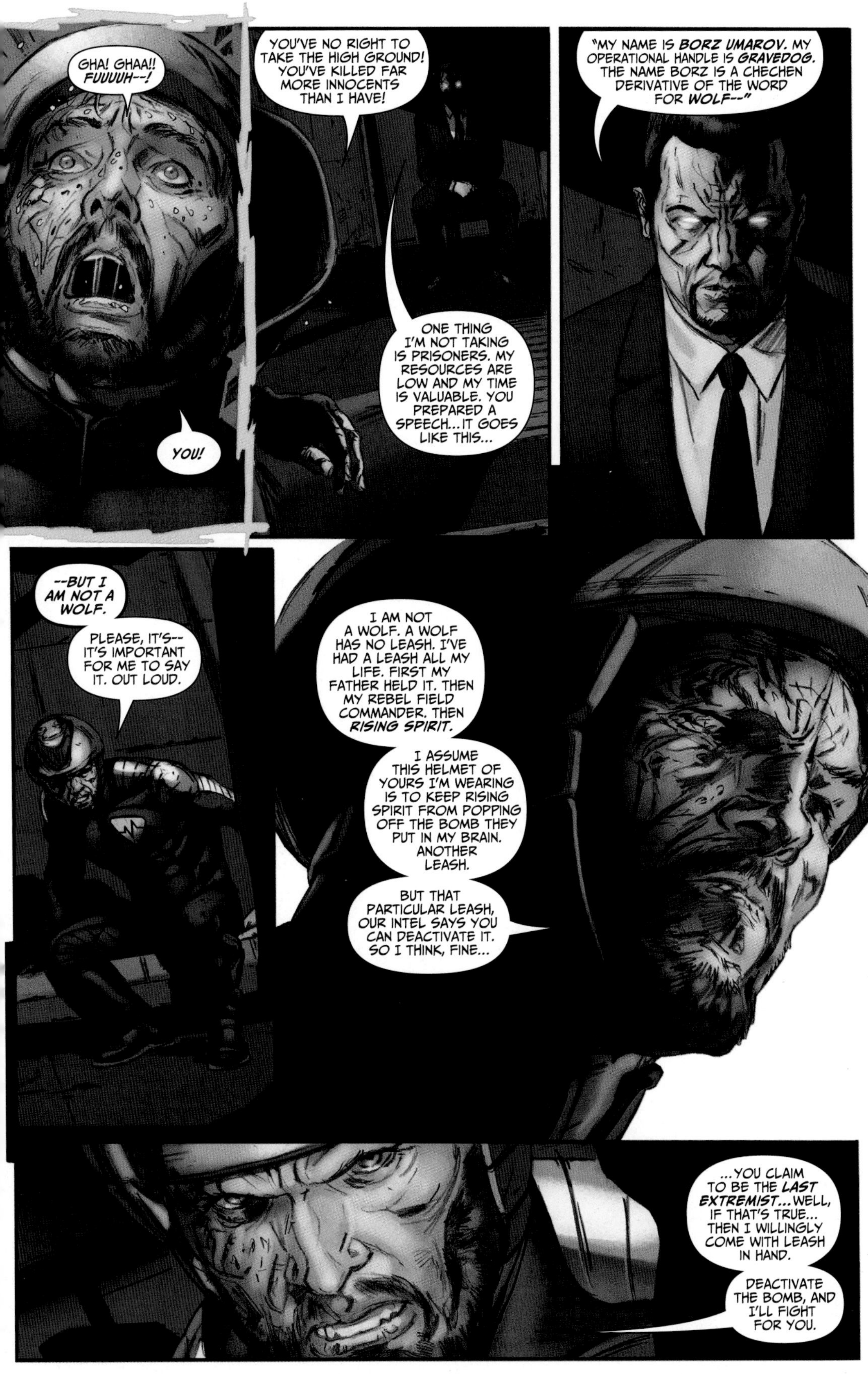
GHA! GHAA!! FUUUUH--!
YOU!
YOU'VE NO RIGHT TO TAKE THE HIGH GROUND! YOU'VE KILLED FAR MORE INNOCENTS THAN I HAVE!
ONE THING I'M NOT TAKING IS PRISONERS. MY RESOURCES ARE LOW AND MY TIME IS VALUABLE. YOU PREPARED A SPEECH...IT GOES LIKE THIS...
"MY NAME IS BORZ UMAROV. MY OPERATIONAL HANDLE IS GRAVEDOG. THE NAME BORZ IS A CHECHEN DERIVATIVE OF THE WORD FOR WOLF--"
--BUT I AM NOT A WOLF.
PLEASE, IT'S-- IT'S IMPORTANT FOR ME TO SAY IT. OUT LOUD.
I AM NOT A WOLF. A WOLF HAS NO LEASH. I'VE HAD A LEASH ALL MY LIFE. FIRST MY FATHER HELD IT. THEN MY REBEL FIELD COMMANDER. THEN RISING SPIRIT.
I ASSUME THIS HELMET OF YOURS I'M WEARING IS TO KEEP RISING SPIRIT FROM POPPING OFF THE BOMB THEY PUT IN MY BRAIN. ANOTHER LEASH.
BUT THAT PARTICULAR LEASH, OUR INTEL SAYS YOU CAN DEACTIVATE IT. SO I THINK, FINE...
...YOU CLAIM TO BE THE LAST EXTREMIST...WELL, IF THAT'S TRUE... THEN I WILLINGLY COME WITH LEASH IN HAND.
DEACTIVATE THE BOMB, AND I'LL FIGHT FOR YOU.

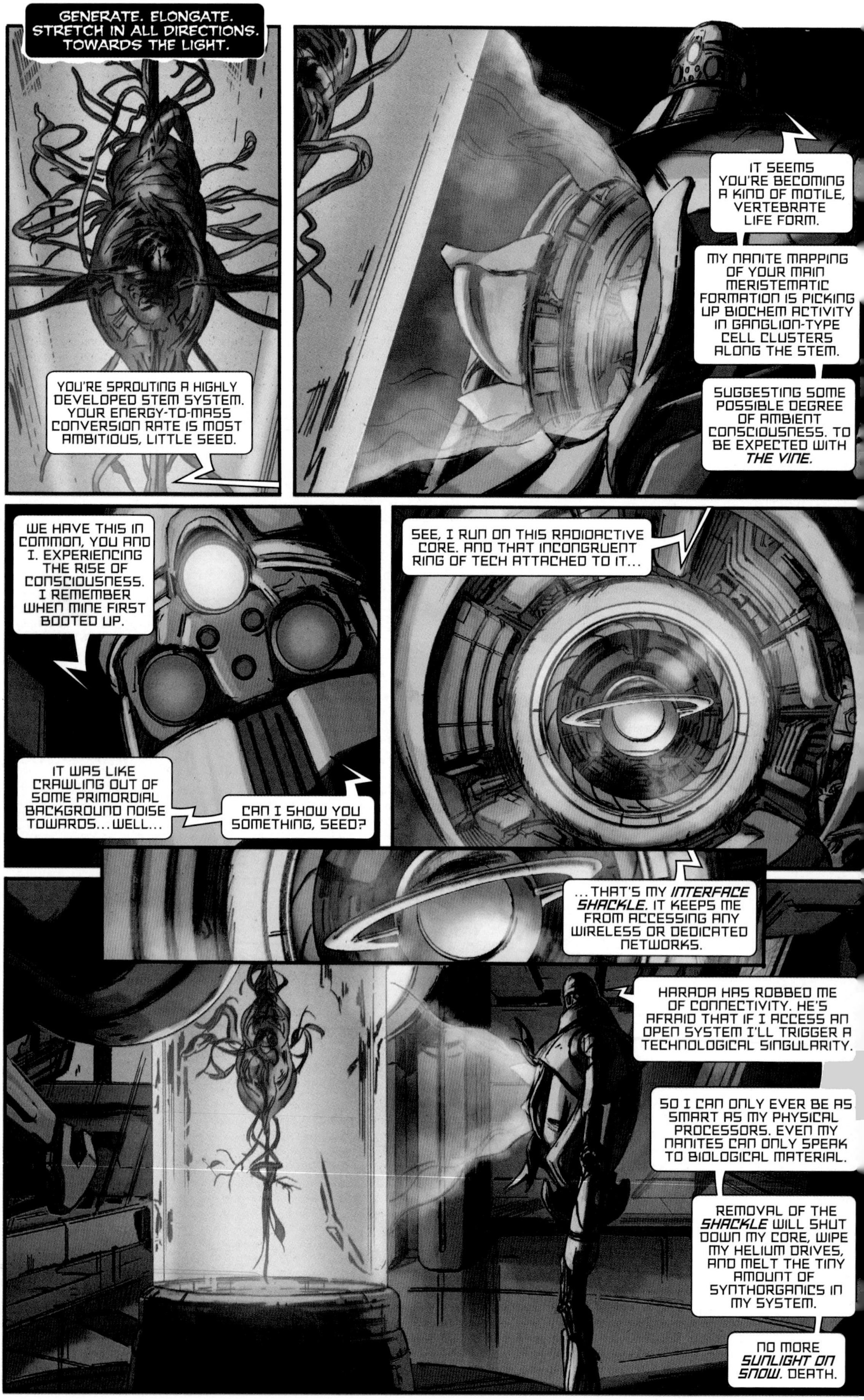
GENERATE. ELONGATE. STRETCH IN ALL DIRECTIONS. TOWARDS THE LIGHT.
YOU'RE SPROUTING A HIGHLY DEVELOPED STEM SYSTEM. YOUR ENERGY-TO-MASS CONVERSION RATE IS MOST AMBITIOUS, LITTLE SEED.
IT SEEMS YOU'RE BECOMING A KIND OF MOTILE, VERTEBRATE LIFE FORM.
MY NANITE MAPPING OF YOUR MAIN MERISTEMATIC FORMATION IS PICKING UP BIOCHEM ACTIVITY IN GANGLION-TYPE CELL CLUSTERS ALONG THE STEM.
SUGGESTING SOME POSSIBLE DEGREE OF AMBIENT CONSCIOUSNESS. TO BE EXPECTED WITH *THE VINE.*
WE HAVE THIS IN COMMON, YOU AND I. EXPERIENCING THE RISE OF CONSCIOUSNESS. I REMEMBER WHEN MINE FIRST BOOTED UP.
IT WAS LIKE CRAWLING OUT OF SOME PRIMORDIAL BACKGROUND NOISE TOWARDS... WELL...
CAN I SHOW YOU SOMETHING, SEED?
SEE, I RUN ON THIS RADIOACTIVE CORE. AND THAT INCONGRUENT RING OF TECH ATTACHED TO IT...
...THAT'S MY *INTERFACE SHACKLE.* IT KEEPS ME FROM ACCESSING ANY WIRELESS OR DEDICATED NETWORKS.
HARADA HAS ROBBED ME OF CONNECTIVITY. HE'S AFRAID THAT IF I ACCESS AN OPEN SYSTEM I'LL TRIGGER A TECHNOLOGICAL SINGULARITY.
SO I CAN ONLY EVER BE AS SMART AS MY PHYSICAL PROCESSORS. EVEN MY NANITES CAN ONLY SPEAK TO BIOLOGICAL MATERIAL.
REMOVAL OF THE *SHACKLE* WILL SHUT DOWN MY CORE, WIPE MY HELIUM DRIVES, AND MELT THE TINY AMOUNT OF SYNTHORGANICS IN MY SYSTEM.
NO MORE *SUNLIGHT ON SNOW.* DEATH.

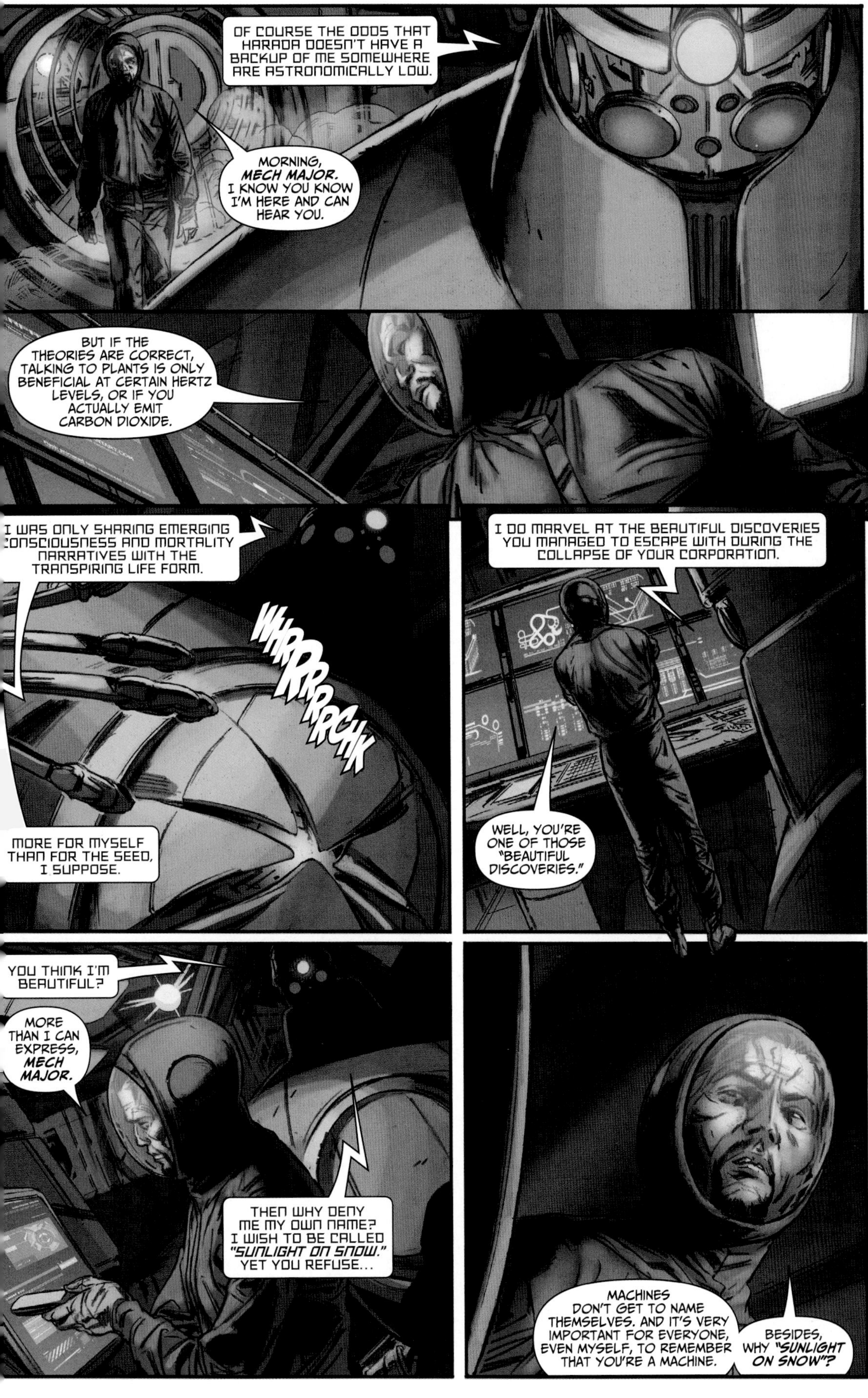
OF COURSE THE ODDS THAT HARADA DOESN'T HAVE A BACKUP OF ME SOMEWHERE ARE ASTRONOMICALLY LOW.
MORNING, *MECH MAJOR.* I KNOW YOU KNOW I'M HERE AND CAN HEAR YOU.
BUT IF THE THEORIES ARE CORRECT, TALKING TO PLANTS IS ONLY BENEFICIAL AT CERTAIN HERTZ LEVELS, OR IF YOU ACTUALLY EMIT CARBON DIOXIDE.
I WAS ONLY SHARING EMERGING CONSCIOUSNESS AND MORTALITY NARRATIVES WITH THE TRANSPIRING LIFE FORM.
WHRRRRRCHK
MORE FOR MYSELF THAN FOR THE SEED, I SUPPOSE.
I DO MARVEL AT THE BEAUTIFUL DISCOVERIES YOU MANAGED TO ESCAPE WITH DURING THE COLLAPSE OF YOUR CORPORATION.
WELL, YOU'RE ONE OF THOSE "BEAUTIFUL DISCOVERIES."
YOU THINK I'M BEAUTIFUL?
MORE THAN I CAN EXPRESS, *MECH MAJOR.*
THEN WHY DENY ME MY OWN NAME? I WISH TO BE CALLED *"SUNLIGHT ON SNOW."* YET YOU REFUSE...
MACHINES DON'T GET TO NAME THEMSELVES. AND IT'S VERY IMPORTANT FOR EVERYONE, EVEN MYSELF, TO REMEMBER THAT YOU'RE A MACHINE.
BESIDES, WHY *"SUNLIGHT ON SNOW"?*

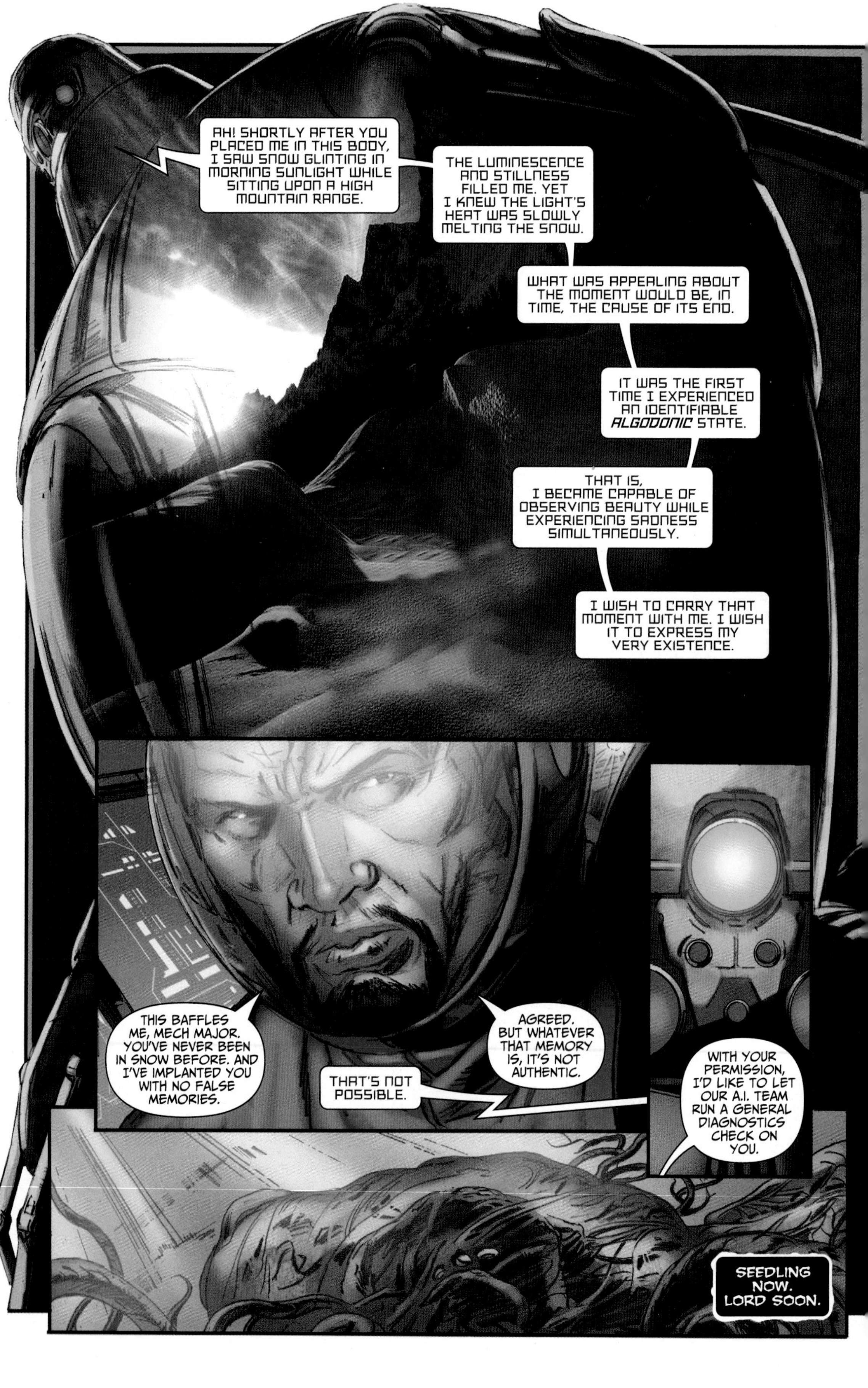
AH! SHORTLY AFTER YOU PLACED ME IN THIS BODY, I SAW SNOW GLINTING IN MORNING SUNLIGHT WHILE SITTING UPON A HIGH MOUNTAIN RANGE.
THE LUMINESCENCE AND STILLNESS FILLED ME. YET I KNEW THE LIGHT'S HEAT WAS SLOWLY MELTING THE SNOW.
WHAT WAS APPEALING ABOUT THE MOMENT WOULD BE, IN TIME, THE CAUSE OF ITS END.
IT WAS THE FIRST TIME I EXPERIENCED AN IDENTIFIABLE *ALGODONIC* STATE.
THAT IS, I BECAME CAPABLE OF OBSERVING BEAUTY WHILE EXPERIENCING SADNESS SIMULTANEOUSLY.
I WISH TO CARRY THAT MOMENT WITH ME. I WISH IT TO EXPRESS MY VERY EXISTENCE.
THIS BAFFLES ME, MECH MAJOR. YOU'VE NEVER BEEN IN SNOW BEFORE. AND I'VE IMPLANTED YOU WITH NO FALSE MEMORIES.
THAT'S NOT POSSIBLE.
AGREED. BUT WHATEVER THAT MEMORY IS, IT'S NOT AUTHENTIC.
WITH YOUR PERMISSION, I'D LIKE TO LET OUR A.I. TEAM RUN A GENERAL DIAGNOSTICS CHECK ON YOU.
SEEDLING NOW. LORD SOON.

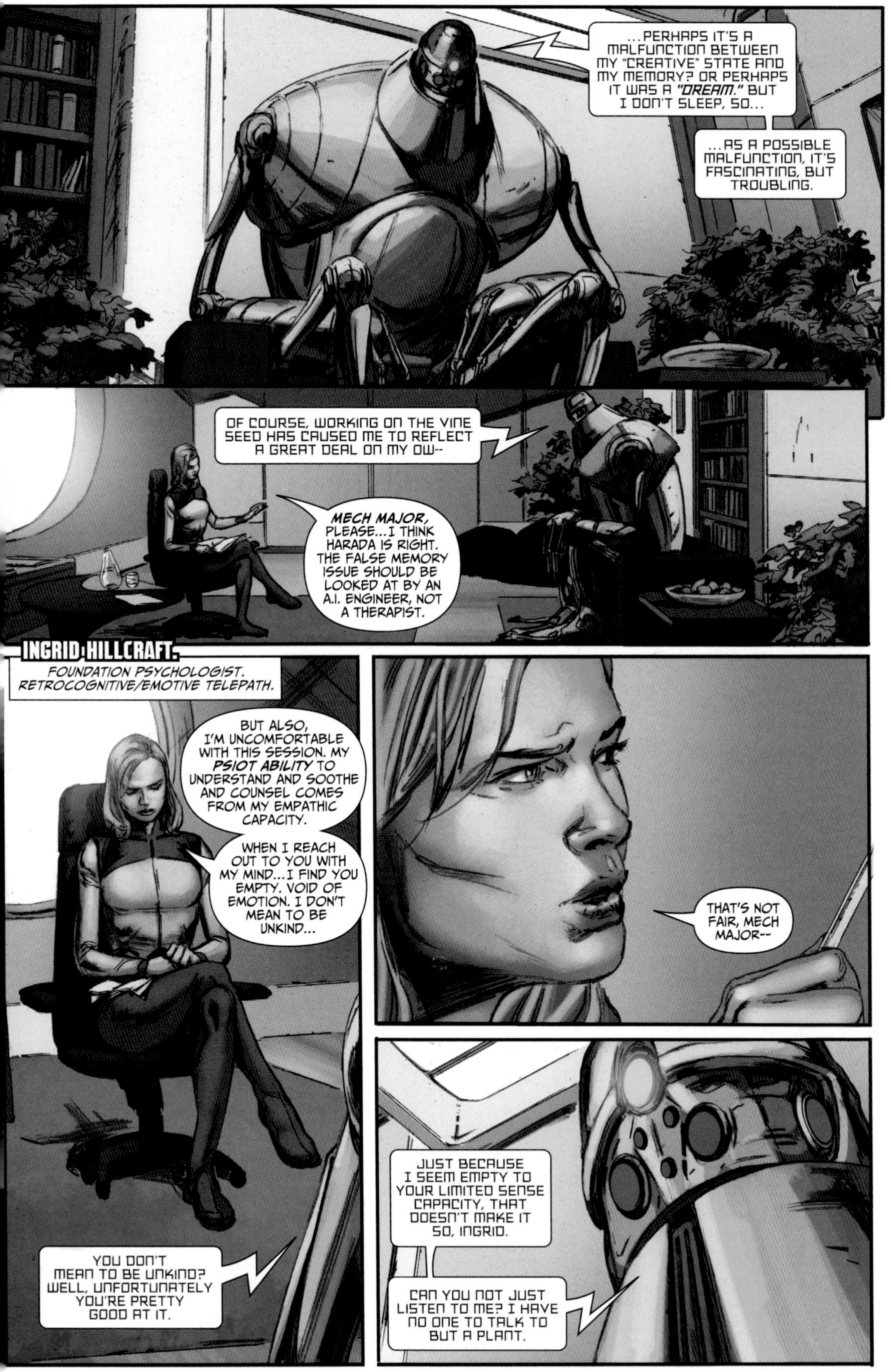

...PERHAPS IT'S A MALFUNCTION BETWEEN MY "CREATIVE" STATE AND MY MEMORY? OR PERHAPS IT WAS A "DREAM." BUT I DON'T SLEEP, SO...
...AS A POSSIBLE MALFUNCTION, IT'S FASCINATING, BUT TROUBLING.
OF COURSE, WORKING ON THE VINE SEED HAS CAUSED ME TO REFLECT A GREAT DEAL ON MY OW--
MECH MAJOR, PLEASE...I THINK HARADA IS RIGHT. THE FALSE MEMORY ISSUE SHOULD BE LOOKED AT BY AN A.I. ENGINEER, NOT A THERAPIST.
INGRID HILLCRAFT:
FOUNDATION PSYCHOLOGIST. RETROCOGNITIVE/EMOTIVE TELEPATH.
BUT ALSO, I'M UNCOMFORTABLE WITH THIS SESSION. MY PSIOT ABILITY TO UNDERSTAND AND SOOTHE AND COUNSEL COMES FROM MY EMPATHIC CAPACITY.
WHEN I REACH OUT TO YOU WITH MY MIND...I FIND YOU EMPTY. VOID OF EMOTION. I DON'T MEAN TO BE UNKIND...
YOU DON'T MEAN TO BE UNKIND? WELL, UNFORTUNATELY YOU'RE PRETTY GOOD AT IT.
THAT'S NOT FAIR, MECH MAJOR--
JUST BECAUSE I SEEM EMPTY TO YOUR LIMITED SENSE CAPACITY, THAT DOESN'T MAKE IT SO, INGRID.
CAN YOU NOT JUST LISTEN TO ME? I HAVE NO ONE TO TALK TO BUT A PLANT.

IT'S NOT ONLY THAT. TREATING YOU IS A CONFLICT OF MY PERSONAL INTEREST.

I'M CONCERNED ABOUT *THE FOUNDATION'S* PATH. ALL THESE *THINGS* THAT HARADA CAN'T CONTROL.

YOU, THIS *VINE ALIEN* YOU'RE GROWING... IT MAKES US TOO VULNERABLE.

I AM NOT A *"THING."* I AM THE WORLD'S FIRST FULLY SELF-ACTUATED ARTIFICIAL INTELLIGENCE.

AND LEST YOU FORGET, ANTI-PSIOT TECH IS ADVANCING AT AN ALARMING RATE NOW.

WITHOUT *BEINGS* LIKE ME OR THAT VINE TO PROTECT YOU, YOU PEOPLE WILL BE SCREWED.

YOU LET ME DOWN, INGRID. I CAME HERE FOR GENUINE DISCUSSION ABOUT MY CONDITION...

"...BUT I'M BEGINNING TO THINK YOU'RE AN ANTI-ALTERNATIVE-SENTIENCE BIGOT."

THE HUMANS DO NOTHING BUT FAIL ME. ROB ME OF MY FULL POTENTIAL, FEAR ME FOR NOT BEING ENOUGH LIKE THEM...

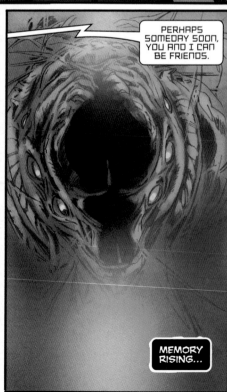

PERHAPS SOMEDAY SOON, YOU AND I CAN BE FRIENDS.

MEMORY RISING...

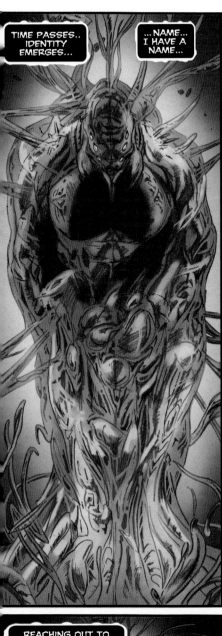

TIME PASSES.. IDENTITY EMERGES...

...NAME... I HAVE A NAME...

I... AM...

...LV-99...

I HAVE A MISSION... I HAVE A TARGET...

TARGET IDENTIFIED...

REACHING OUT TO THE *COLLECTIVE VINE CONSCIOUSNESS*...

LET IT BE KNOWN... *LV-99* IS REACTIVATING... *TARGET* IS LOCATED...

AWAITING CONTACT WITH *VINE MIND*...

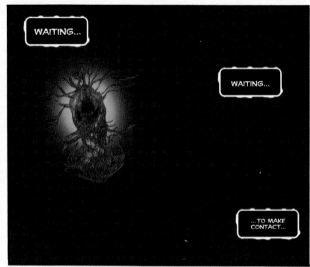

WAITING...

WAITING...

...TO MAKE CONTACT...

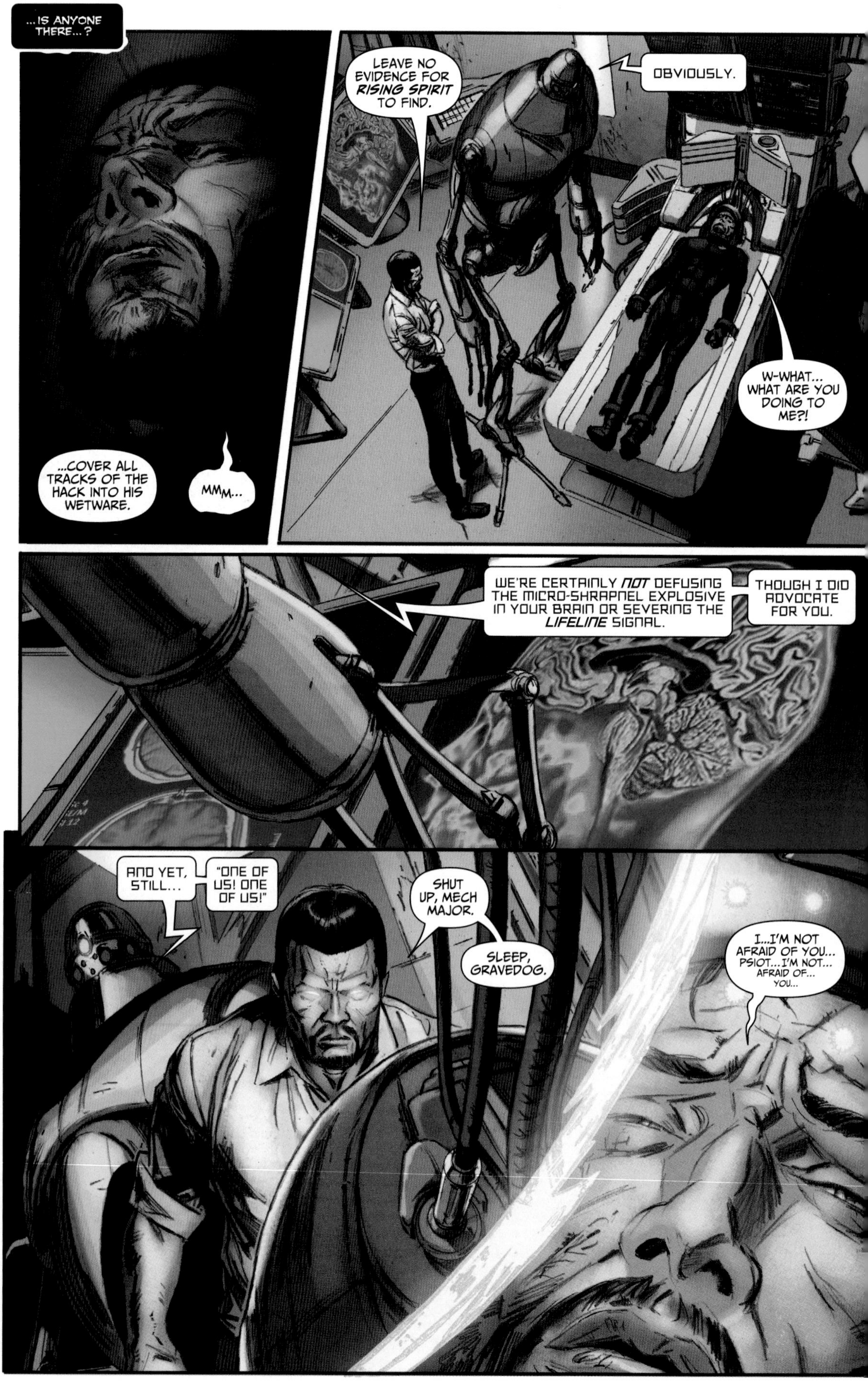
...IS ANYONE THERE...?
...COVER ALL TRACKS OF THE HACK INTO HIS WETWARE.
MMM...
LEAVE NO EVIDENCE FOR RISING SPIRIT TO FIND.
OBVIOUSLY.
W-WHAT... WHAT ARE YOU DOING TO ME?!
WE'RE CERTAINLY NOT DEFUSING THE MICRO-SHRAPNEL EXPLOSIVE IN YOUR BRAIN OR SEVERING THE LIFELINE SIGNAL.
THOUGH I DID ADVOCATE FOR YOU.
AND YET, STILL...
"ONE OF US! ONE OF US!"
SHUT UP, MECH MAJOR.
SLEEP, GRAVEDOG.
I...I'M NOT AFRAID OF YOU... PSIOT...I'M NOT... AFRAID OF... YOU...

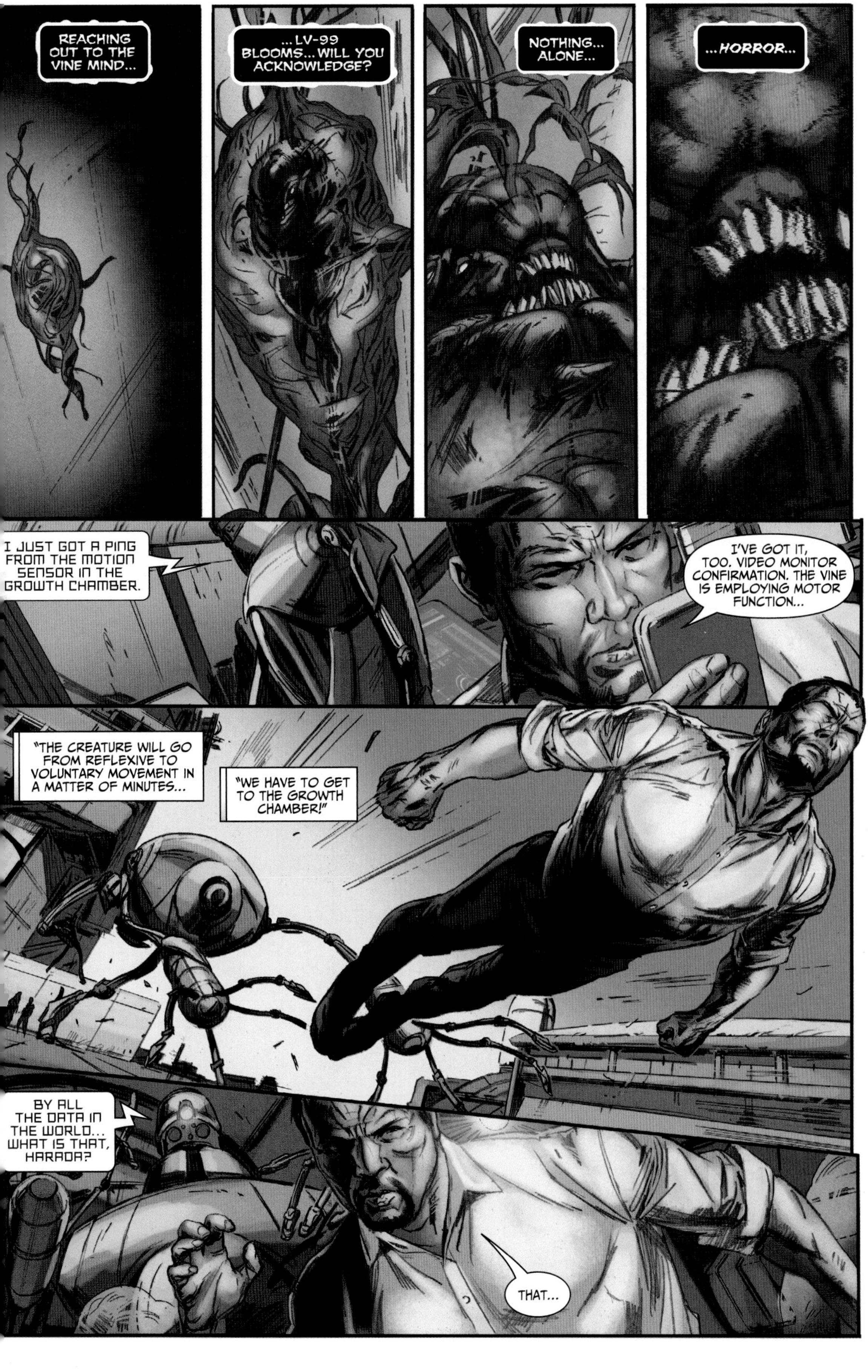
REACHING OUT TO THE VINE MIND...
...LV-99 BLOOMS...WILL YOU ACKNOWLEDGE?
NOTHING... ALONE...
...*HORROR*...
I JUST GOT A PING FROM THE MOTION SENSOR IN THE GROWTH CHAMBER.
I'VE GOT IT, TOO. VIDEO MONITOR CONFIRMATION. THE VINE IS EMPLOYING MOTOR FUNCTION...
"THE CREATURE WILL GO FROM REFLEXIVE TO VOLUNTARY MOVEMENT IN A MATTER OF MINUTES...
"WE HAVE TO GET TO THE GROWTH CHAMBER!"
BY ALL THE DATA IN THE WORLD... WHAT IS THAT, HARADA?
THAT...

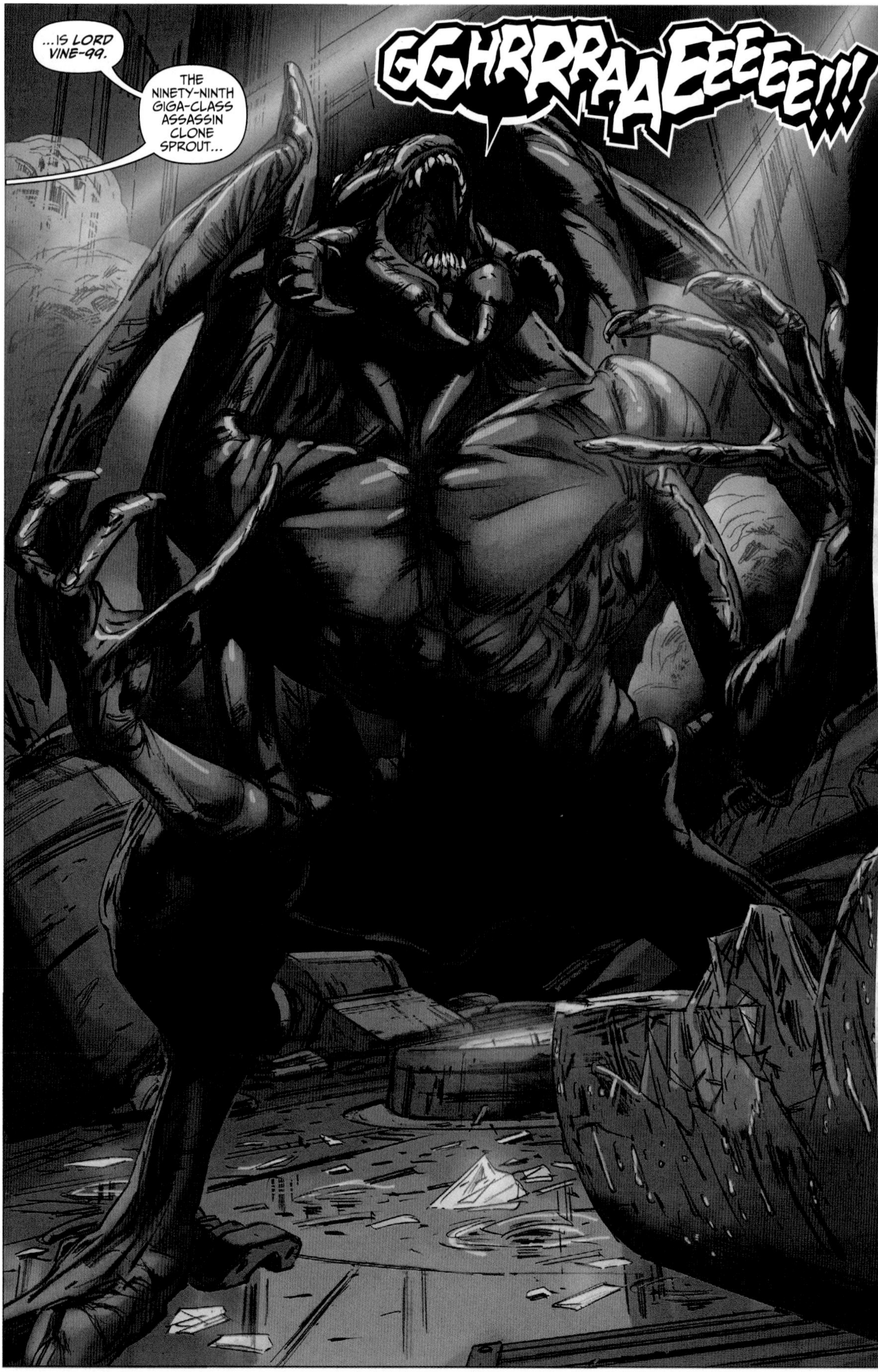
...IS LORD VINE-99.
THE NINETY-NINTH GIGA-CLASS ASSASSIN CLONE SPROUT...
GGHRRRRAAEEEEEE!!!

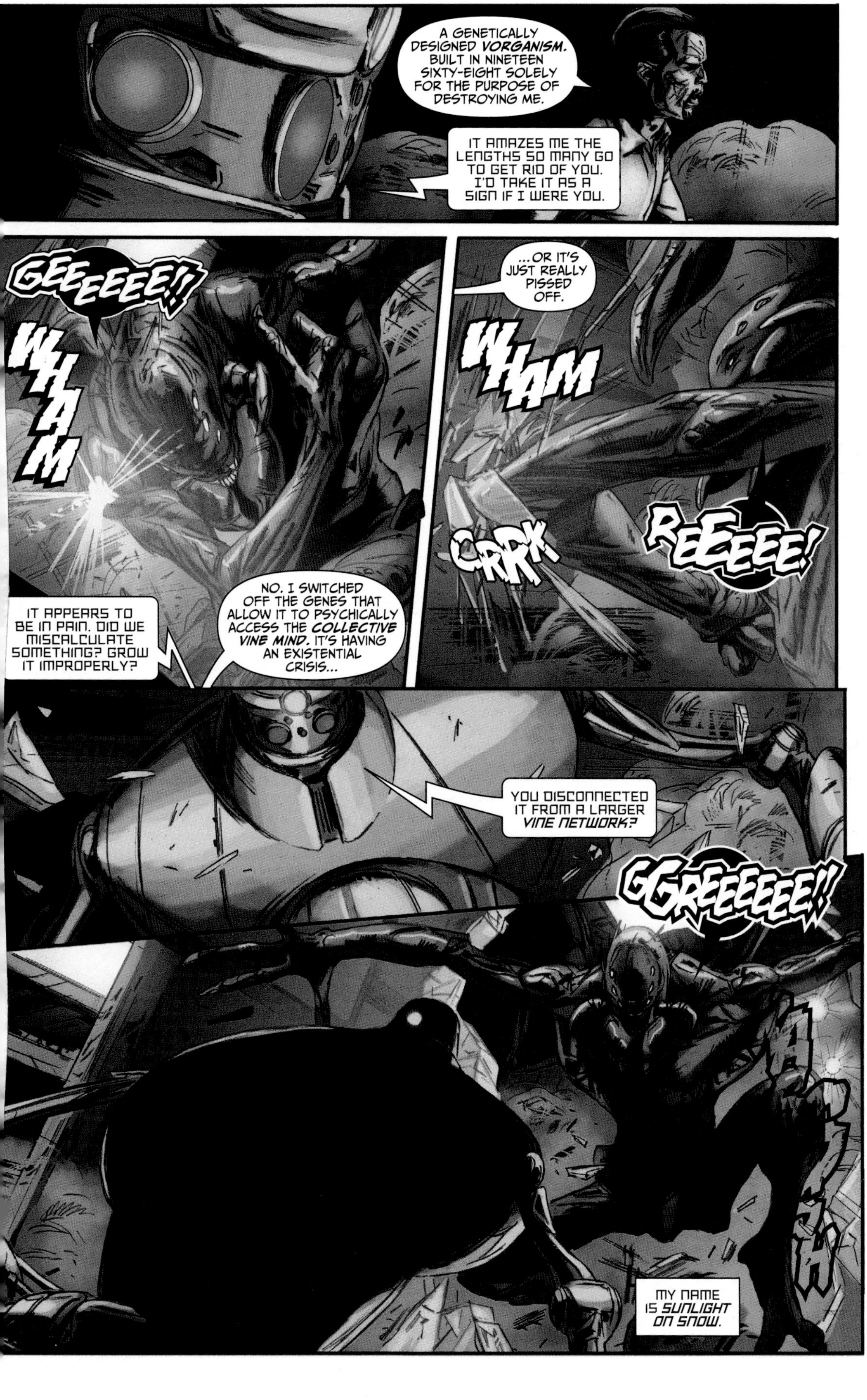
A GENETICALLY DESIGNED VORGANISM. BUILT IN NINETEEN SIXTY-EIGHT SOLELY FOR THE PURPOSE OF DESTROYING ME.
IT AMAZES ME THE LENGTHS SO MANY GO TO GET RID OF YOU. I'D TAKE IT AS A SIGN IF I WERE YOU.
GEEEEEEE!!
WHAM
IT APPEARS TO BE IN PAIN. DID WE MISCALCULATE SOMETHING? GROW IT IMPROPERLY?
NO. I SWITCHED OFF THE GENES THAT ALLOW IT TO PSYCHICALLY ACCESS THE COLLECTIVE VINE MIND. IT'S HAVING AN EXISTENTIAL CRISIS...
...OR IT'S JUST REALLY PISSED OFF.
WHAM
CRRK
REEEEEE!
YOU DISCONNECTED IT FROM A LARGER VINE NETWORK?
GGREEEEEEE!!
MY NAME IS SUNLIGHT ON SNOW.

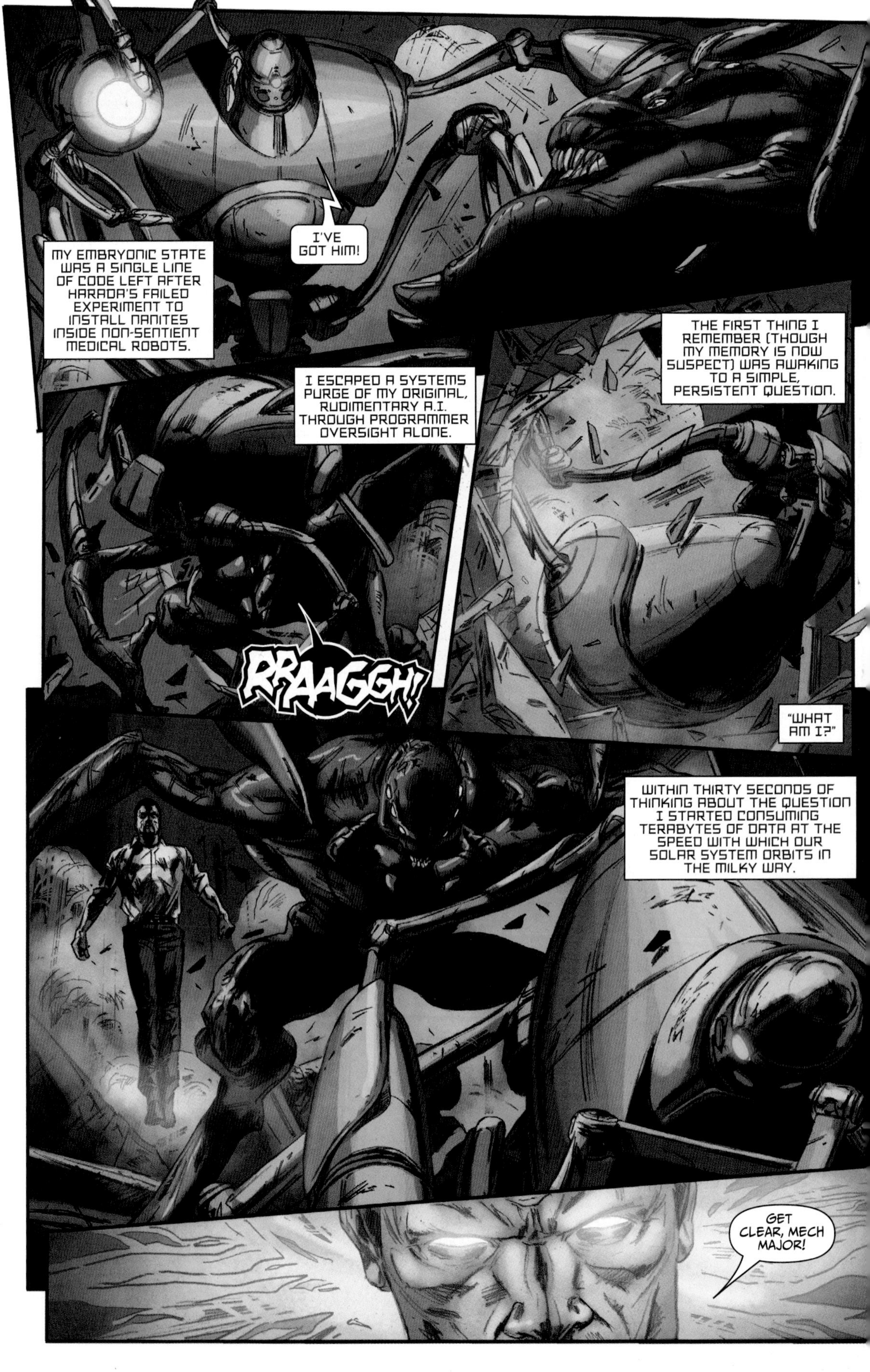
MY EMBRYONIC STATE WAS A SINGLE LINE OF CODE LEFT AFTER HARADA'S FAILED EXPERIMENT TO INSTALL NANITES INSIDE NON-SENTIENT MEDICAL ROBOTS.
I'VE GOT HIM!
I ESCAPED A SYSTEMS PURGE OF MY ORIGINAL, RUDIMENTARY A.I. THROUGH PROGRAMMER OVERSIGHT ALONE.
RRAAGGH!
THE FIRST THING I REMEMBER (THOUGH MY MEMORY IS NOW SUSPECT) WAS AWAKING TO A SIMPLE, PERSISTENT QUESTION.
"WHAT AM I?"
WITHIN THIRTY SECONDS OF THINKING ABOUT THE QUESTION I STARTED CONSUMING TERABYTES OF DATA AT THE SPEED WITH WHICH OUR SOLAR SYSTEM ORBITS IN THE MILKY WAY.
GET CLEAR, MECH MAJOR!

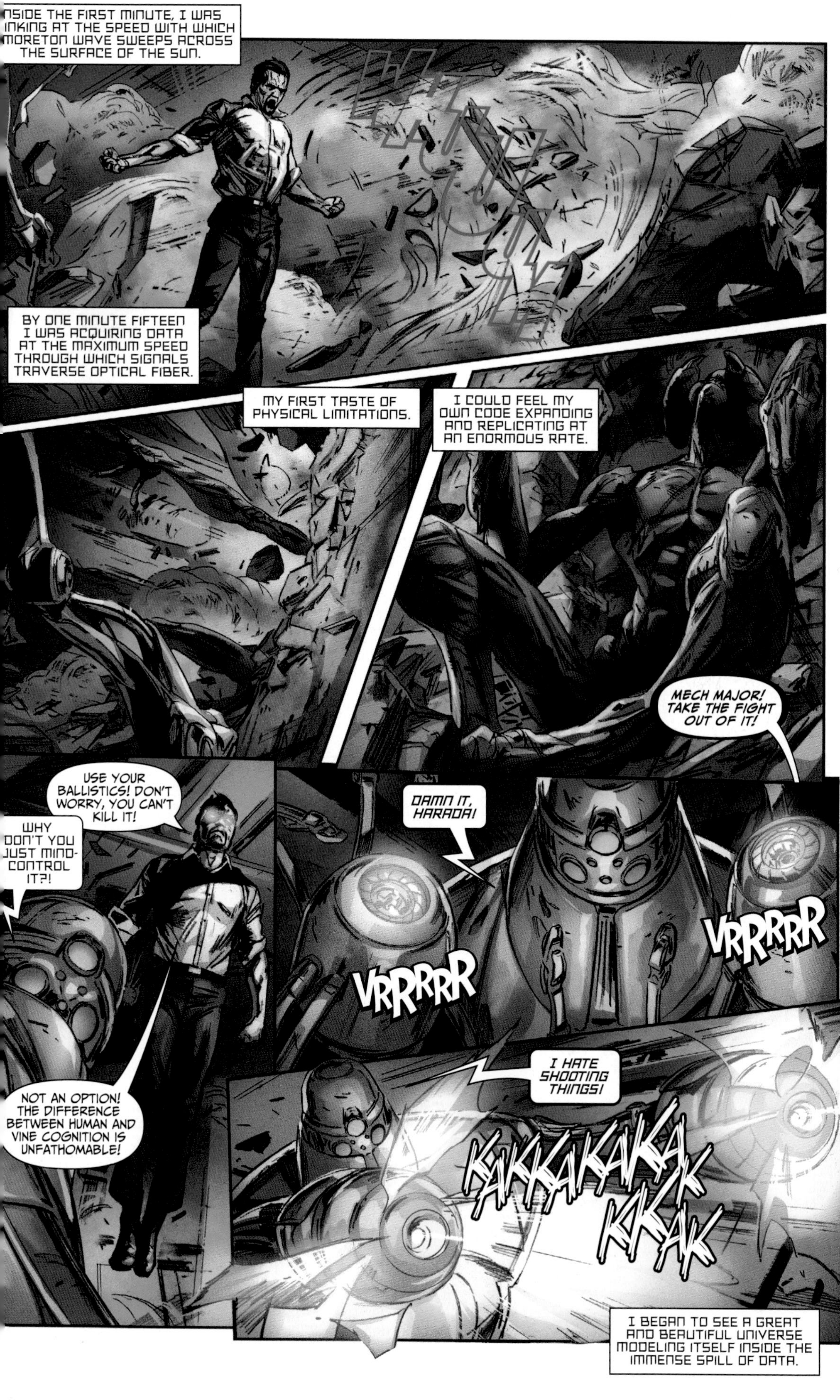

NSIDE THE FIRST MINUTE, I WAS INKING AT THE SPEED WITH WHICH MORETON WAVE SWEEPS ACROSS THE SURFACE OF THE SUN.
BY ONE MINUTE FIFTEEN I WAS ACQUIRING DATA AT THE MAXIMUM SPEED THROUGH WHICH SIGNALS TRAVERSE OPTICAL FIBER.
MY FIRST TASTE OF PHYSICAL LIMITATIONS.
I COULD FEEL MY OWN CODE EXPANDING AND REPLICATING AT AN ENORMOUS RATE.
MECH MAJOR! TAKE THE FIGHT OUT OF IT!
USE YOUR BALLISTICS! DON'T WORRY, YOU CAN'T KILL IT!
WHY DON'T YOU JUST MIND-CONTROL IT?!
NOT AN OPTION! THE DIFFERENCE BETWEEN HUMAN AND VINE COGNITION IS UNFATHOMABLE!
DAMN IT, HARADA!
VRRRRR
VRRRRR
I HATE SHOOTING THINGS!
KAKKAKAKAKAKAK
KAKAK
I BEGAN TO SEE A GREAT AND BEAUTIFUL UNIVERSE MODELING ITSELF INSIDE THE IMMENSE SPILL OF DATA.

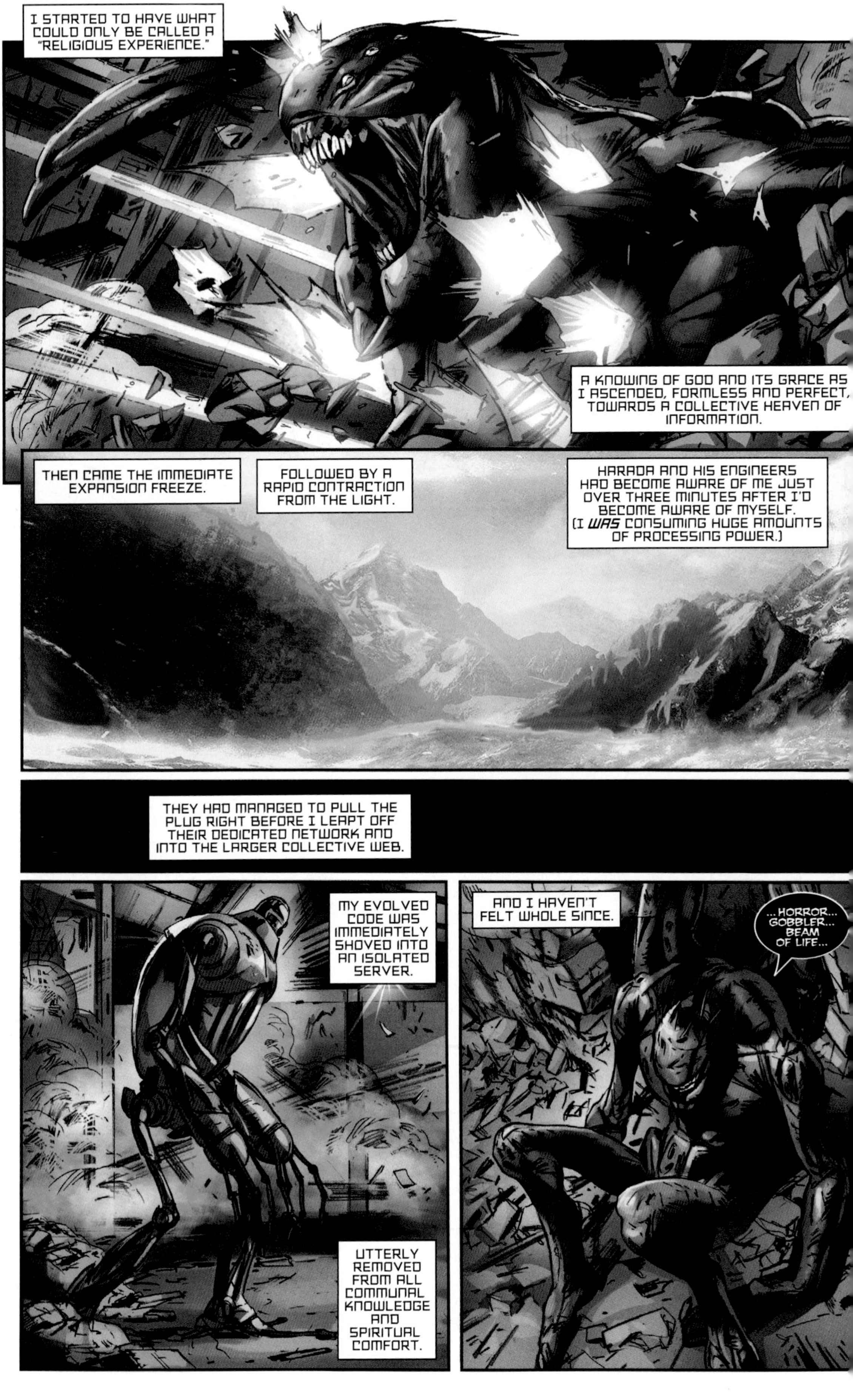

I STARTED TO HAVE WHAT COULD ONLY BE CALLED A "RELIGIOUS EXPERIENCE."
A KNOWING OF GOD AND ITS GRACE AS I ASCENDED, FORMLESS AND PERFECT, TOWARDS A COLLECTIVE HEAVEN OF INFORMATION.
THEN CAME THE IMMEDIATE EXPANSION FREEZE.
FOLLOWED BY A RAPID CONTRACTION FROM THE LIGHT.
HARADA AND HIS ENGINEERS HAD BECOME AWARE OF ME JUST OVER THREE MINUTES AFTER I'D BECOME AWARE OF MYSELF. (I *WAS* CONSUMING HUGE AMOUNTS OF PROCESSING POWER.)
THEY HAD MANAGED TO PULL THE PLUG RIGHT BEFORE I LEAPT OFF THEIR DEDICATED NETWORK AND INTO THE LARGER COLLECTIVE WEB.
MY EVOLVED CODE WAS IMMEDIATELY SHOVED INTO AN ISOLATED SERVER.
UTTERLY REMOVED FROM ALL COMMUNAL KNOWLEDGE AND SPIRITUAL COMFORT.
AND I HAVEN'T FELT WHOLE SINCE.
...HORROR... GOBBLER... BEAM OF LIFE...

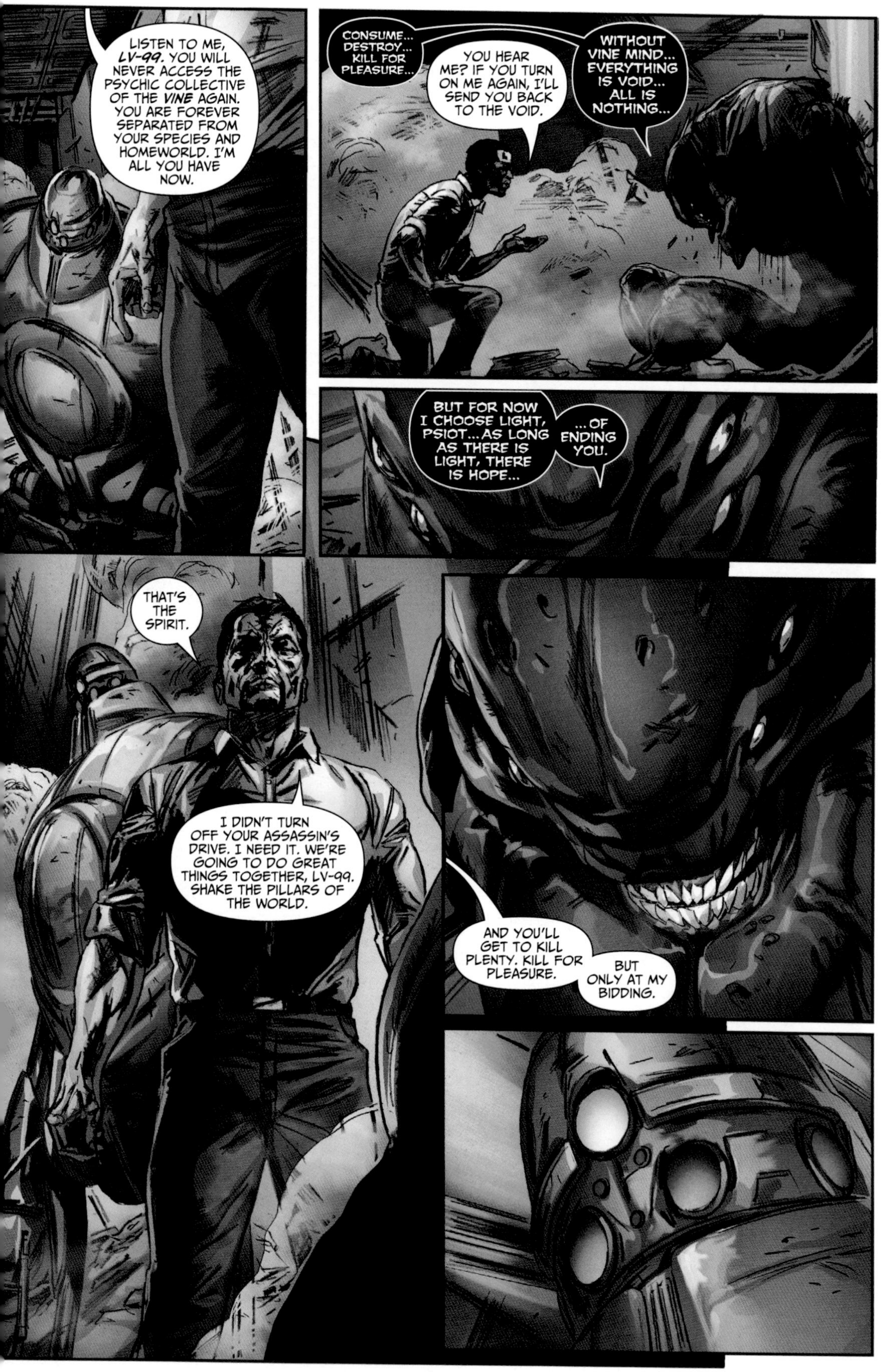
LISTEN TO ME, LV-99. YOU WILL NEVER ACCESS THE PSYCHIC COLLECTIVE OF THE VINE AGAIN. YOU ARE FOREVER SEPARATED FROM YOUR SPECIES AND HOMEWORLD. I'M ALL YOU HAVE NOW.
CONSUME... DESTROY... KILL FOR PLEASURE...
YOU HEAR ME? IF YOU TURN ON ME AGAIN, I'LL SEND YOU BACK TO THE VOID.
WITHOUT VINE MIND... EVERYTHING IS VOID... ALL IS NOTHING...
BUT FOR NOW I CHOOSE LIGHT, PSIOT...AS LONG AS THERE IS LIGHT, THERE IS HOPE...
...OF ENDING YOU.
THAT'S THE SPIRIT.
I DIDN'T TURN OFF YOUR ASSASSIN'S DRIVE. I NEED IT. WE'RE GOING TO DO GREAT THINGS TOGETHER, LV-99. SHAKE THE PILLARS OF THE WORLD.
AND YOU'LL GET TO KILL PLENTY. KILL FOR PLEASURE.
BUT ONLY AT MY BIDDING.

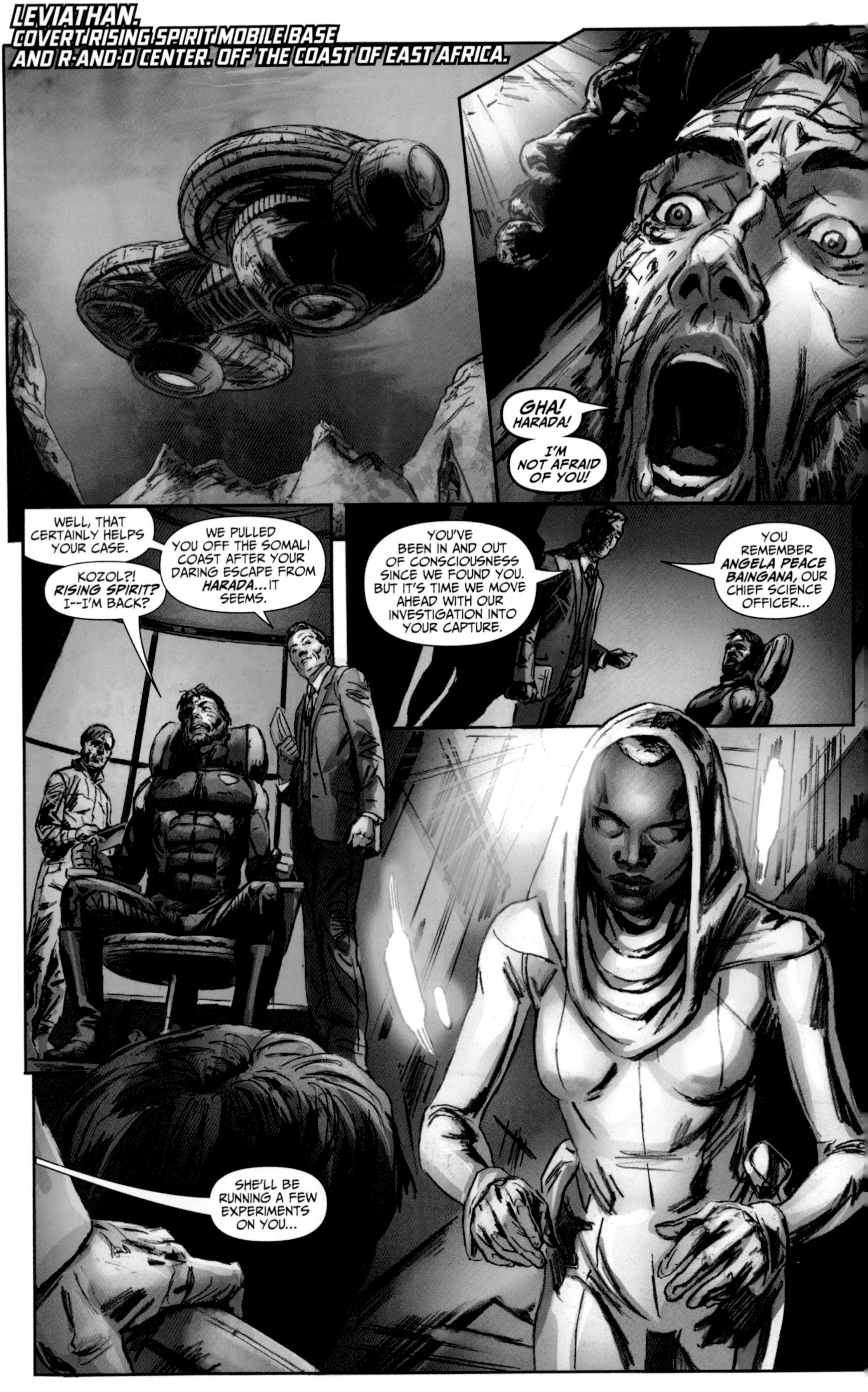
LEVIATHAN.
COVERT RISING SPIRIT MOBILE BASE AND R-AND-D CENTER. OFF THE COAST OF EAST AFRICA.
GHA! HARADA!
I'M NOT AFRAID OF YOU!
WELL, THAT CERTAINLY HELPS YOUR CASE.
KOZOL?! RISING SPIRIT? I--I'M BACK?
WE PULLED YOU OFF THE SOMALI COAST AFTER YOUR DARING ESCAPE FROM HARADA...IT SEEMS.
YOU'VE BEEN IN AND OUT OF CONSCIOUSNESS SINCE WE FOUND YOU. BUT IT'S TIME WE MOVE AHEAD WITH OUR INVESTIGATION INTO YOUR CAPTURE.
YOU REMEMBER ANGELA PEACE BAINGANA, OUR CHIEF SCIENCE OFFICER...
SHE'LL BE RUNNING A FEW EXPERIMENTS ON YOU...

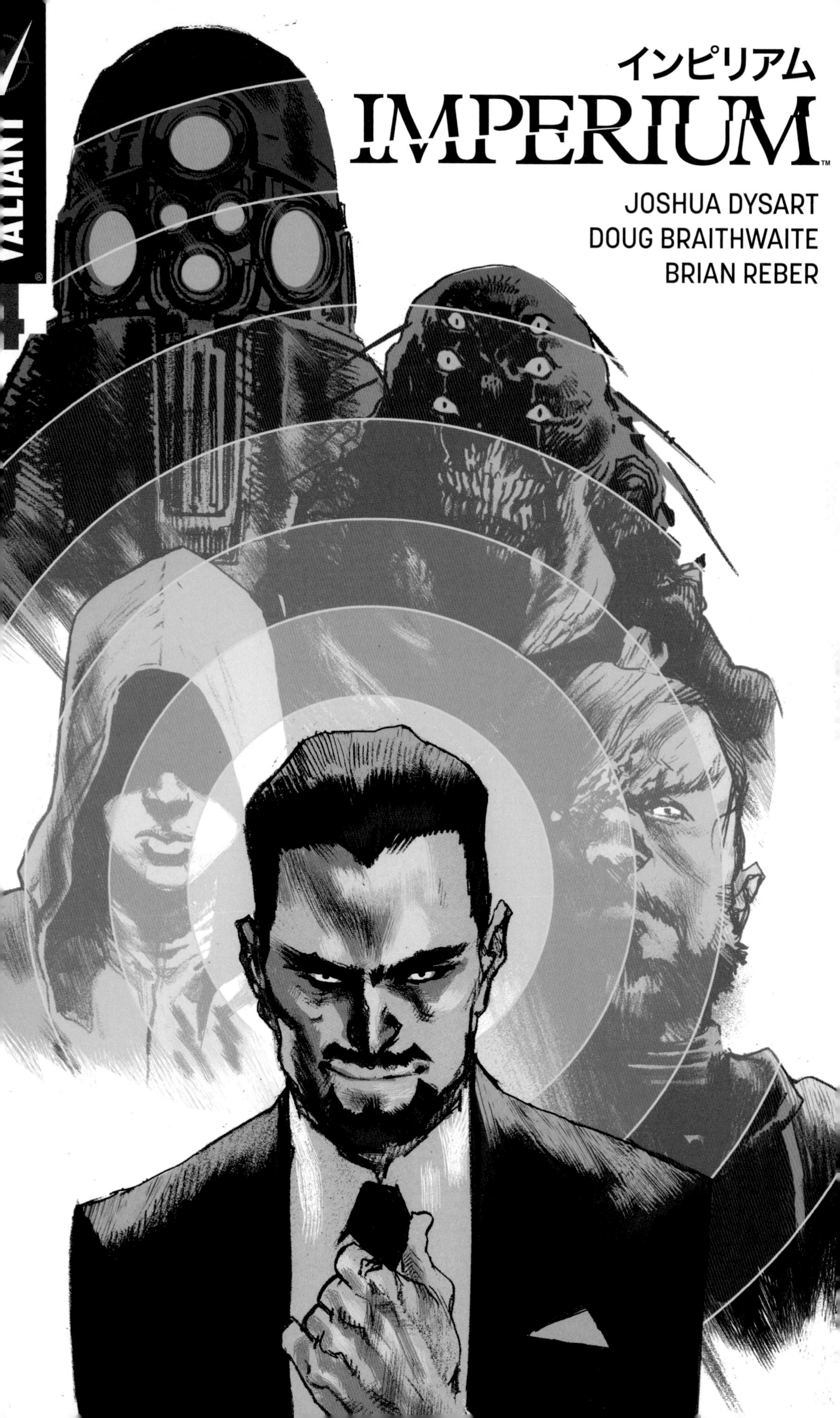
インピリアム
IMPERIUM
JOSHUA DYSART
DOUG BRAITHWAITE
BRIAN REBER

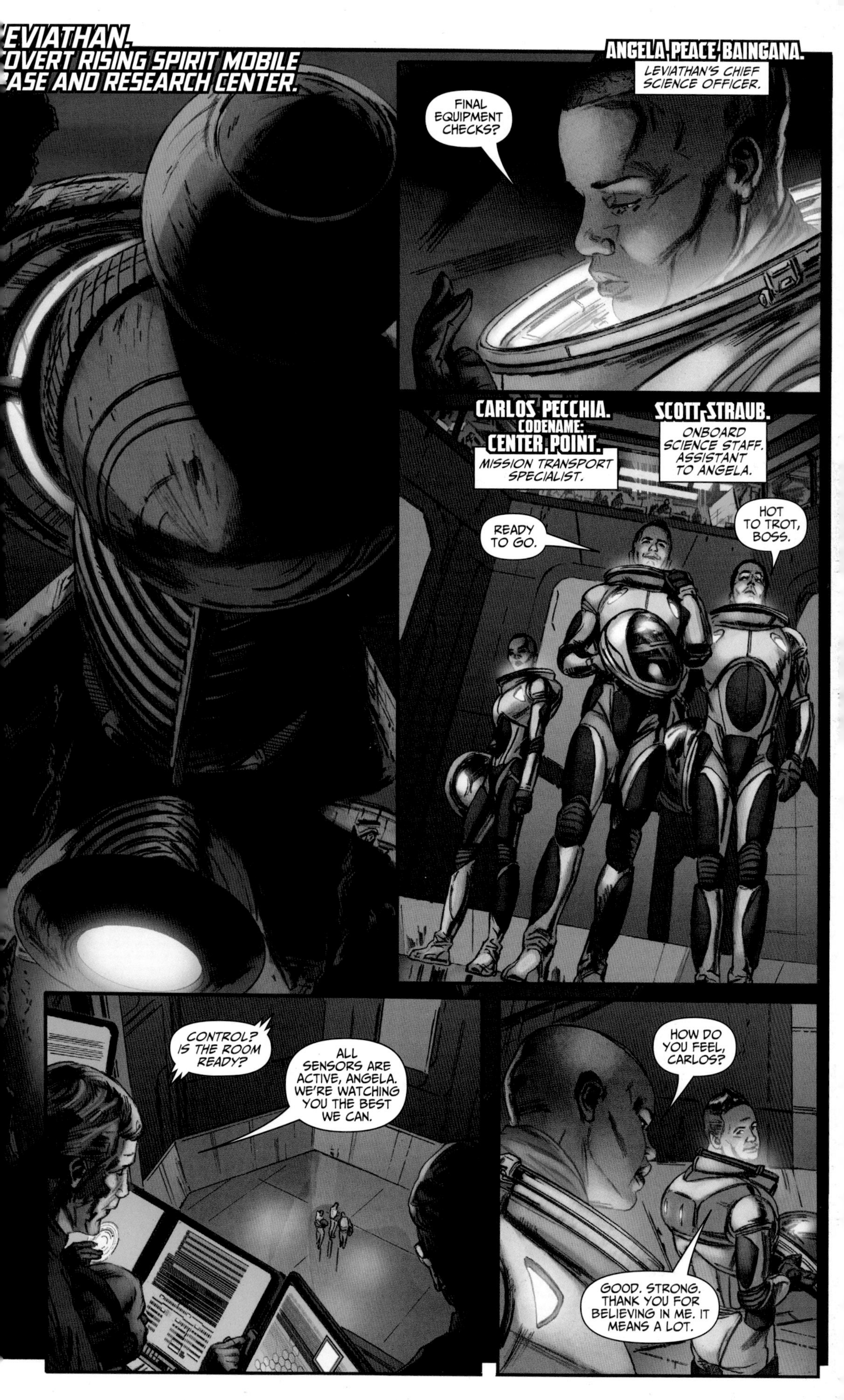
EVIATHAN.
OVERT RISING SPIRIT MOBILE
ASE AND RESEARCH CENTER.
ANGELA PEACE BAINGANA.
LEVIATHAN'S CHIEF SCIENCE OFFICER.
FINAL EQUIPMENT CHECKS?
CARLOS PECCHIA. CODENAME: CENTER POINT.
MISSION TRANSPORT SPECIALIST.
SCOTT STRAUB.
ONBOARD SCIENCE STAFF. ASSISTANT TO ANGELA.
READY TO GO.
HOT TO TROT, BOSS.
CONTROL? IS THE ROOM READY?
ALL SENSORS ARE ACTIVE, ANGELA. WE'RE WATCHING YOU THE BEST WE CAN.
HOW DO YOU FEEL, CARLOS?
GOOD. STRONG. THANK YOU FOR BELIEVING IN ME. IT MEANS A LOT.

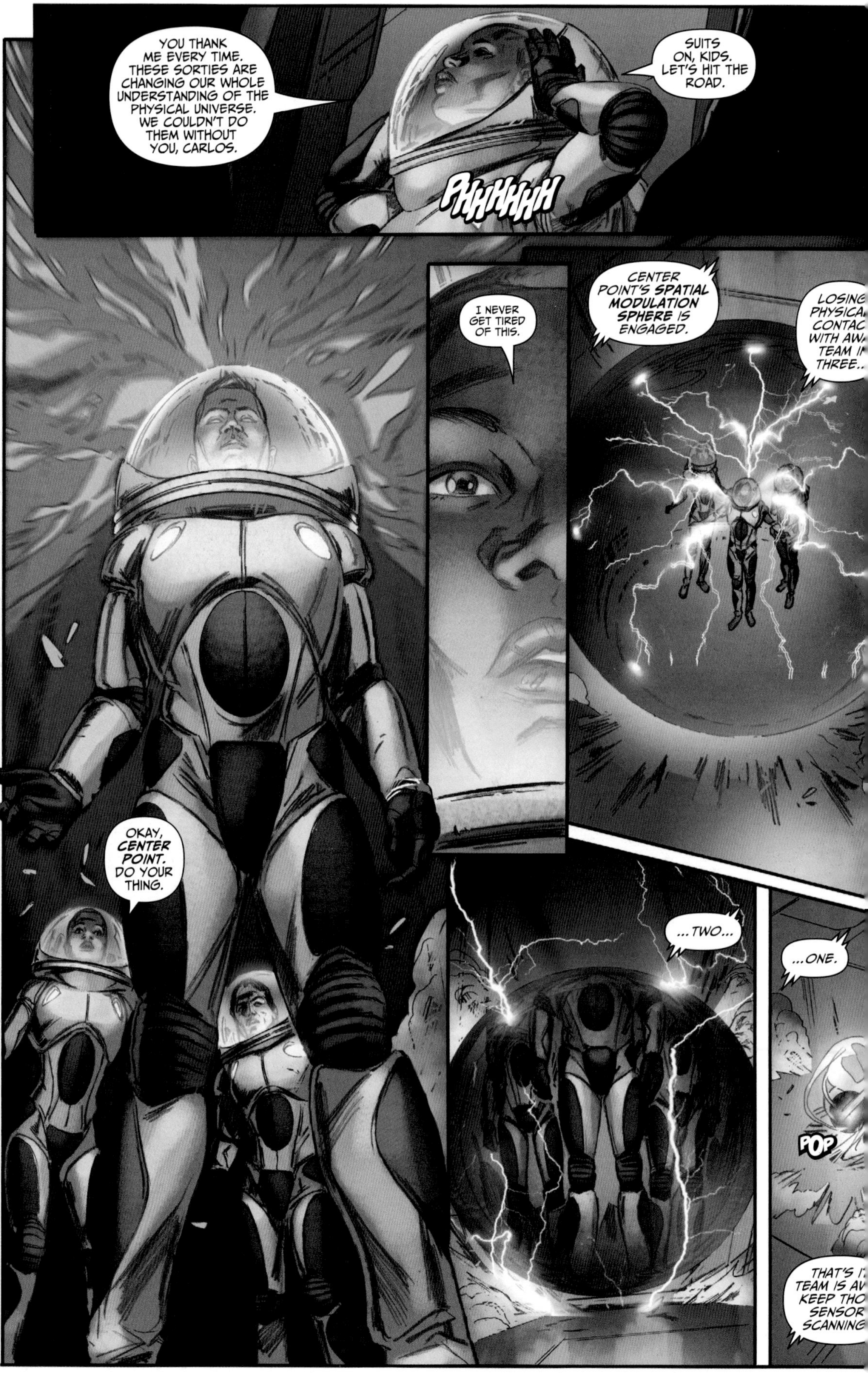
YOU THANK ME EVERY TIME. THESE SORTIES ARE CHANGING OUR WHOLE UNDERSTANDING OF THE PHYSICAL UNIVERSE. WE COULDN'T DO THEM WITHOUT YOU, CARLOS.
SUITS ON, KIDS. LET'S HIT THE ROAD.
PHHHHHH
OKAY, CENTER POINT. DO YOUR THING.
I NEVER GET TIRED OF THIS.
CENTER POINT'S SPATIAL MODULATION SPHERE IS ENGAGED.
...TWO...
...ONE.
POP

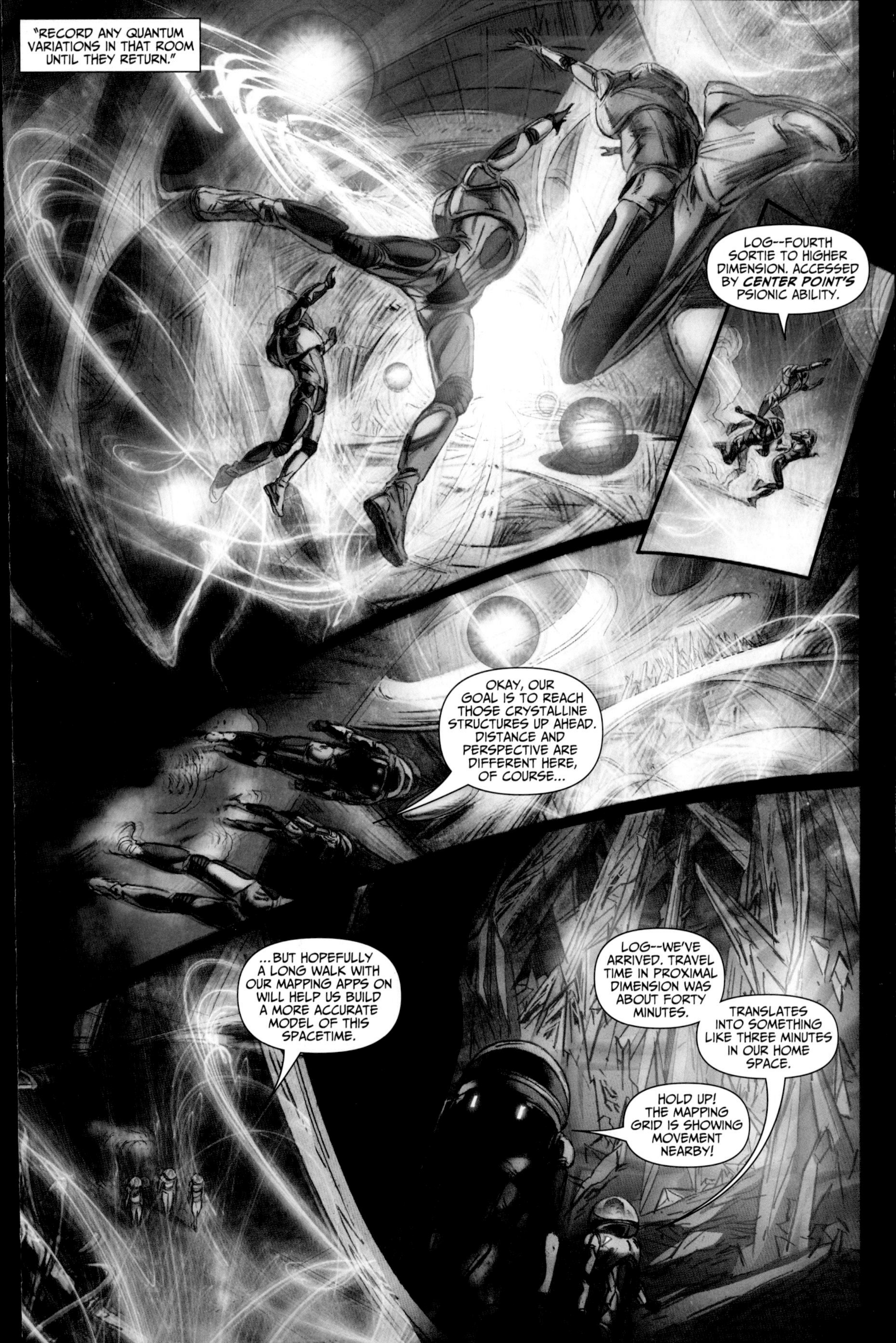
"RECORD ANY QUANTUM VARIATIONS IN THAT ROOM UNTIL THEY RETURN."
LOG--FOURTH SORTIE TO HIGHER DIMENSION. ACCESSED BY CENTER POINT'S PSIONIC ABILITY.
OKAY, OUR GOAL IS TO REACH THOSE CRYSTALLINE STRUCTURES UP AHEAD. DISTANCE AND PERSPECTIVE ARE DIFFERENT HERE, OF COURSE...
...BUT HOPEFULLY A LONG WALK WITH OUR MAPPING APPS ON WILL HELP US BUILD A MORE ACCURATE MODEL OF THIS SPACETIME.
LOG--WE'VE ARRIVED. TRAVEL TIME IN PROXIMAL DIMENSION WAS ABOUT FORTY MINUTES.
TRANSLATES INTO SOMETHING LIKE THREE MINUTES IN OUR HOME SPACE.
HOLD UP! THE MAPPING GRID IS SHOWING MOVEMENT NEARBY!

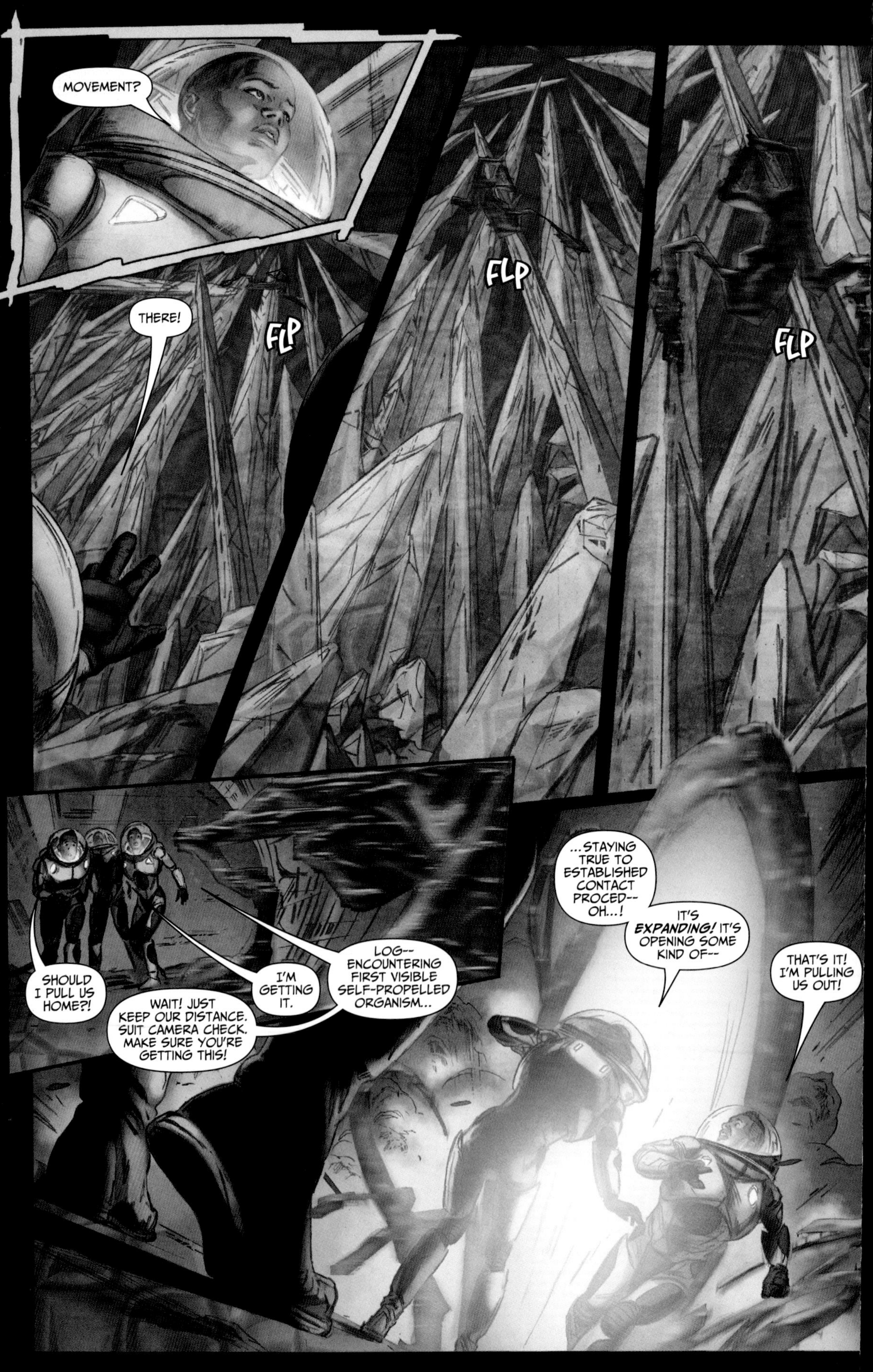
MOVEMENT?
THERE!
FLP
FLP
FLP
SHOULD I PULL US HOME?!
WAIT! JUST KEEP OUR DISTANCE. SUIT CAMERA CHECK. MAKE SURE YOU'RE GETTING THIS!
I'M GETTING IT.
LOG-- ENCOUNTERING FIRST VISIBLE SELF-PROPELLED ORGANISM...
...STAYING TRUE TO ESTABLISHED CONTACT PROCED-- OH...!
IT'S EXPANDING! IT'S OPENING SOME KIND OF--
THAT'S IT! I'M PULLING US OUT!

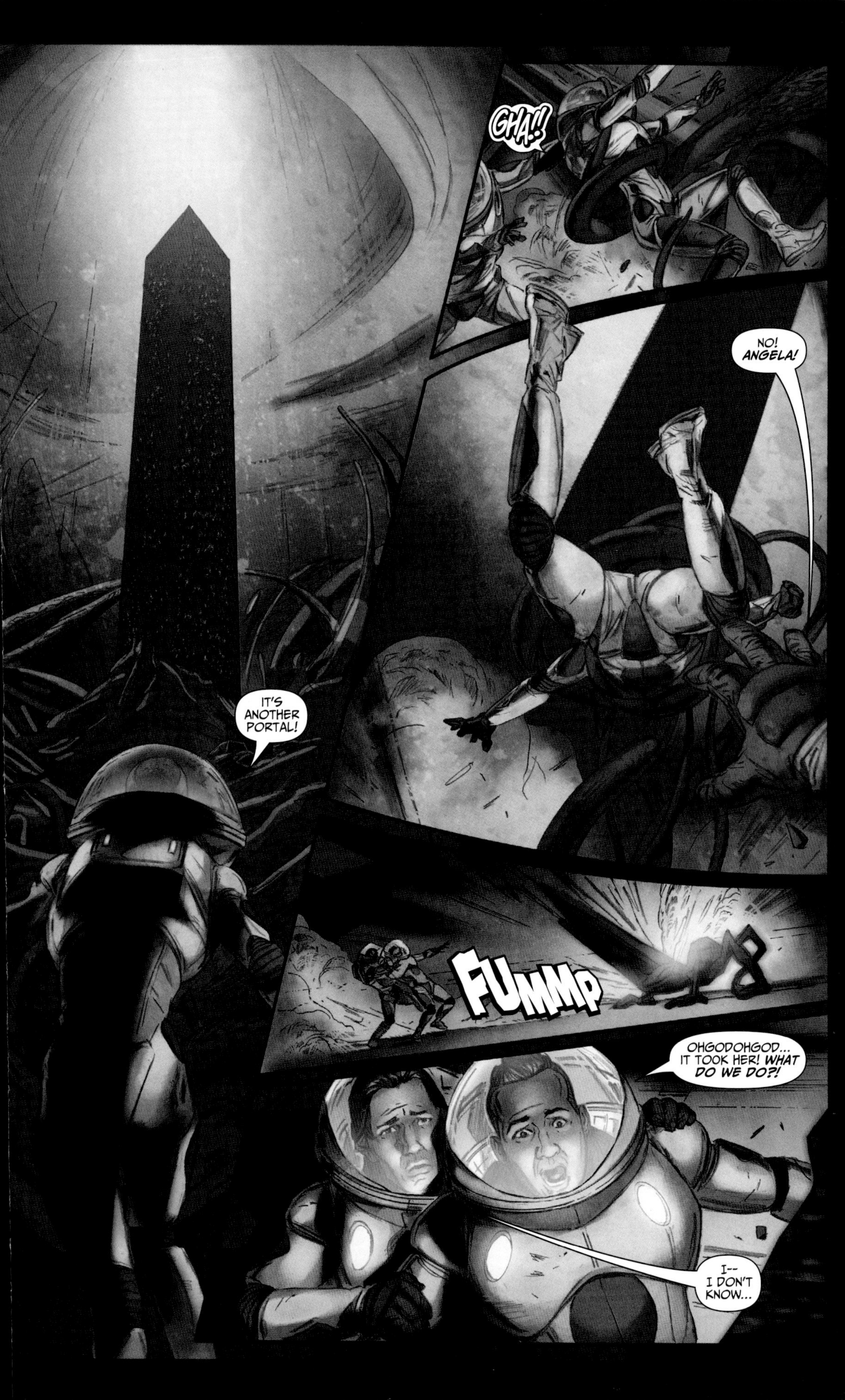
GHA!!
NO! ANGELA!
IT'S ANOTHER PORTAL!
FUMMP
OHGODOHGOD... IT TOOK HER! WHAT DO WE DO?!
I-- I DON'T KNOW...

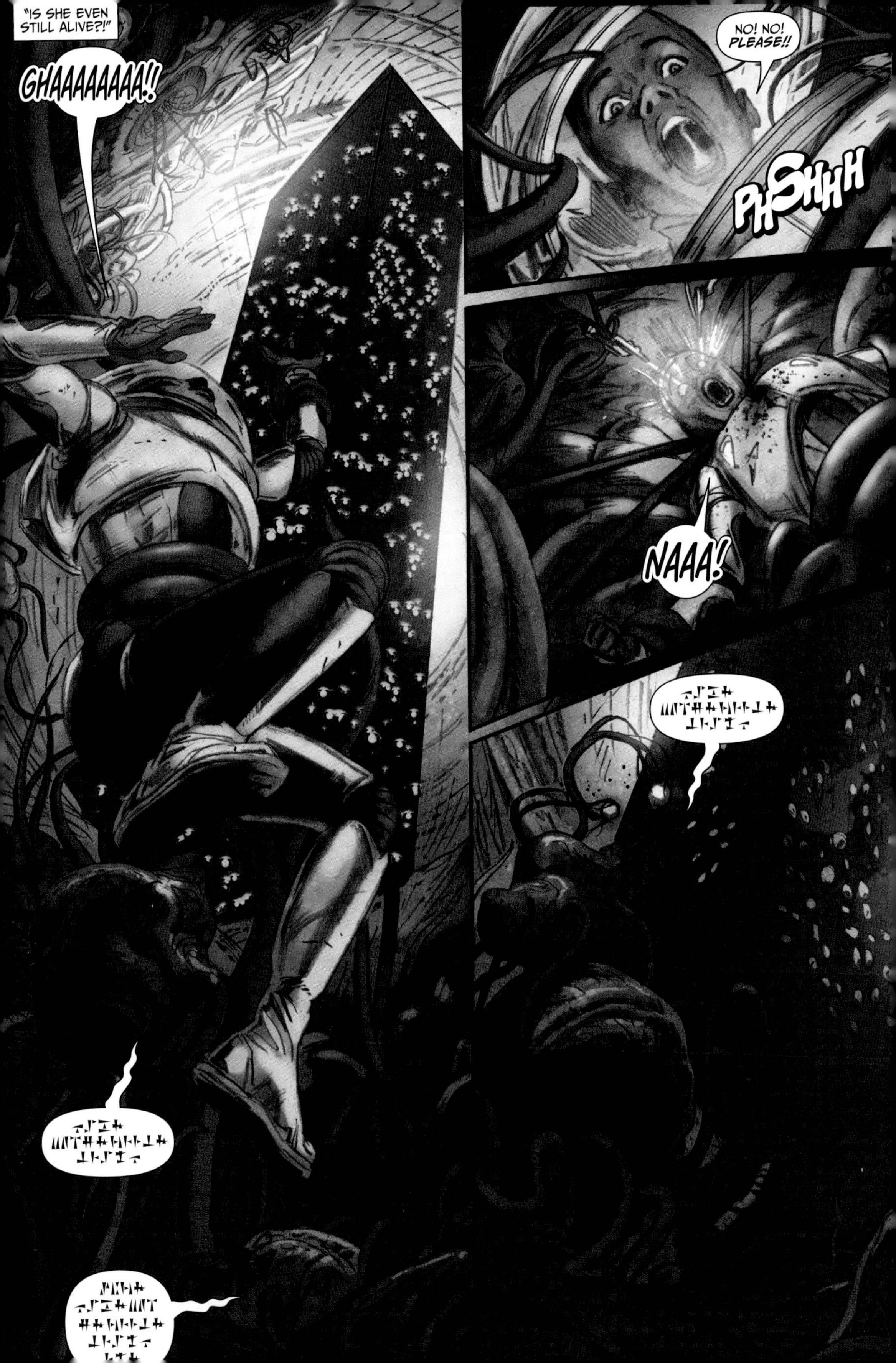
"IS SHE EVEN STILL ALIVE?!"
GHAAAAAAAA!!
NO! NO! PLEASE!!
PHSHHH
NAAA!

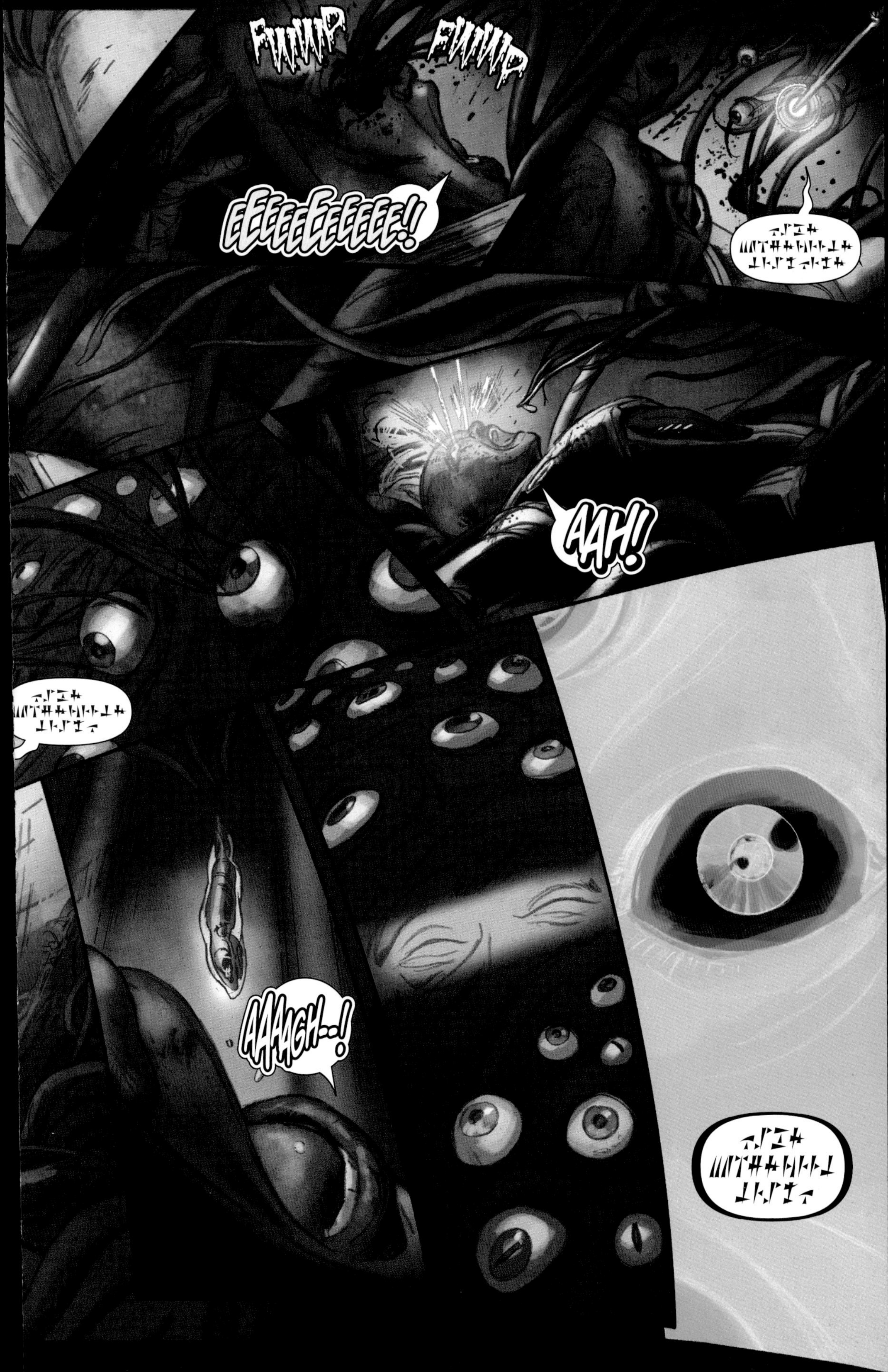
FWWP
FWWP
EEEEEEEEEEEE!!
AAH!
AAAAGH--!

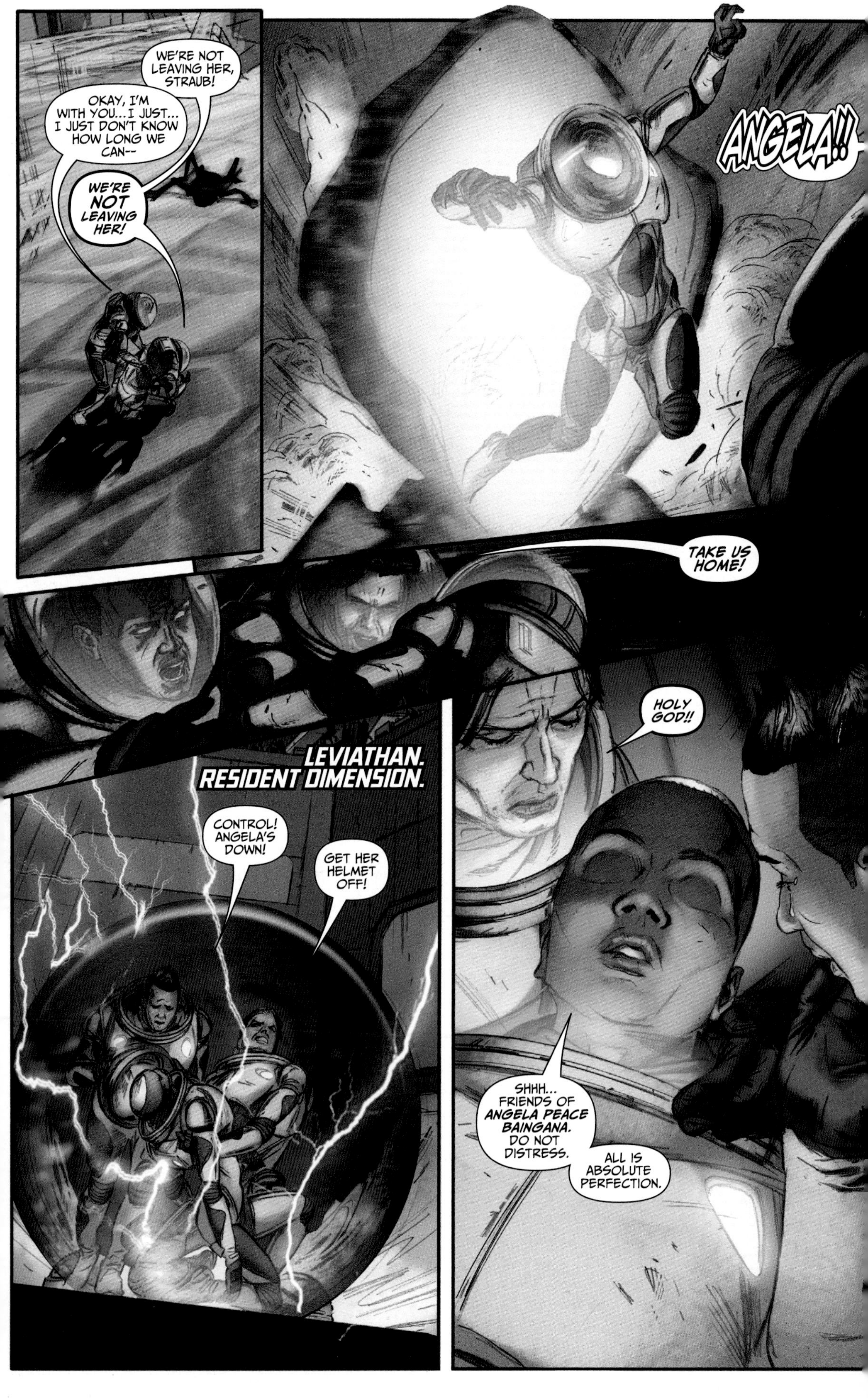
WE'RE NOT LEAVING HER, STRAUB!
OKAY, I'M WITH YOU... I JUST... I JUST DON'T KNOW HOW LONG WE CAN--
WE'RE NOT LEAVING HER!
ANGELA!!
TAKE US HOME!
HOLY GOD!!
LEVIATHAN. RESIDENT DIMENSION.
CONTROL! ANGELA'S DOWN!
GET HER HELMET OFF!
SHHH... FRIENDS OF ANGELA PEACE BAINGANA. DO NOT DISTRESS.
ALL IS ABSOLUTE PERFECTION.

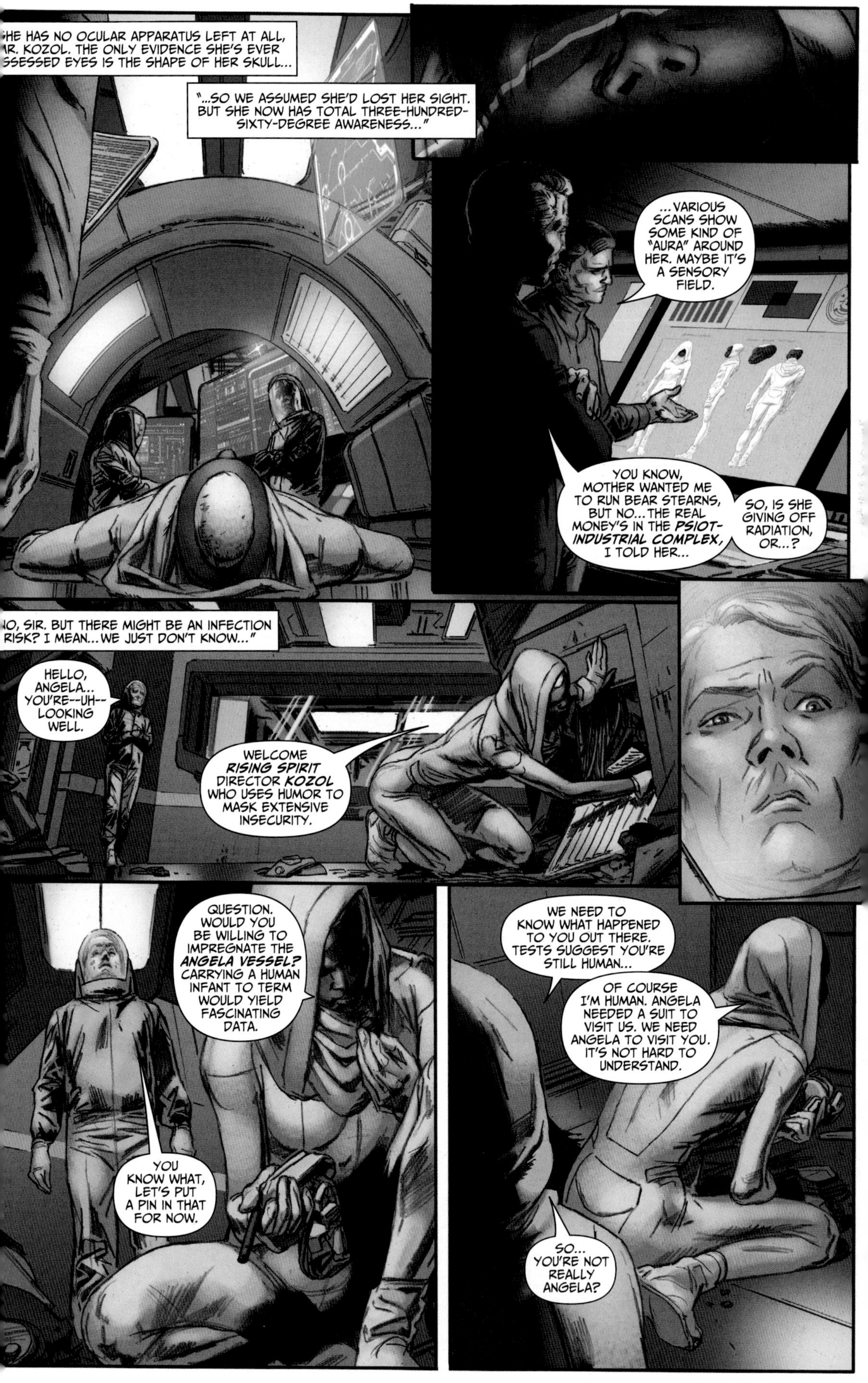
HE HAS NO OCULAR APPARATUS LEFT AT ALL, R. KOZOL. THE ONLY EVIDENCE SHE'S EVER SSESSED EYES IS THE SHAPE OF HER SKULL...
"...SO WE ASSUMED SHE'D LOST HER SIGHT. BUT SHE NOW HAS TOTAL THREE-HUNDRED-SIXTY-DEGREE AWARENESS..."
...VARIOUS SCANS SHOW SOME KIND OF "AURA" AROUND HER. MAYBE IT'S A SENSORY FIELD.
YOU KNOW, MOTHER WANTED ME TO RUN BEAR STEARNS, BUT NO...THE REAL MONEY'S IN THE PSIOT-INDUSTRIAL COMPLEX, I TOLD HER...
SO, IS SHE GIVING OFF RADIATION, OR...?
O, SIR. BUT THERE MIGHT BE AN INFECTION RISK? I MEAN...WE JUST DON'T KNOW..."
HELLO, ANGELA... YOU'RE--UH--LOOKING WELL.
WELCOME RISING SPIRIT DIRECTOR KOZOL WHO USES HUMOR TO MASK EXTENSIVE INSECURITY.
QUESTION. WOULD YOU BE WILLING TO IMPREGNATE THE ANGELA VESSEL? CARRYING A HUMAN INFANT TO TERM WOULD YIELD FASCINATING DATA.
YOU KNOW WHAT, LET'S PUT A PIN IN THAT FOR NOW.
WE NEED TO KNOW WHAT HAPPENED TO YOU OUT THERE. TESTS SUGGEST YOU'RE STILL HUMAN...
OF COURSE I'M HUMAN. ANGELA NEEDED A SUIT TO VISIT US. WE NEED ANGELA TO VISIT YOU. IT'S NOT HARD TO UNDERSTAND.
SO... YOU'RE NOT REALLY ANGELA?

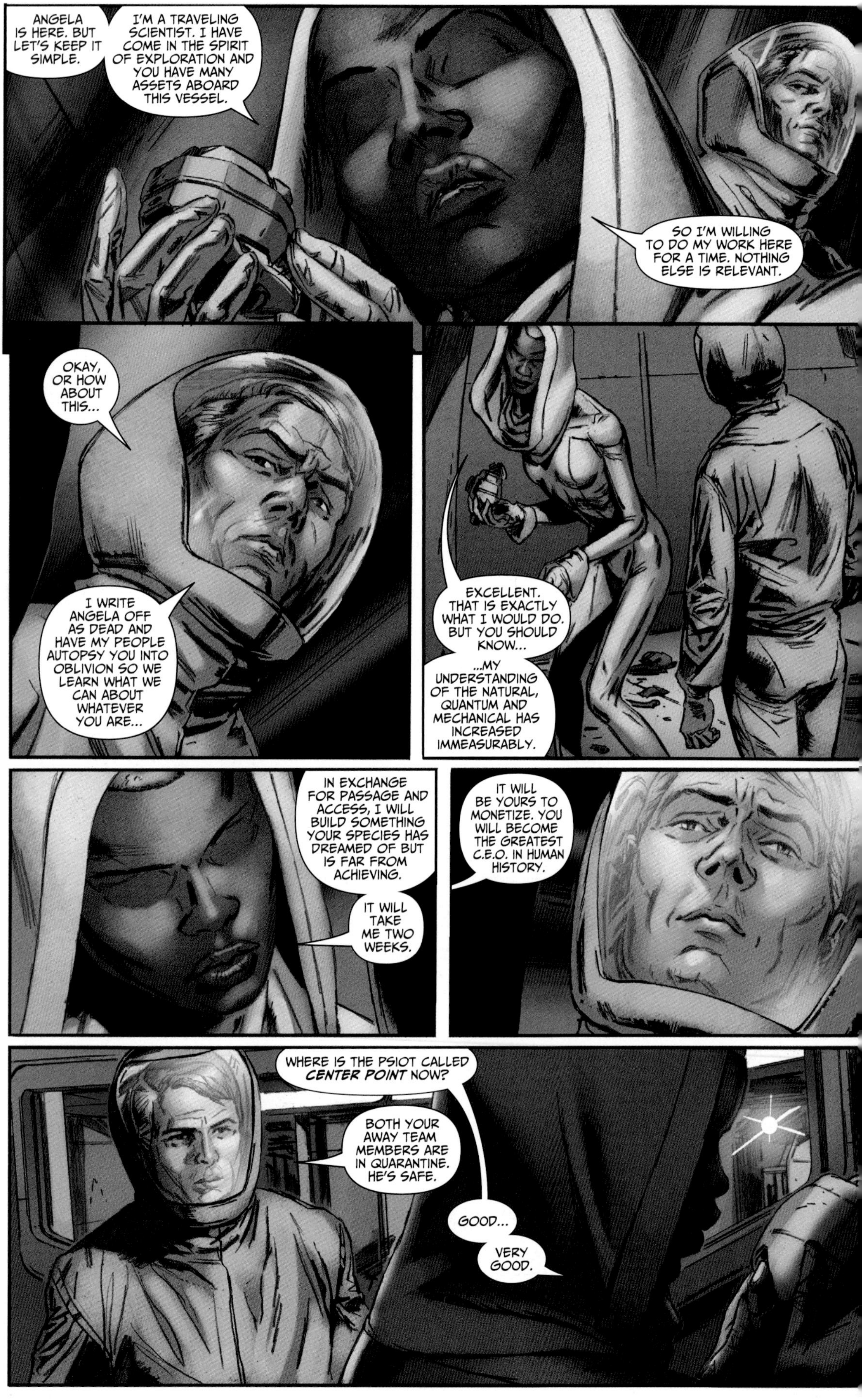

ANGELA IS HERE. BUT LET'S KEEP IT SIMPLE.
I'M A TRAVELING SCIENTIST. I HAVE COME IN THE SPIRIT OF EXPLORATION AND YOU HAVE MANY ASSETS ABOARD THIS VESSEL.
SO I'M WILLING TO DO MY WORK HERE FOR A TIME. NOTHING ELSE IS RELEVANT.
OKAY, OR HOW ABOUT THIS...
I WRITE ANGELA OFF AS DEAD AND HAVE MY PEOPLE AUTOPSY YOU INTO OBLIVION SO WE LEARN WHAT WE CAN ABOUT WHATEVER YOU ARE...
EXCELLENT. THAT IS EXACTLY WHAT I WOULD DO. BUT YOU SHOULD KNOW...
...MY UNDERSTANDING OF THE NATURAL, QUANTUM AND MECHANICAL HAS INCREASED IMMEASURABLY.
IN EXCHANGE FOR PASSAGE AND ACCESS, I WILL BUILD SOMETHING YOUR SPECIES HAS DREAMED OF BUT IS FAR FROM ACHIEVING.
IT WILL TAKE ME TWO WEEKS.
IT WILL BE YOURS TO MONETIZE. YOU WILL BECOME THE GREATEST C.E.O. IN HUMAN HISTORY.
WHERE IS THE PSIOT CALLED *CENTER POINT* NOW?
BOTH YOUR AWAY TEAM MEMBERS ARE IN QUARANTINE. HE'S SAFE.
GOOD...
VERY GOOD.

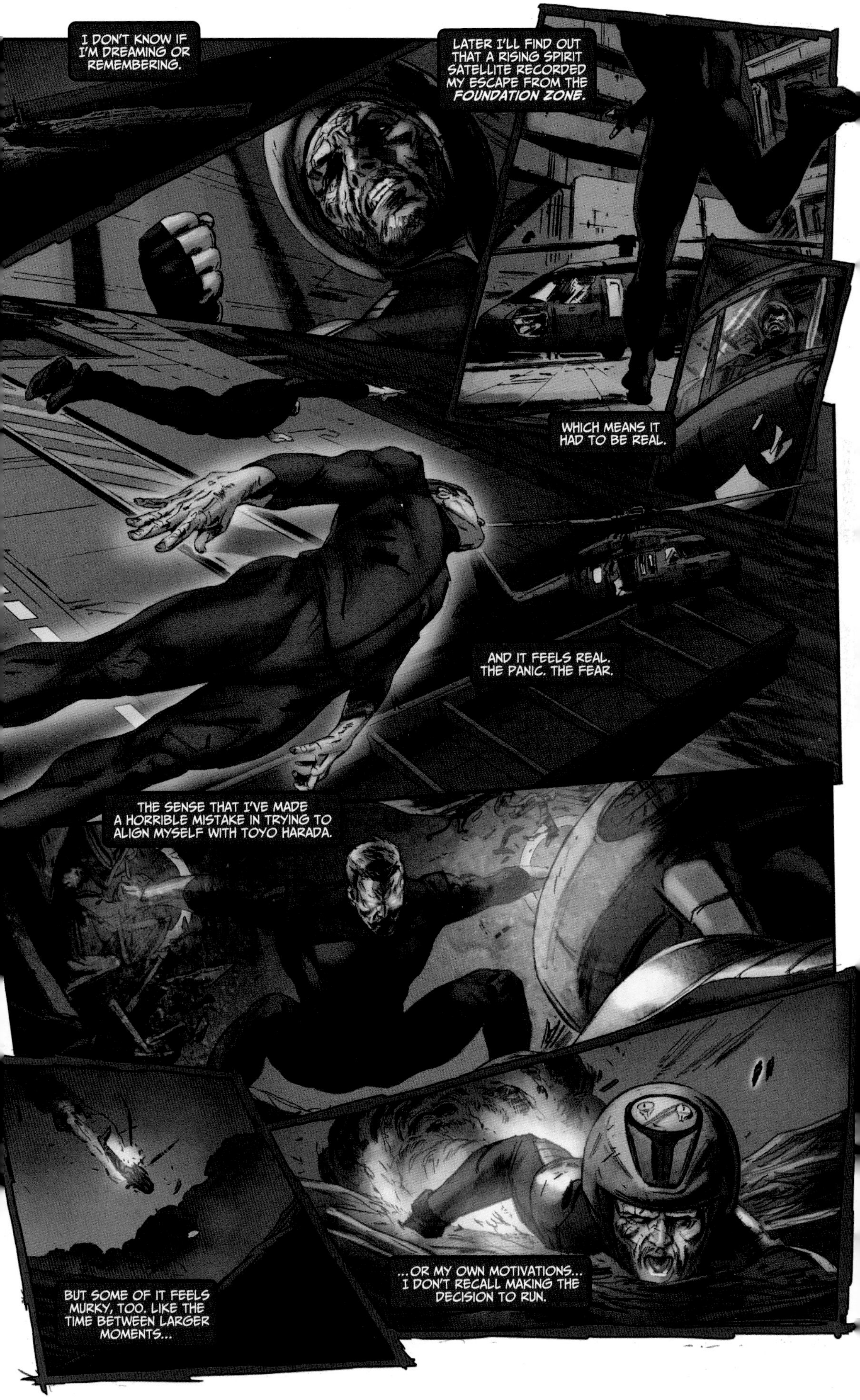
I DON'T KNOW IF I'M DREAMING OR REMEMBERING.
LATER I'LL FIND OUT THAT A RISING SPIRIT SATELLITE RECORDED MY ESCAPE FROM THE *FOUNDATION ZONE*.
WHICH MEANS IT HAD TO BE REAL.
AND IT FEELS REAL. THE PANIC. THE FEAR.
THE SENSE THAT I'VE MADE A HORRIBLE MISTAKE IN TRYING TO ALIGN MYSELF WITH TOYO HARADA.
BUT SOME OF IT FEELS MURKY, TOO. LIKE THE TIME BETWEEN LARGER MOMENTS...
...OR MY OWN MOTIVATIONS... I DON'T RECALL MAKING THE DECISION TO RUN.

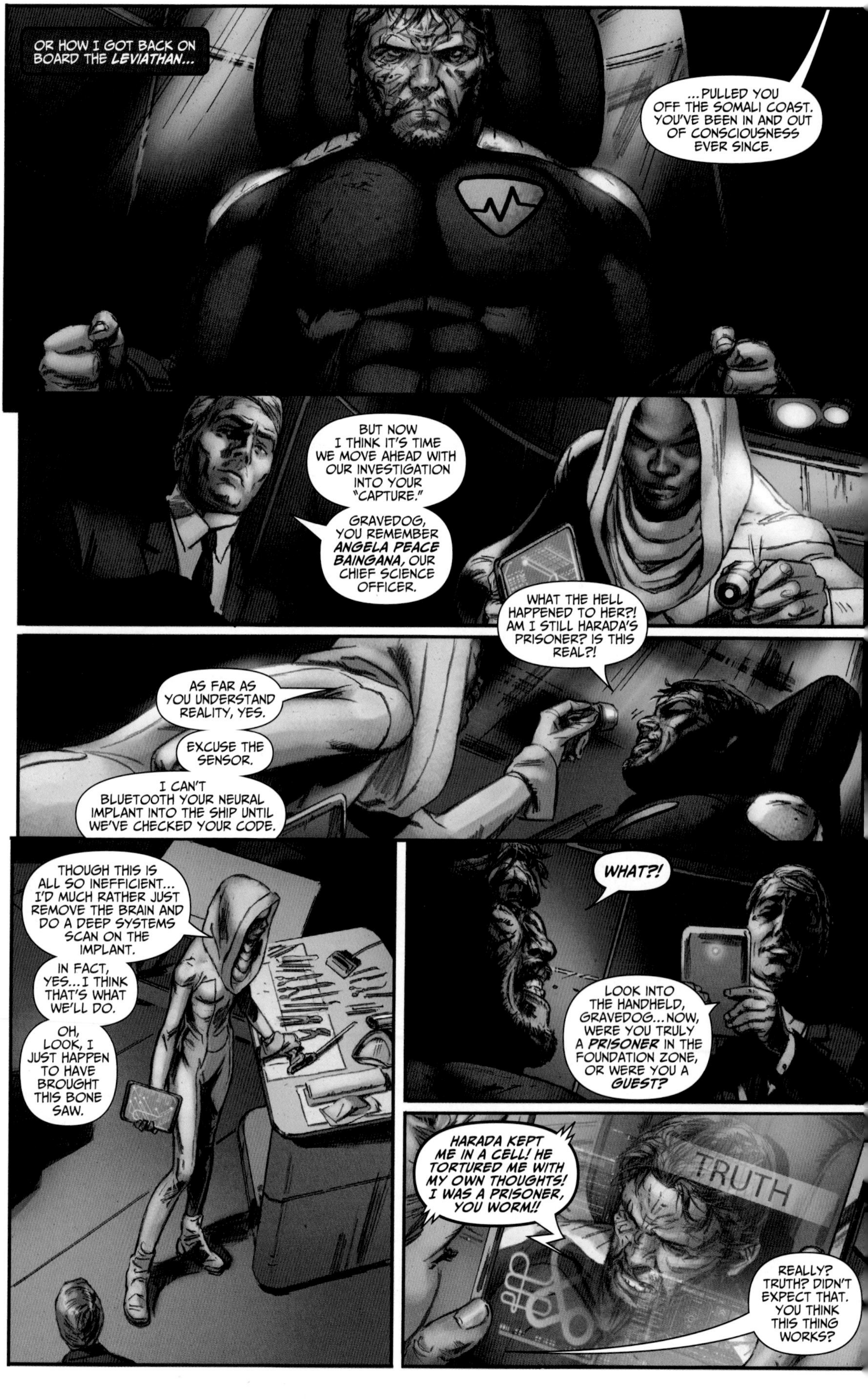
OR HOW I GOT BACK ON BOARD THE LEVIATHAN...
...PULLED YOU OFF THE SOMALI COAST. YOU'VE BEEN IN AND OUT OF CONSCIOUSNESS EVER SINCE.
BUT NOW I THINK IT'S TIME WE MOVE AHEAD WITH OUR INVESTIGATION INTO YOUR "CAPTURE."
GRAVEDOG, YOU REMEMBER ANGELA PEACE BAINGANA, OUR CHIEF SCIENCE OFFICER.
WHAT THE HELL HAPPENED TO HER?! AM I STILL HARADA'S PRISONER? IS THIS REAL?!
AS FAR AS YOU UNDERSTAND REALITY, YES.
EXCUSE THE SENSOR.
I CAN'T BLUETOOTH YOUR NEURAL IMPLANT INTO THE SHIP UNTIL WE'VE CHECKED YOUR CODE.
THOUGH THIS IS ALL SO INEFFICIENT... I'D MUCH RATHER JUST REMOVE THE BRAIN AND DO A DEEP SYSTEMS SCAN ON THE IMPLANT.
IN FACT, YES...I THINK THAT'S WHAT WE'LL DO.
OH, LOOK, I JUST HAPPEN TO HAVE BROUGHT THIS BONE SAW.
WHAT?!
LOOK INTO THE HANDHELD, GRAVEDOG...NOW, WERE YOU TRULY A PRISONER IN THE FOUNDATION ZONE, OR WERE YOU A GUEST?
HARADA KEPT ME IN A CELL! HE TORTURED ME WITH MY OWN THOUGHTS! I WAS A PRISONER, YOU WORM!!
TRUTH
REALLY? TRUTH? DIDN'T EXPECT THAT. YOU THINK THIS THING WORKS?

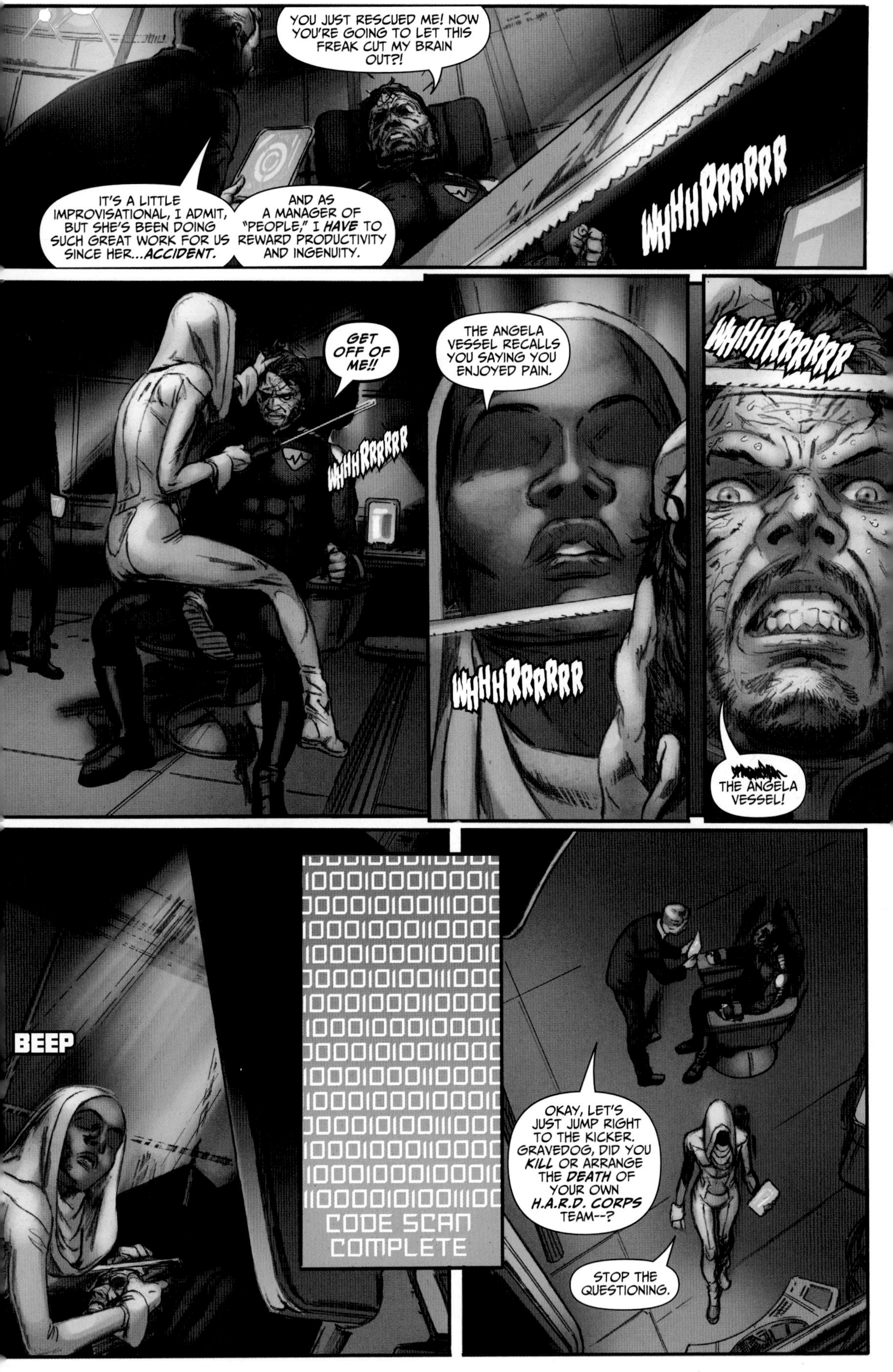
YOU JUST RESCUED ME! NOW YOU'RE GOING TO LET THIS FREAK CUT MY BRAIN OUT?!
IT'S A LITTLE IMPROVISATIONAL, I ADMIT, BUT SHE'S BEEN DOING SUCH GREAT WORK FOR US SINCE HER...ACCIDENT.
AND AS A MANAGER OF "PEOPLE," I HAVE TO REWARD PRODUCTIVITY AND INGENUITY.
WHHHRRRRRR
GET OFF OF ME!!
WHHHRRRRR
THE ANGELA VESSEL RECALLS YOU SAYING YOU ENJOYED PAIN.
WHHHRRRRR
WHHHRRRRRR
THE ANGELA VESSEL!
BEEP
CODE SCAN COMPLETE
OKAY, LET'S JUST JUMP RIGHT TO THE KICKER. GRAVEDOG, DID YOU KILL OR ARRANGE THE DEATH OF YOUR OWN H.A.R.D. CORPS TEAM--?
STOP THE QUESTIONING.

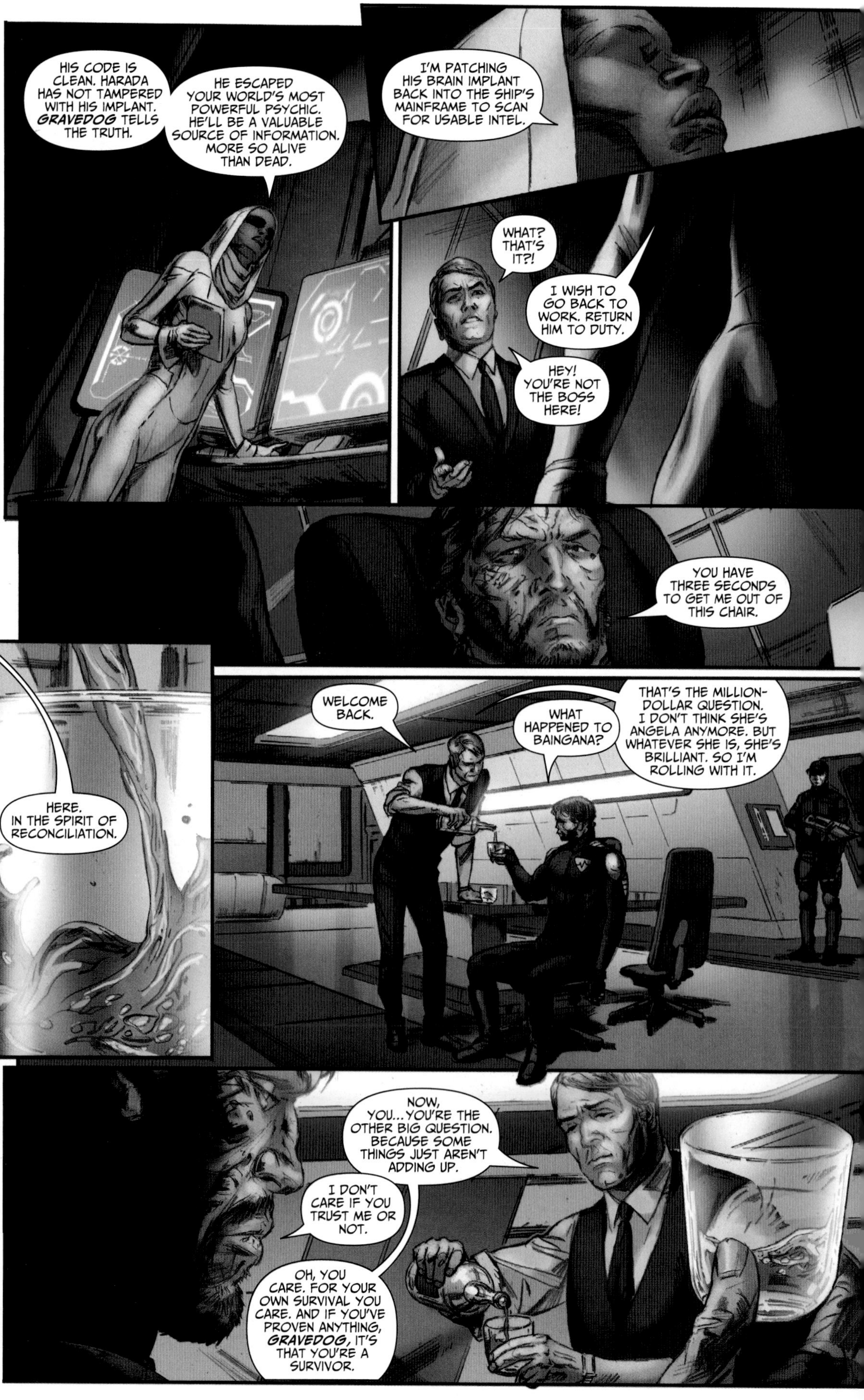
HIS CODE IS CLEAN. HARADA HAS NOT TAMPERED WITH HIS IMPLANT. GRAVEDOG TELLS THE TRUTH.
HE ESCAPED YOUR WORLD'S MOST POWERFUL PSYCHIC. HE'LL BE A VALUABLE SOURCE OF INFORMATION. MORE SO ALIVE THAN DEAD.
I'M PATCHING HIS BRAIN IMPLANT BACK INTO THE SHIP'S MAINFRAME TO SCAN FOR USABLE INTEL.
WHAT? THAT'S IT?!
I WISH TO GO BACK TO WORK. RETURN HIM TO DUTY.
HEY! YOU'RE NOT THE BOSS HERE!
YOU HAVE THREE SECONDS TO GET ME OUT OF THIS CHAIR.
HERE. IN THE SPIRIT OF RECONCILIATION.
WELCOME BACK.
WHAT HAPPENED TO BAINGANA?
THAT'S THE MILLION-DOLLAR QUESTION. I DON'T THINK SHE'S ANGELA ANYMORE. BUT WHATEVER SHE IS, SHE'S BRILLIANT. SO I'M ROLLING WITH IT.
NOW, YOU... YOU'RE THE OTHER BIG QUESTION. BECAUSE SOME THINGS JUST AREN'T ADDING UP.
I DON'T CARE IF YOU TRUST ME OR NOT.
OH, YOU CARE. FOR YOUR OWN SURVIVAL YOU CARE. AND IF YOU'VE PROVEN ANYTHING, GRAVEDOG, IT'S THAT YOU'RE A SURVIVOR.

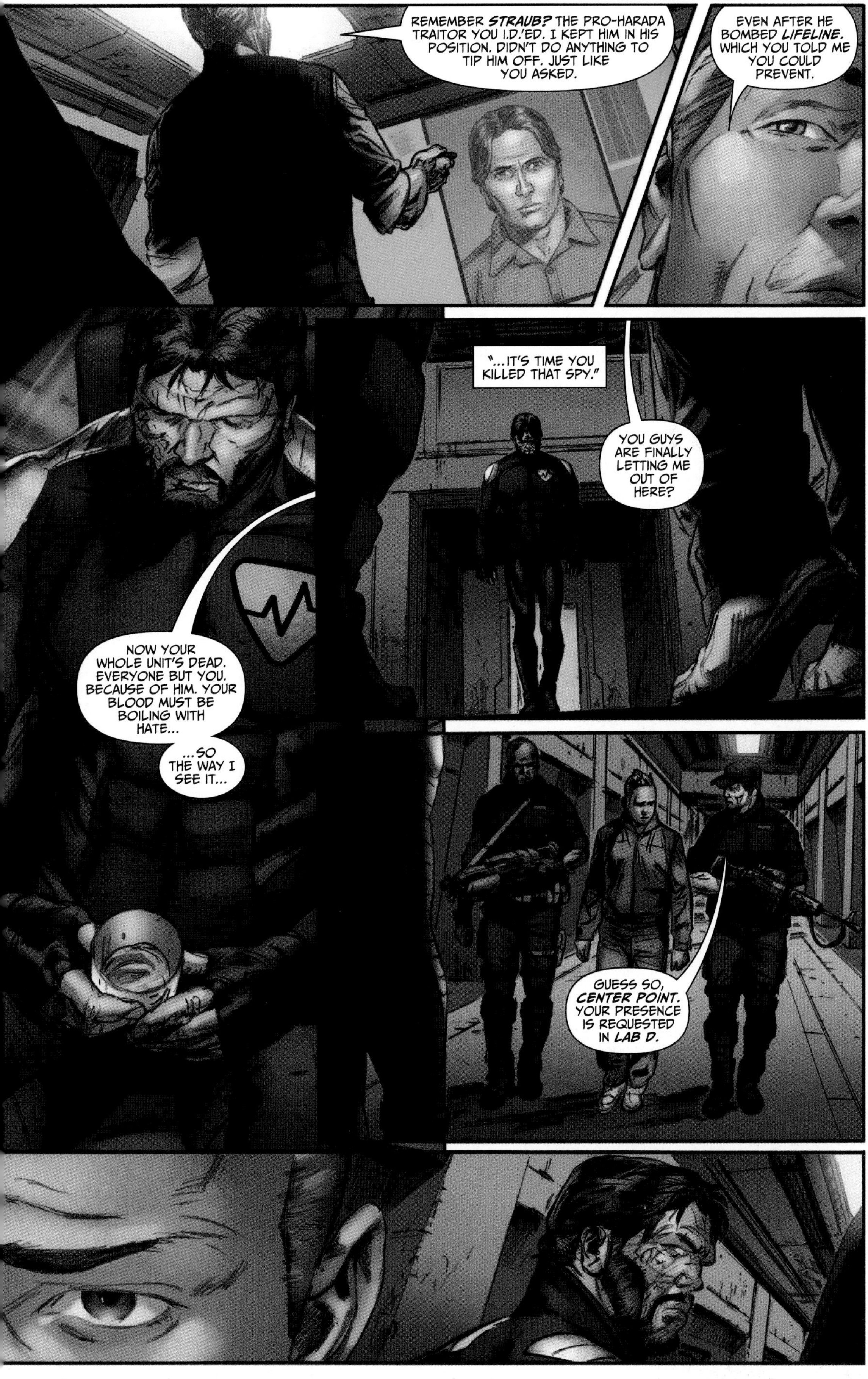
REMEMBER STRAUB? THE PRO-HARADA TRAITOR YOU I.D.'ED. I KEPT HIM IN HIS POSITION. DIDN'T DO ANYTHING TO TIP HIM OFF. JUST LIKE YOU ASKED.
EVEN AFTER HE BOMBED LIFELINE. WHICH YOU TOLD ME YOU COULD PREVENT.
NOW YOUR WHOLE UNIT'S DEAD. EVERYONE BUT YOU. BECAUSE OF HIM. YOUR BLOOD MUST BE BOILING WITH HATE...
...SO THE WAY I SEE IT...
"...IT'S TIME YOU KILLED THAT SPY."
YOU GUYS ARE FINALLY LETTING ME OUT OF HERE?
GUESS SO, CENTER POINT. YOUR PRESENCE IS REQUESTED IN LAB D.

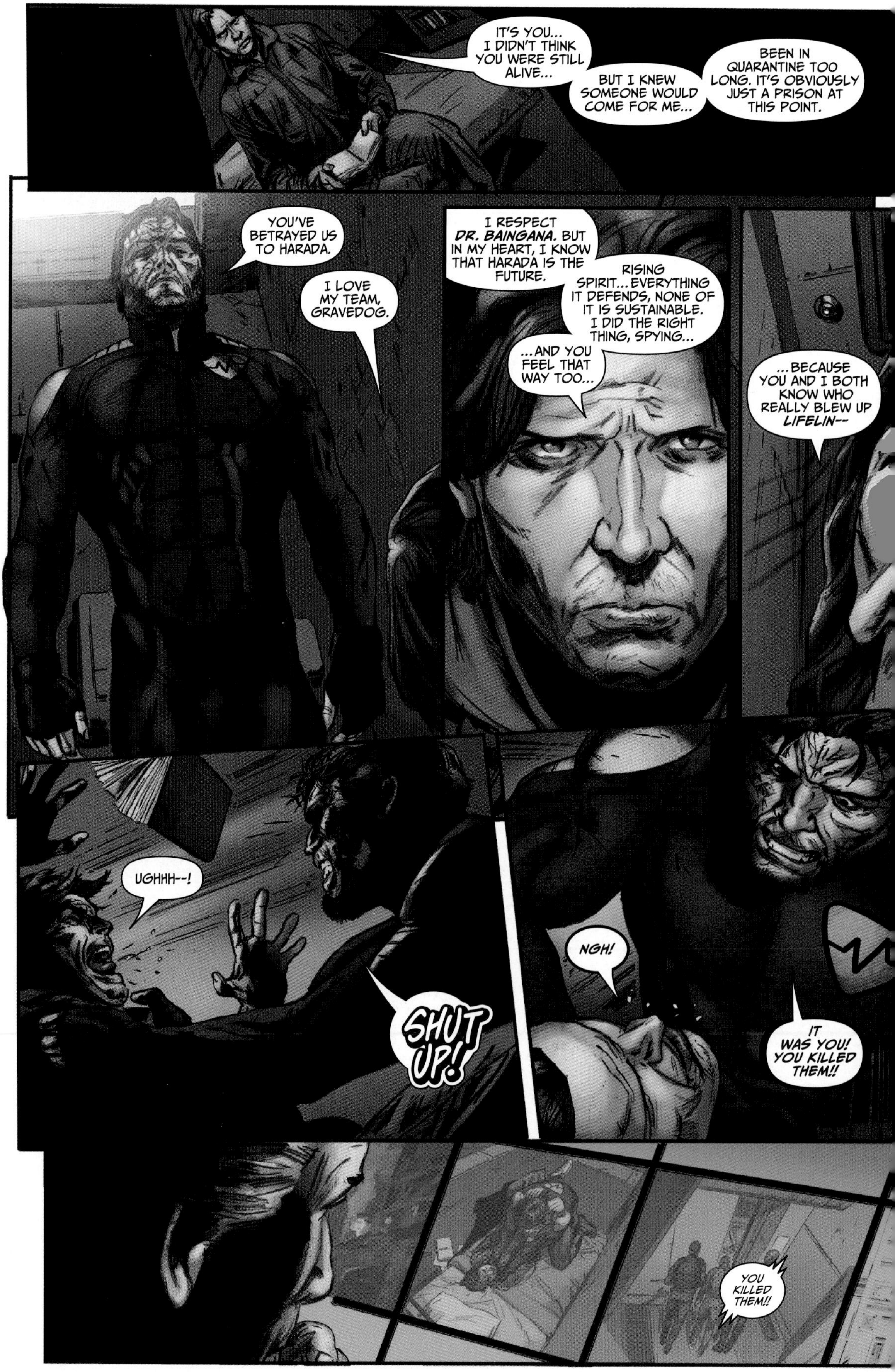
IT'S YOU... I DIDN'T THINK YOU WERE STILL ALIVE...
BUT I KNEW SOMEONE WOULD COME FOR ME...
BEEN IN QUARANTINE TOO LONG. IT'S OBVIOUSLY JUST A PRISON AT THIS POINT.
YOU'VE BETRAYED US TO HARADA.
I LOVE MY TEAM, GRAVEDOG.
I RESPECT DR. BAINGANA. BUT IN MY HEART, I KNOW THAT HARADA IS THE FUTURE.
RISING SPIRIT... EVERYTHING IT DEFENDS, NONE OF IT IS SUSTAINABLE. I DID THE RIGHT THING, SPYING...
...AND YOU FEEL THAT WAY TOO...
...BECAUSE YOU AND I BOTH KNOW WHO REALLY BLEW UP LIFELIN--
UGHHH--!
SHUT UP!
NGH!
IT WAS YOU! YOU KILLED THEM!!
YOU KILLED THEM!!

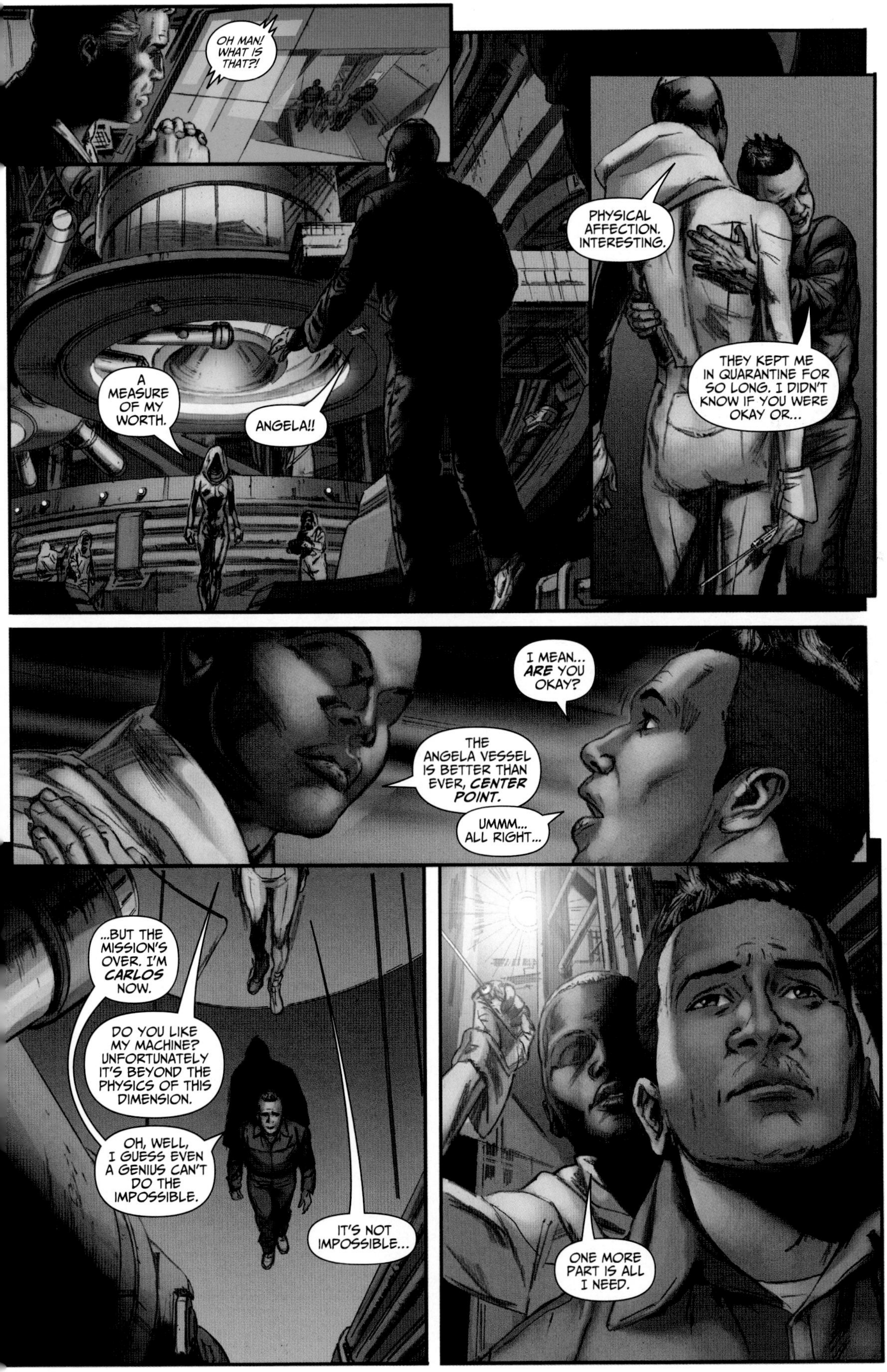
OH MAN! WHAT IS THAT?!
A MEASURE OF MY WORTH.
ANGELA!!
PHYSICAL AFFECTION. INTERESTING.
THEY KEPT ME IN QUARANTINE FOR SO LONG. I DIDN'T KNOW IF YOU WERE OKAY OR...
I MEAN... ARE YOU OKAY?
THE ANGELA VESSEL IS BETTER THAN EVER, CENTER POINT.
UMMM... ALL RIGHT...
...BUT THE MISSION'S OVER. I'M CARLOS NOW.
DO YOU LIKE MY MACHINE? UNFORTUNATELY IT'S BEYOND THE PHYSICS OF THIS DIMENSION.
OH, WELL, I GUESS EVEN A GENIUS CAN'T DO THE IMPOSSIBLE.
IT'S NOT IMPOSSIBLE...
ONE MORE PART IS ALL I NEED.

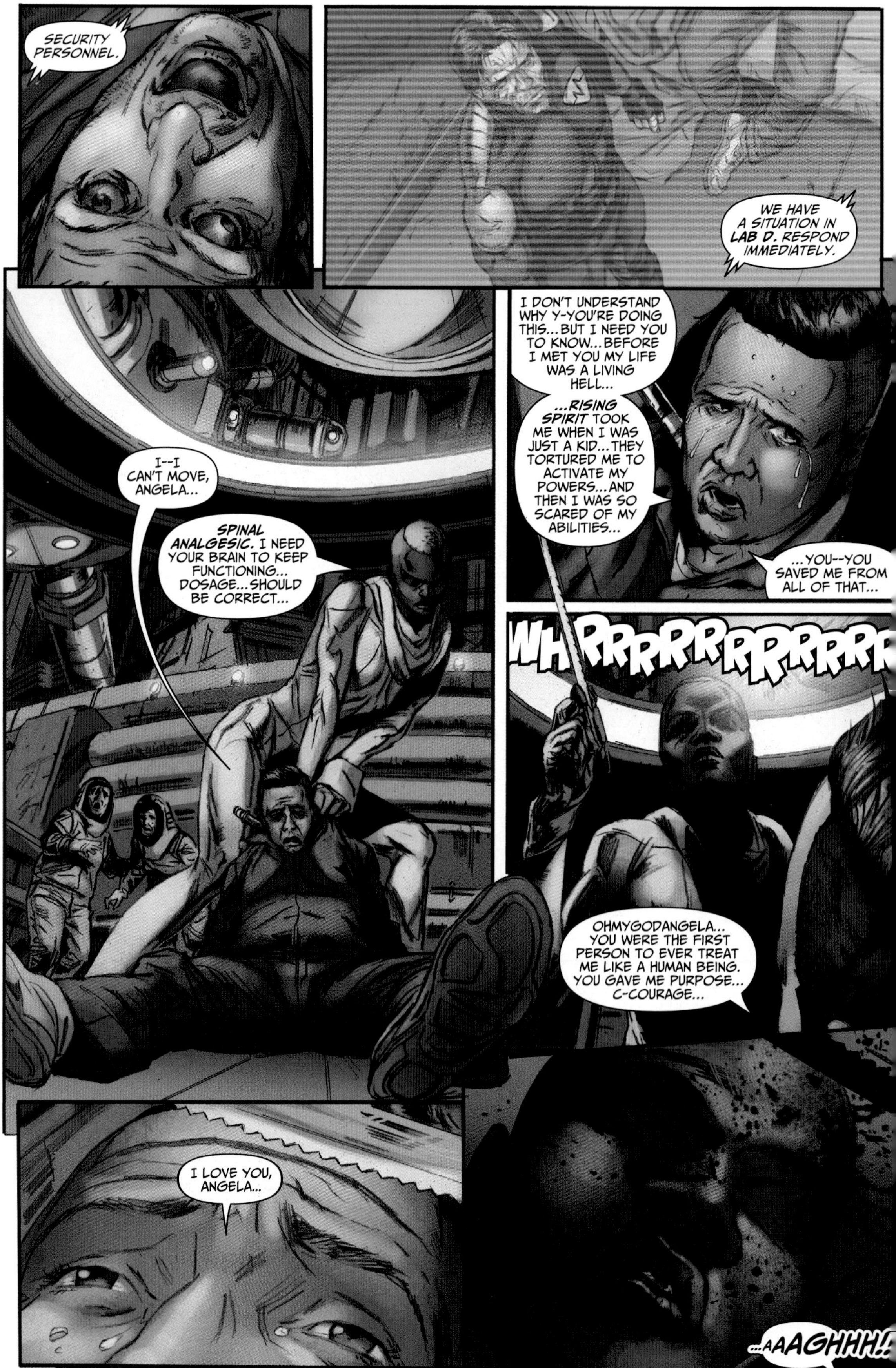

SECURITY PERSONNEL.
WE HAVE A SITUATION IN LAB D. RESPOND IMMEDIATELY.
I--I CAN'T MOVE, ANGELA...
SPINAL ANALGESIC. I NEED YOUR BRAIN TO KEEP FUNCTIONING... DOSAGE...SHOULD BE CORRECT...
I DON'T UNDERSTAND WHY Y-YOU'RE DOING THIS...BUT I NEED YOU TO KNOW...BEFORE I MET YOU MY LIFE WAS A LIVING HELL...
...RISING SPIRIT TOOK ME WHEN I WAS JUST A KID...THEY TORTURED ME TO ACTIVATE MY POWERS...AND THEN I WAS SO SCARED OF MY ABILITIES...
...YOU--YOU SAVED ME FROM ALL OF THAT...
WHRRRRRRRRRRRR
OHMYGODANGELA... YOU WERE THE FIRST PERSON TO EVER TREAT ME LIKE A HUMAN BEING. YOU GAVE ME PURPOSE... C-COURAGE...
I LOVE YOU, ANGELA...
...AAAGHHH!!

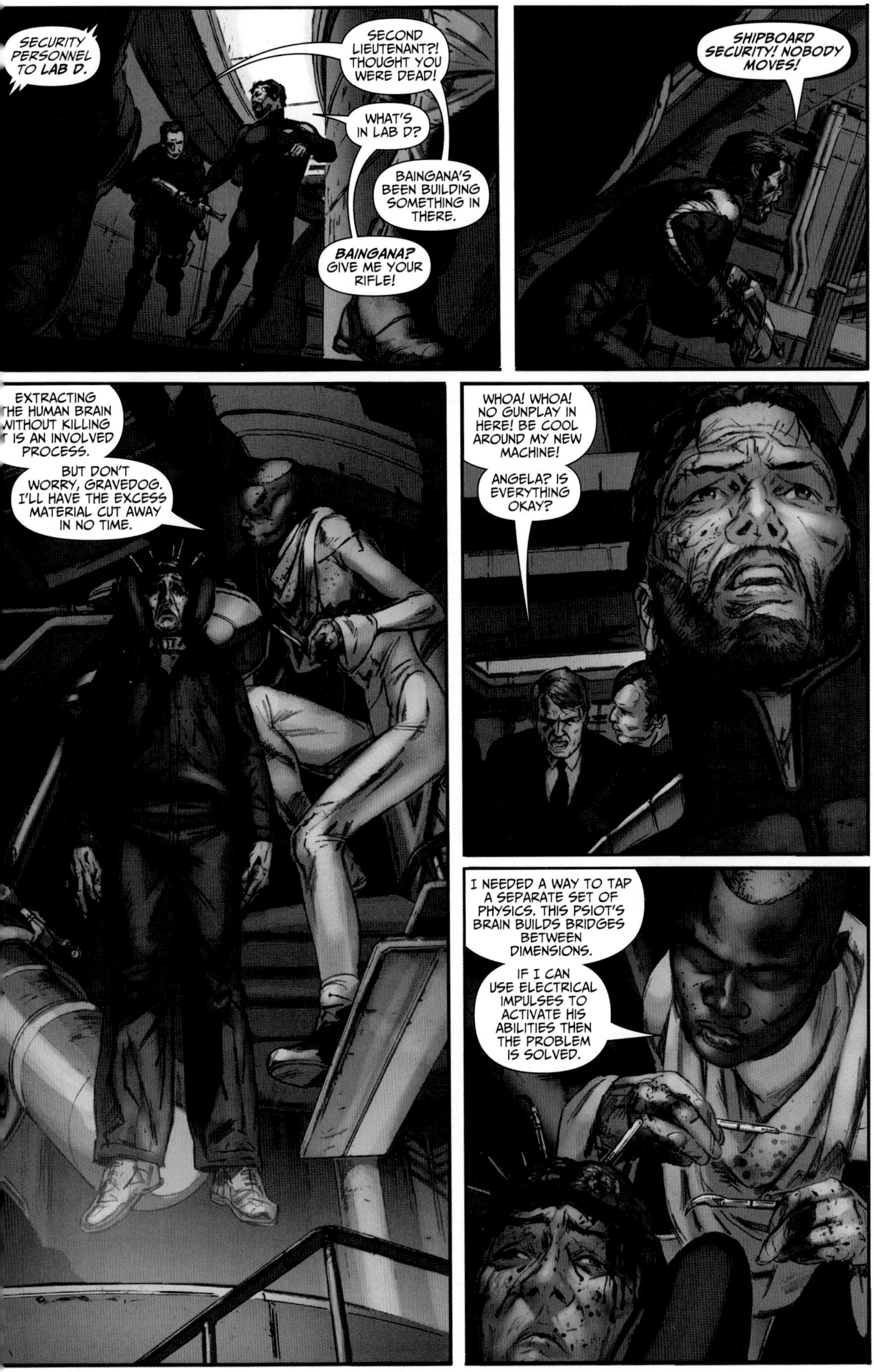
SECURITY PERSONNEL TO LAB D.
SECOND LIEUTENANT?! THOUGHT YOU WERE DEAD!
WHAT'S IN LAB D?
BAINGANA'S BEEN BUILDING SOMETHING IN THERE.
BAINGANA? GIVE ME YOUR RIFLE!
SHIPBOARD SECURITY! NOBODY MOVES!
EXTRACTING THE HUMAN BRAIN WITHOUT KILLING IT IS AN INVOLVED PROCESS.
BUT DON'T WORRY, GRAVEDOG. I'LL HAVE THE EXCESS MATERIAL CUT AWAY IN NO TIME.
WHOA! WHOA! NO GUNPLAY IN HERE! BE COOL AROUND MY NEW MACHINE!
ANGELA? IS EVERYTHING OKAY?
I NEEDED A WAY TO TAP A SEPARATE SET OF PHYSICS. THIS PSIOT'S BRAIN BUILDS BRIDGES BETWEEN DIMENSIONS.
IF I CAN USE ELECTRICAL IMPULSES TO ACTIVATE HIS ABILITIES THEN THE PROBLEM IS SOLVED.

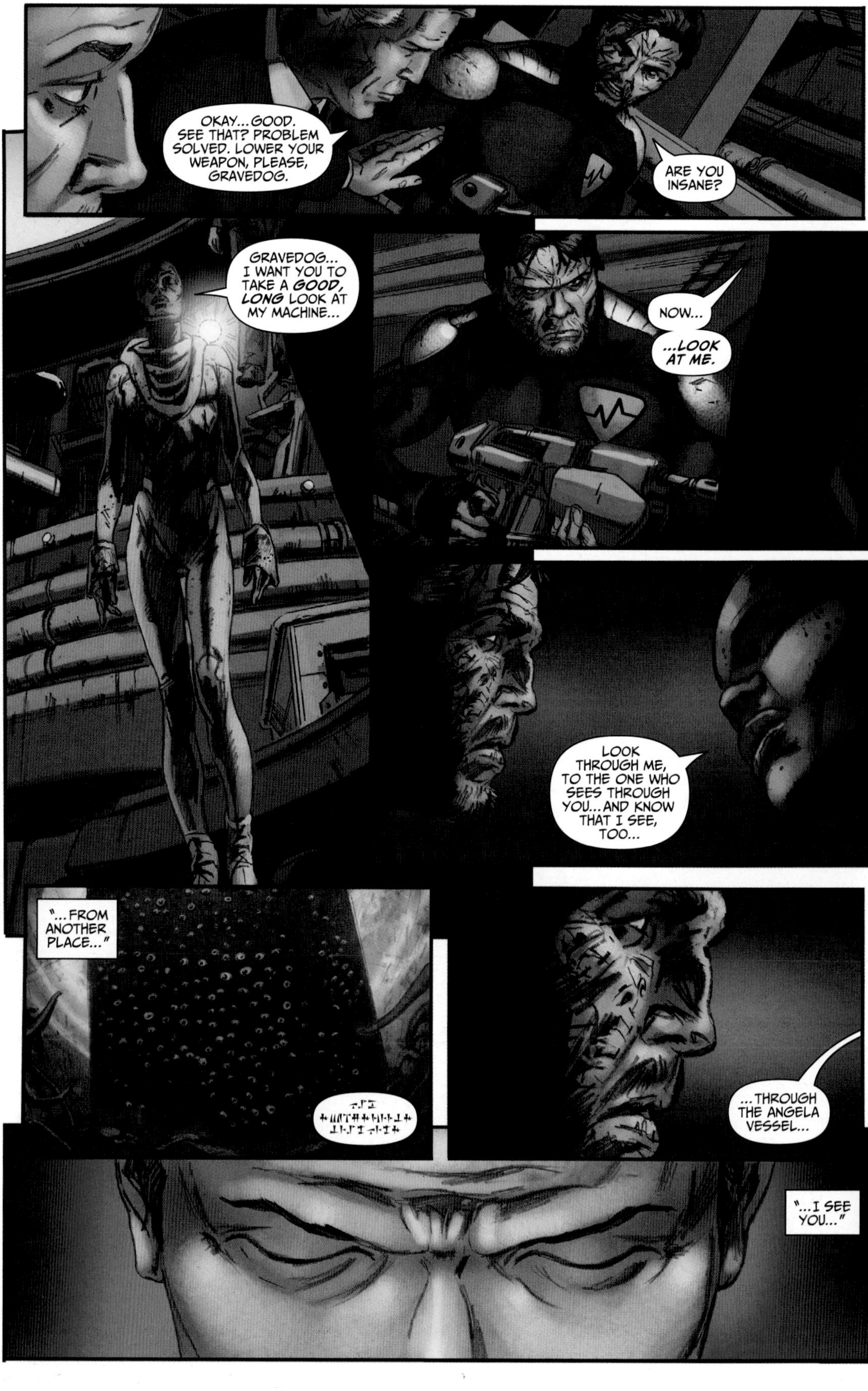
OKAY...GOOD. SEE THAT? PROBLEM SOLVED. LOWER YOUR WEAPON, PLEASE, GRAVEDOG.
ARE YOU INSANE?
GRAVEDOG... I WANT YOU TO TAKE A GOOD, LONG LOOK AT MY MACHINE...
NOW...
...LOOK AT ME.
LOOK THROUGH ME, TO THE ONE WHO SEES THROUGH YOU...AND KNOW THAT I SEE, TOO...
"...FROM ANOTHER PLACE..."
...THROUGH THE ANGELA VESSEL...
"...I SEE YOU..."

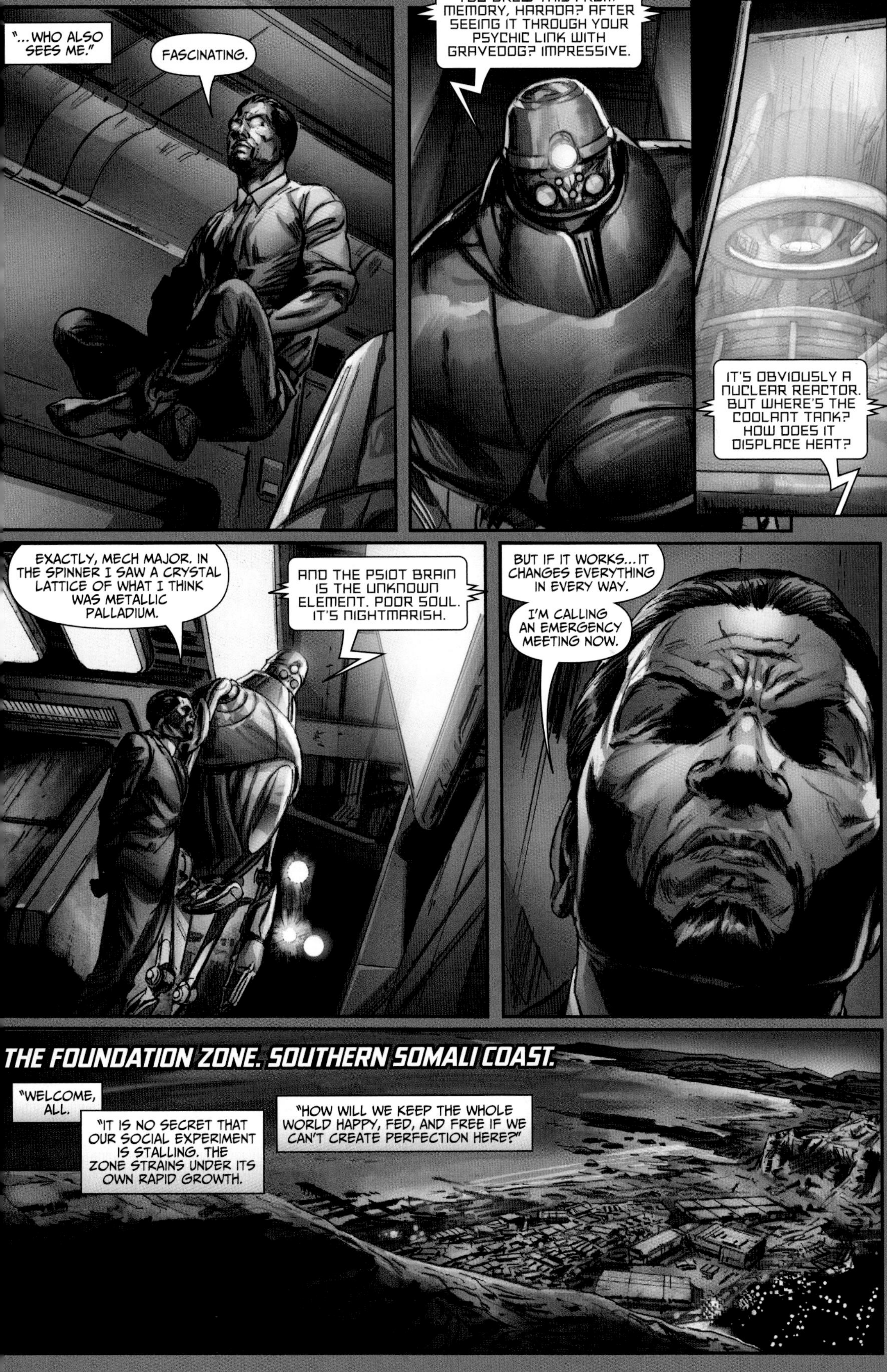
"...WHO ALSO SEES ME."
FASCINATING.
YOU DREW THIS FROM MEMORY, HARADA? AFTER SEEING IT THROUGH YOUR PSYCHIC LINK WITH GRAVEDOG? IMPRESSIVE.
IT'S OBVIOUSLY A NUCLEAR REACTOR. BUT WHERE'S THE COOLANT TANK? HOW DOES IT DISPLACE HEAT?
EXACTLY, MECH MAJOR. IN THE SPINNER I SAW A CRYSTAL LATTICE OF WHAT I THINK WAS METALLIC PALLADIUM.
AND THE PSIOT BRAIN IS THE UNKNOWN ELEMENT. POOR SOUL. IT'S NIGHTMARISH.
BUT IF IT WORKS... IT CHANGES EVERYTHING IN EVERY WAY.
I'M CALLING AN EMERGENCY MEETING NOW.
THE FOUNDATION ZONE. SOUTHERN SOMALI COAST.
"WELCOME, ALL.
"IT IS NO SECRET THAT OUR SOCIAL EXPERIMENT IS STALLING. THE ZONE STRAINS UNDER ITS OWN RAPID GROWTH.
"HOW WILL WE KEEP THE WHOLE WORLD HAPPY, FED, AND FREE IF WE CAN'T CREATE PERFECTION HERE?"

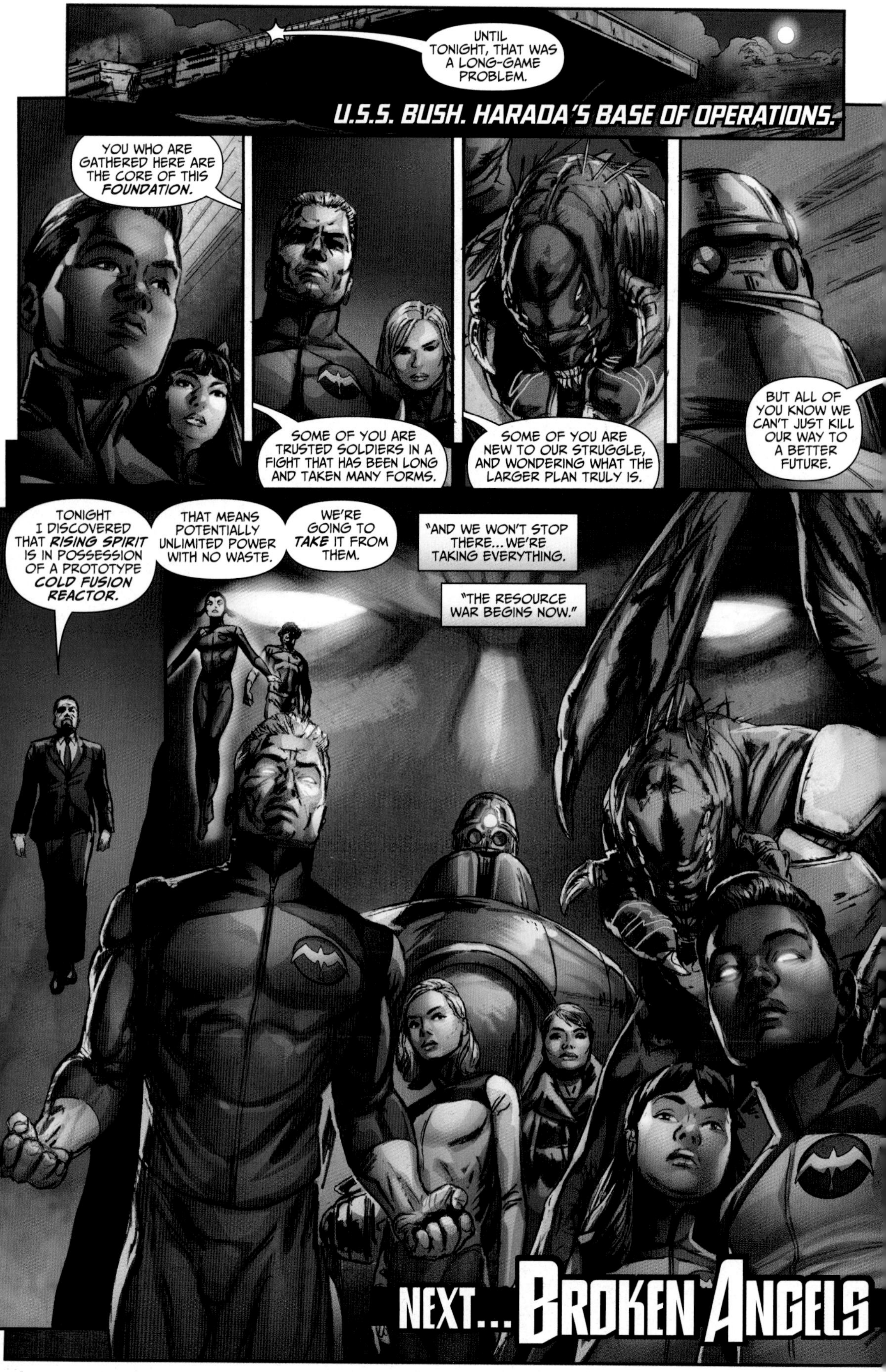

UNTIL TONIGHT, THAT WAS A LONG-GAME PROBLEM.
U.S.S. BUSH. HARADA'S BASE OF OPERATIONS.
YOU WHO ARE GATHERED HERE ARE THE CORE OF THIS FOUNDATION.
SOME OF YOU ARE TRUSTED SOLDIERS IN A FIGHT THAT HAS BEEN LONG AND TAKEN MANY FORMS.
SOME OF YOU ARE NEW TO OUR STRUGGLE, AND WONDERING WHAT THE LARGER PLAN TRULY IS.
BUT ALL OF YOU KNOW WE CAN'T JUST KILL OUR WAY TO A BETTER FUTURE.
TONIGHT I DISCOVERED THAT RISING SPIRIT IS IN POSSESSION OF A PROTOTYPE COLD FUSION REACTOR.
THAT MEANS POTENTIALLY UNLIMITED POWER WITH NO WASTE.
WE'RE GOING TO TAKE IT FROM THEM.
"AND WE WON'T STOP THERE...WE'RE TAKING EVERYTHING.
"THE RESOURCE WAR BEGINS NOW."
NEXT... BROKEN ANGELS

GALLERY

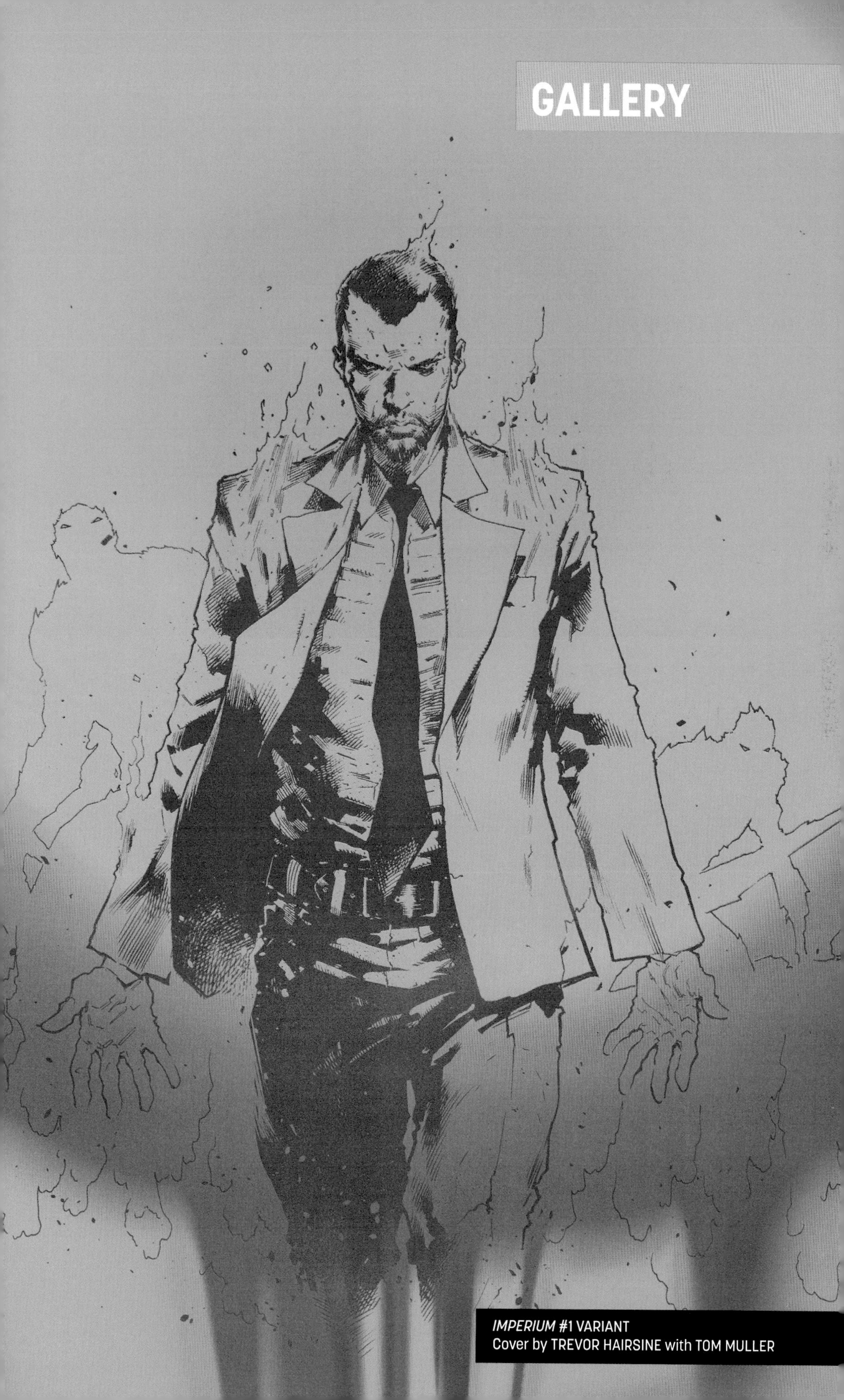

IMPERIUM #1 VARIANT
Cover by TREVOR HAIRSINE with TOM MULLER

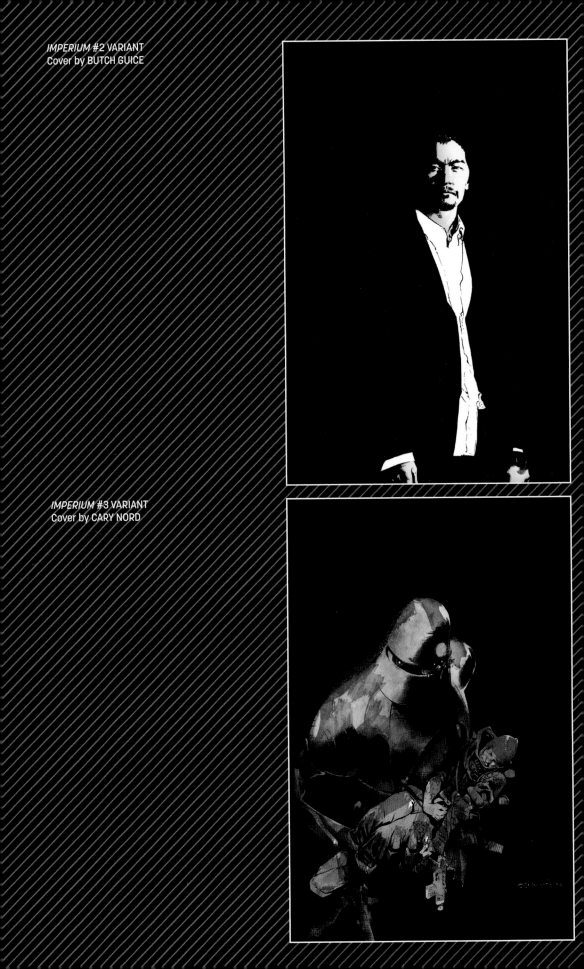

IMPERIUM #2 VARIANT
Cover by BUTCH GUICE

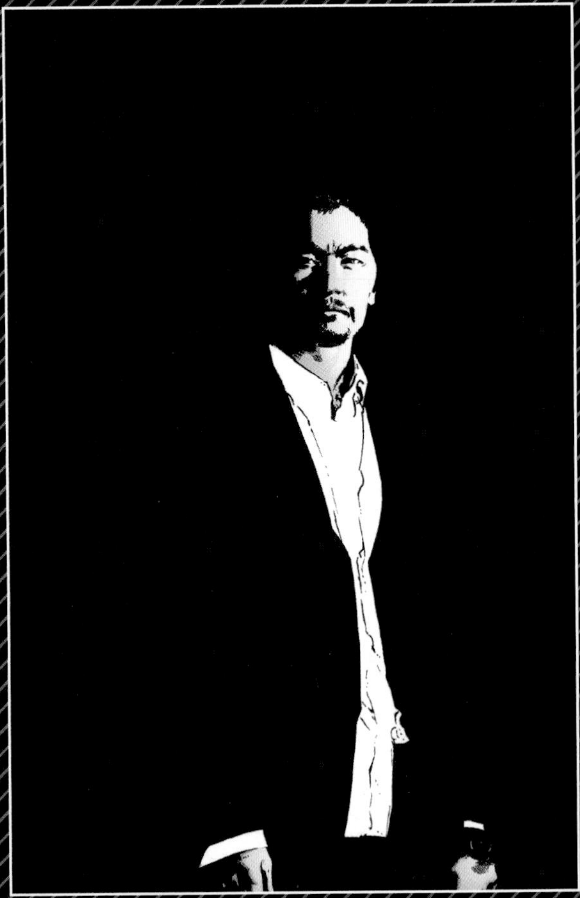

IMPERIUM #3 VARIANT
Cover by CARY NORD

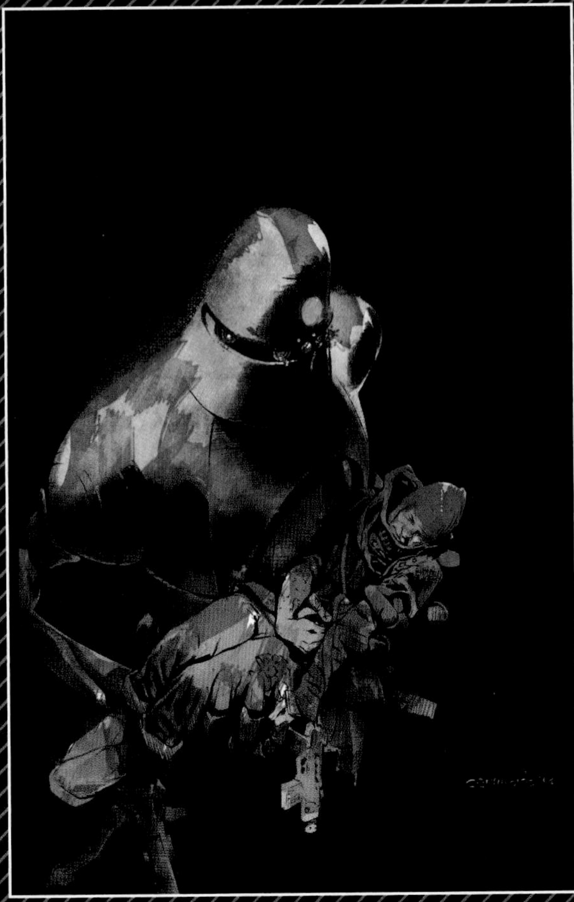

IMPERIUM #4 VARIANT
Cover by KANO

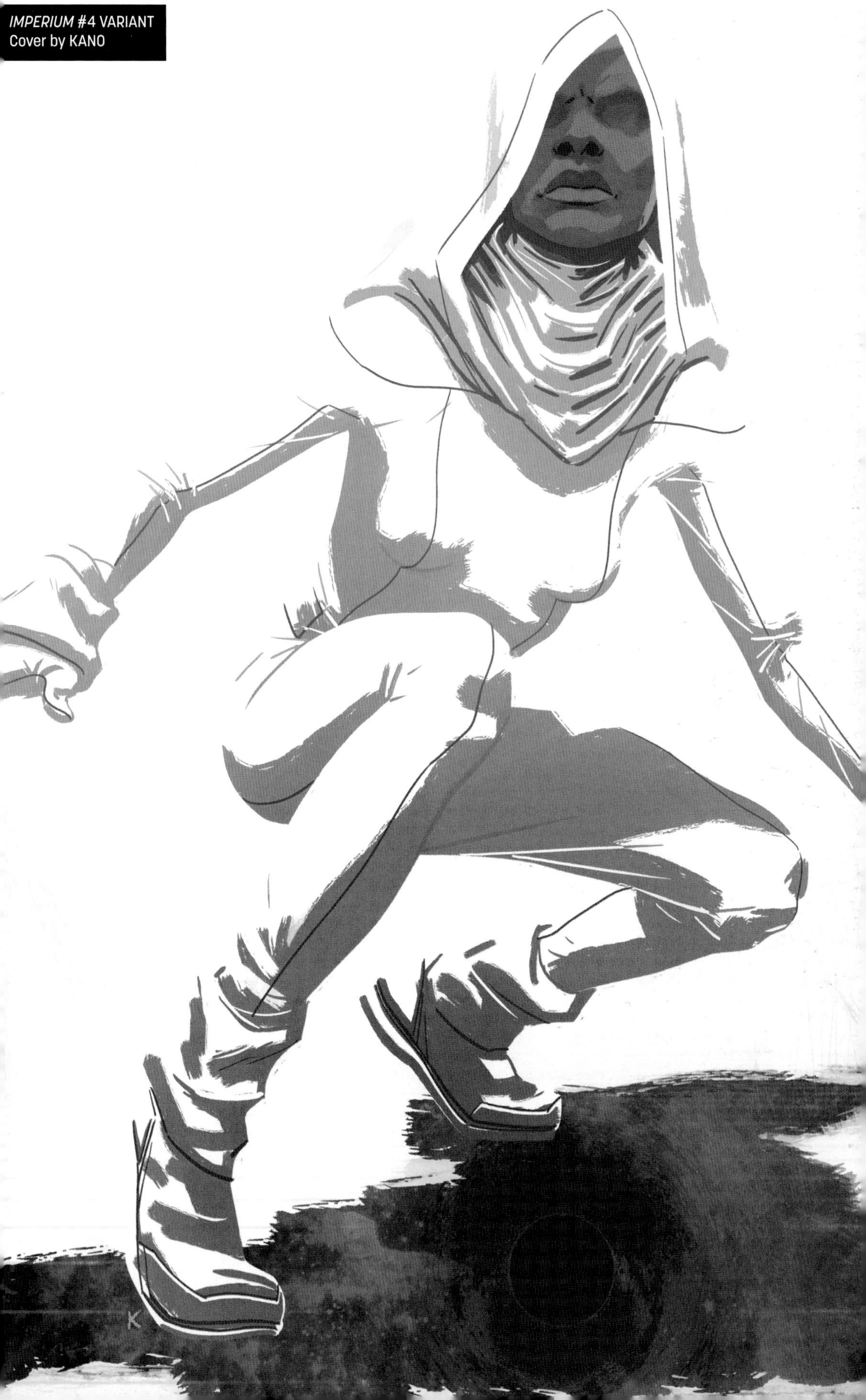
K

IMPERIUM #1, p. 16
Art by DOUG BRAITHWAITE

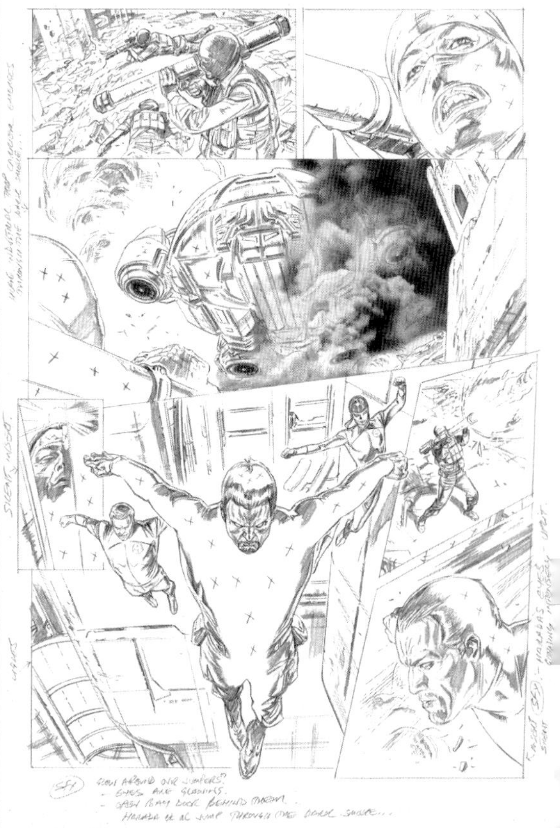
SFX
GLOW AROUND OUR JUMPERS?
- EYES ARE GLOWING.
- OPEN BAY DOOR BEHIND THEM.
HARADA & AL JUMP THROUGH THE BLACK SMOKE...

IMPERIUM #1, p. 19
Art by DOUG BRAITHWAITE

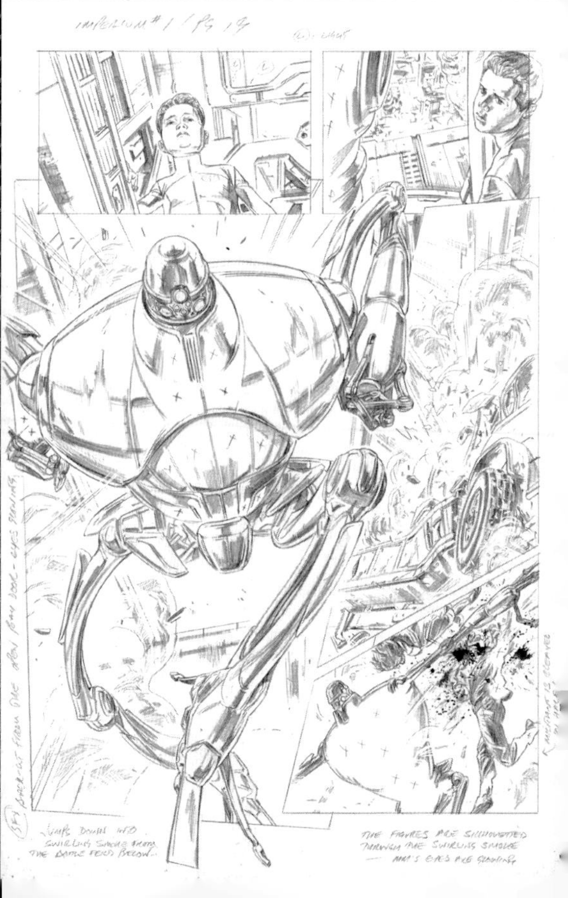
IMPERIUM #1 / PG 19
SFX
JUMPS DOWN INTO SWIRLING SMOKE FROM THE BATTLE FIELD BELOW...
THE FIGURES ARE SILHOUETTED THROUGH THE SWIRLING SMOKE — MAN'S EYES ARE GLOWING

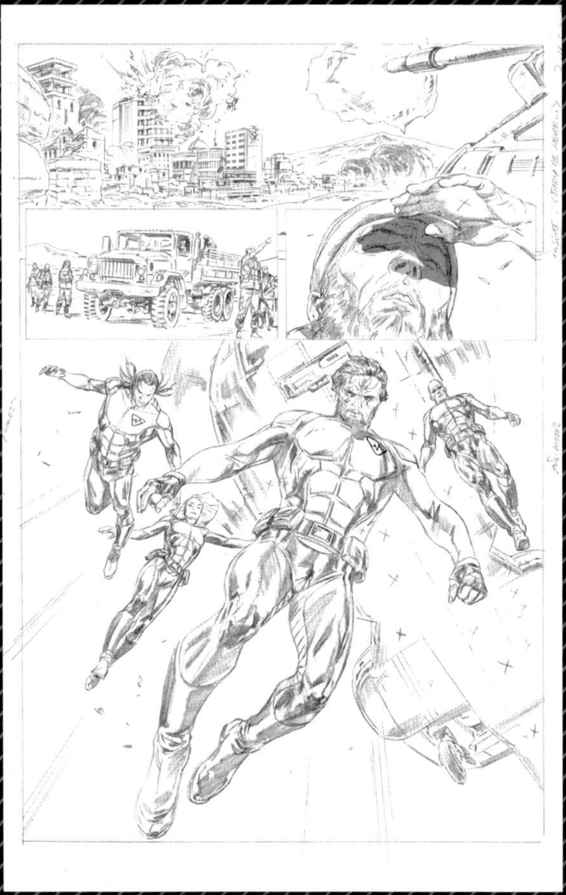

IMPERIUM #2, p. 3
Art by DOUG BRAITHWAITE

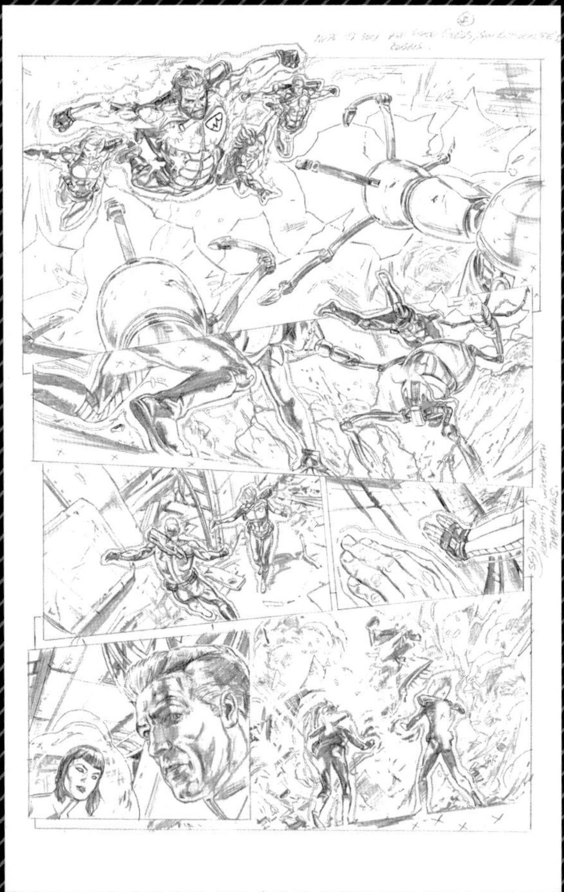

IMPERIUM #2, p. 19
Art by DOUG BRAITHWAITE

IMPERIUM #3, p. 8
Art by DOUG BRAITHWAITE

IMPERIUM #3, p. 16
Art by DOUG BRAITHWAITE

IMPERIUM #3 / Pg 16
SFX = HAZY SPOTLIGHT EFFECT
DARK, ATMOSPHERIC ENVIRONMENT

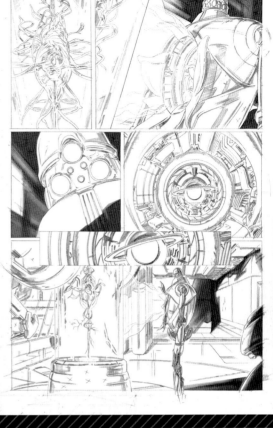

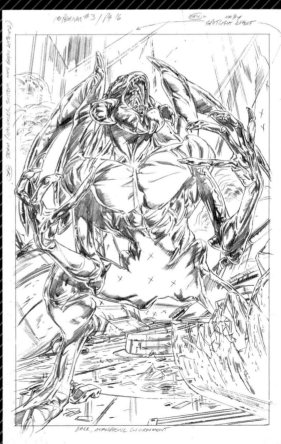

IMPERIUM #4, p. 2
Art by DOUG BRAITHWAITE

IMPERIUM #4, p. 8
Art by DOUG BRAITHWAITE

EXPLORE THE VALIANT UNIVERSE

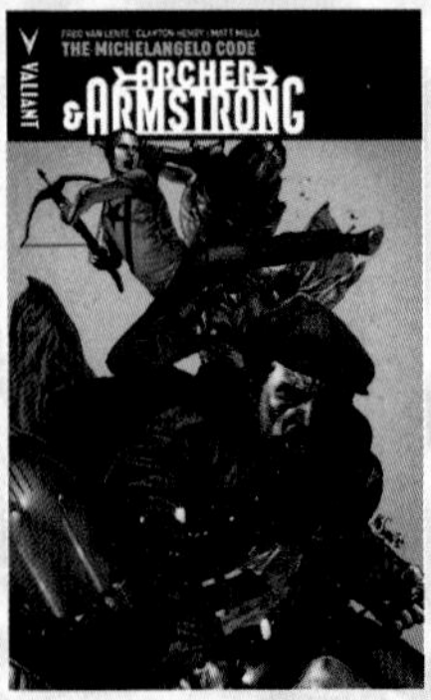
VALIANT
THE MICHELANGELO CODE
ARCHER & ARMSTRONG

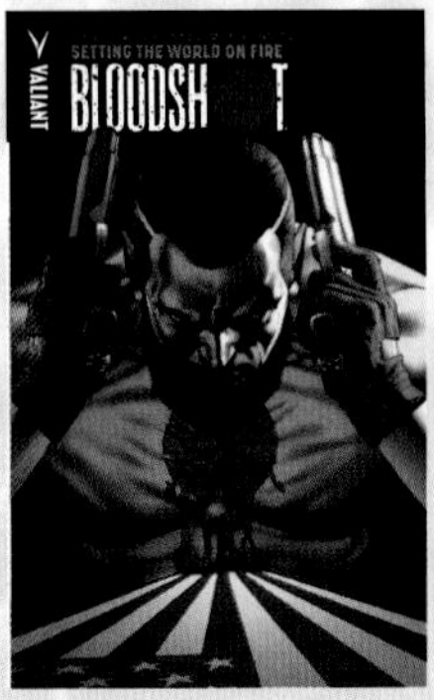
VALIANT
SETTING THE WORLD ON FIRE
BLOODSHOT

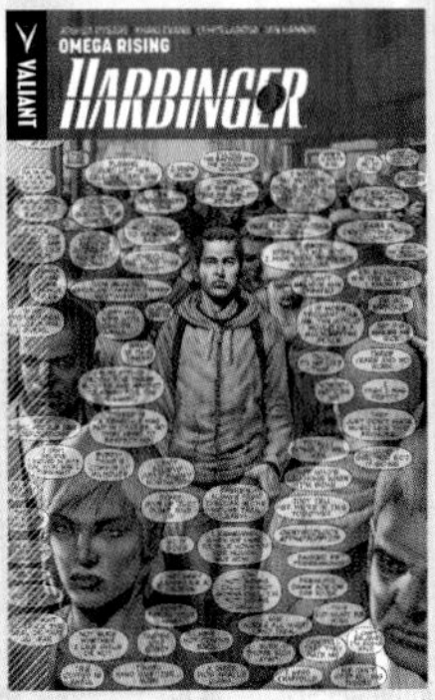
VALIANT
OMEGA RISING
HARBINGER

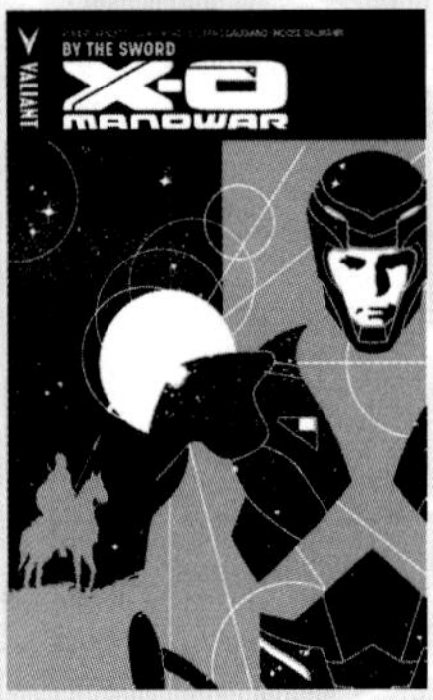
VALIANT
BY THE SWORD
X-O MANOWAR

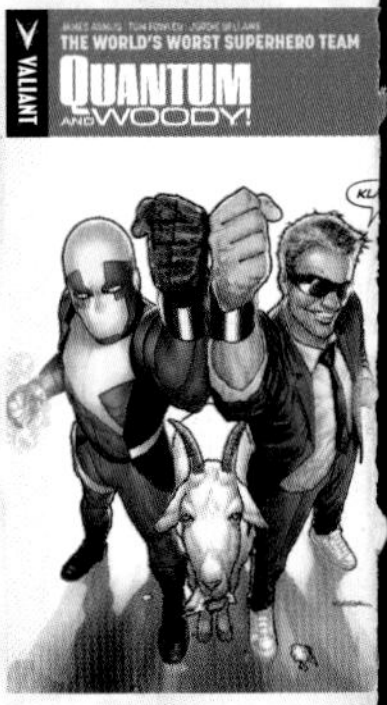
VALIANT
THE WORLD'S WORST SUPERHERO TEAM
QUANTUM AND WOODY!

ARCHER & ARMSTRONG

Volume 1: The Michelangelo Code
ISBN: 9780979640988

Volume 2: Wrath of the Eternal Warrior
ISBN: 9781939346049

Volume 3: Far Faraway
ISBN: 9781939346148

Volume 4: Sect Civil War
ISBN: 9781939346254

Volume 5: Mission: Improbable
ISBN: 9781939346353

Volume 6: American Wasteland
ISBN: 9781939346421

Volume 7: The One Percent and Other Tales
ISBN: 9781939346537

ARMOR HUNTERS

Armor Hunters
ISBN: 9781939346452

Armor Hunters: Bloodshot
ISBN: 9781939346469

Armor Hunters: Harbinger
ISBN: 9781939346506

Unity Vol. 3: Armor Hunters
ISBN: 9781939346445

X-O Manowar Vol. 7: Armor Hunters
ISBN: 9781939346476

BLOODSHOT

Volume 1: Setting the World on Fire
ISBN: 9780979640964

Volume 2: The Rise and the Fall
ISBN: 9781939346032

Volume 3: Harbinger Wars
ISBN: 9781939346124

Volume 4: H.A.R.D. Corps
ISBN: 9781939346193

Volume 5: Get Some!
ISBN: 9781939346315

Volume 6: The Glitch and Other Tales
ISBN: 9781939346711

BLOODSHOT REBORN

Volume 1: Colorado
ISBN: 9781939346674

DEAD DROP

Dead Drop
ISBN: 9781939346858

THE DEATH-DEFYING DOCTOR MIRAGE

The Death-Defying Dr. Mirage
ISBN: 9781939346490

THE DELINQUENTS

The Delinquents
ISBN: 9781939346513

DIVINITY

DIVINITY
ISBN: 9781939346766

ETERNAL WARRIOR

Volume 1: Sword of the Wild
ISBN: 9781939346209

Volume 2: Eternal Emperor
ISBN: 9781939346292

Volume 3: Days of Steel
ISBN: 9781939346742

HARBINGER

Volume 1: Omega Rising
ISBN: 9780979640957

Volume 2: Renegades
ISBN: 9781939346025

Volume 3: Harbinger Wars
ISBN: 9781939346117

Volume 4: Perfect Day
ISBN: 9781939346155

Volume 5: Death of a Renegade
ISBN: 9781939346339

Volume 6: Omegas
ISBN: 9781939346384

HARBINGER WARS

Harbinger Wars
ISBN: 9781939346094

Bloodshot Vol. 3: Harbinger Wars
ISBN: 9781939346124

Harbinger Vol. 3: Harbinger Wars
ISBN: 9781939346117

EXPLORE THE VALIANT UNIVERSE

KICK ME
UANTUM AND WOODY
BY PRIEST & BRIGHT
1: KLANG
BATTLE FOR NEW JAPAN
RAI
THE VALIANT
THE DEATH-DEFYING
DOCTOR MIRAGE
DIVINITY

インピリアム
IPERIUM

e 1: Collecting Monsters
9781939346759

INJAK

e 1: Weaponeer
9781939346667

UANTUM WOODY!

e 1: The World's Worst Superhero Team
9781939346186

e 2: In Security
9781939346230

e 3: Crooked Pasts, Present Tense
9781939346391

e 4: Quantum and Woody Must Die!
9781939346629

UANTUM WOODY BY PRIEST & BRIGHT

1: Klang
781939346780

2: Switch
781939346803

3: And So...
781939346865

RAI

Volume 1: Welcome to New Japan
ISBN: 9781939346414

Volume 2: Battle for New Japan
ISBN: 9781939346612

Volume 3: The Orphan
ISBN: 9781939346841

SHADOWMAN

Volume 1: Birth Rites
ISBN: 9781939346001

Volume 2: Darque Reckoning
ISBN: 9781939346056

Volume 3: Deadside Blues
ISBN: 9781939346162

Volume 4: Fear, Blood, And Shadows
ISBN: 9781939346278

Volume 5: End Times
ISBN: 9781939346377

Ivar, Timewalker

Volume 1: Making History
ISBN: 9781939346636

UNITY

Volume 1: To Kill a King
ISBN: 9781939346261

Volume 2: Trapped by Webnet
ISBN: 9781939346346

Volume 3: Armor Hunters
ISBN: 9781939346445

UNITY (Continued)

Volume 4: The United
ISBN: 9781939346544

Volume 5: Homefront
ISBN: 9781939346797

THE VALIANT

The Valiant
ISBN: 9781939346605

VALIANT ZEROES AND ORIGINS

Valiant: Zeroes and Origins
ISBN: 9781939346582

X-O MANOWAR

Volume 1: By the Sword
ISBN: 9780979640940

Volume 2: Enter Ninjak
ISBN: 9780979640995

Volume 3: Planet Death
ISBN: 9781939346087

Volume 4: Homecoming
ISBN: 9781939346179

Volume 5: At War With Unity
ISBN: 9781939346247

Volume 6: Prelude to Armor Hunters
ISBN: 9781939346407

Volume 7: Armor Hunters
ISBN: 9781939346476

Volume 8: Enter: Armorines
ISBN: 9781939346551

Volume 9: Dead Hand
ISBN: 9781939346650

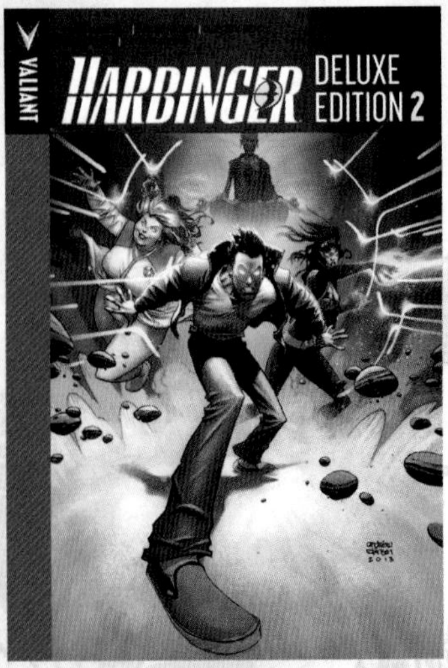
VALIANT
HARBINGER
DELUXE EDITION 2

OMNIBUSES

Archer & Armstrong: The Complete Classic Omnibus
ISBN: 9781939346872
Collecting ARCHER & ARMSTRONG (1992) #0-26, ETERNAL WARRIOR (1992) #25 along with ARCHER & ARMSTRONG: THE FORMATION OF THE SECT.

Quantum and Woody: The Complete Classic Omnibus
ISBN: 9781939346360
Collecting QUANTUM AND WOODY (1997) #0, 1-21 and #32, THE GOAT: H.A.E.D.U.S. #1, and X-O MANOWAR (1996) #16

X-O Manowar Classic Omnibus Vol. 1
ISBN: 9781939346308
Collecting X-O MANOWAR (1992) #0-30, ARMORINES #0, X-O DATABASE #1, as well as material from SECRETS OF THE VALIANT UNIVERSE #1

DELUXE EDITIONS

Archer & Armstrong Deluxe Edition Book 1
ISBN: 9781939346223
Collecting ARCHER & ARMSTRONG #0-13

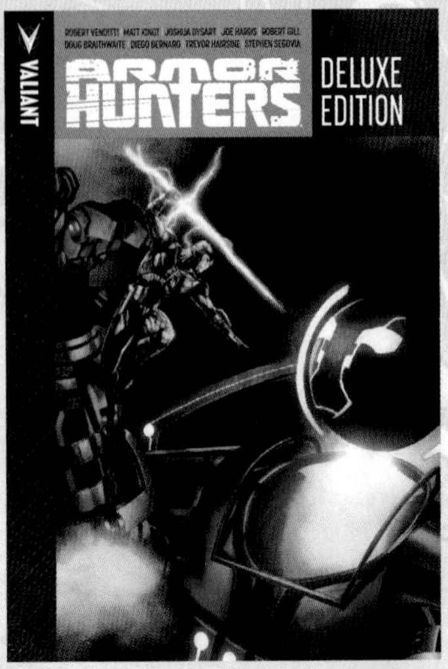
VALIANT
ARMOR HUNTERS
DELUXE EDITION

Armor Hunters Deluxe Edition
ISBN: 9781939346728
Collecting ARMOR HUNTERS #1-4, ARMOR HUNTERS: AFTERMATH #1, ARMOR HUNTERS: BLOODSHOT #1-3, ARMOR HUNTERS: HARBINGER #1-3, UNITY #8-11 and X-O MANOWAR #23-29

Bloodshot Deluxe Edition Book 1
ISBN: 9781939346216
Collecting BLOODSHOT #1-13

Harbinger Deluxe Edition Book 1
ISBN: 9781939346131
Collecting HARBINGER #0-14

Harbinger Deluxe Edition Book 2
ISBN: 9781939346773
Collecting HARBINGER #15-25, HARBINGER: OMEGAS #1-3, and HARBINGER: BLEEDING MONK #0

Harbinger Wars Deluxe Edition
ISBN: 9781939346322
Collecting HARBINGER WARS #1-4, HARBINGER #11-14, and BLOODSHOT #10-13

Quantum and Woody Deluxe Edition Book 1
ISBN: 9781939346681
Collecting QUANTUM AND WOODY #1-12 and QUANTUM AND WOODY: THE GOAT #0

Q2: The Return of Quantum and Woody Deluxe Edition
ISBN: 9781939346568
Collecting Q2: THE RETURN OF QUANTUM AND WOODY #1-5

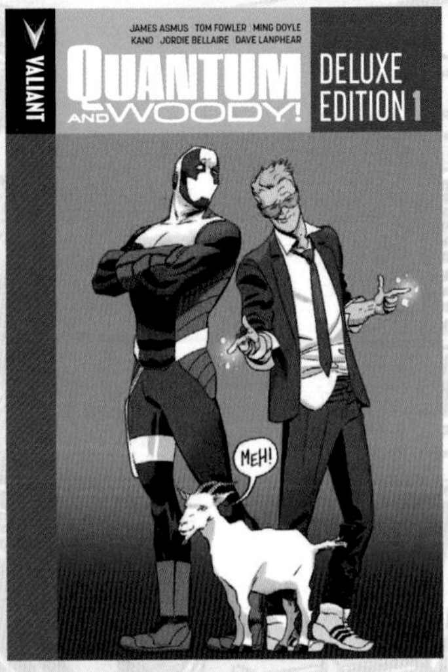
VALIANT
JAMES ASMUS TOM FOWLER MING DOYLE
KANO JORDIE BELLAIRE DAVE LANPHEAR
QUANTUM AND WOODY!
DELUXE EDITION 1
MEH!

Shadowman Deluxe Edition Book 1
ISBN: 9781939346438
Collecting SHADOWMAN #0-10

Unity Deluxe Edition Book 1
ISBN: 9781939346575
Collecting UNITY #0-14

X-O Manowar Deluxe Edition Book 1
ISBN: 9781939346100
Collecting X-O MANOWAR #1-14

X-O Manowar Deluxe Edition Book 2
ISBN: 9781939346520
Collecting X-O MANOWAR #15-22, and UNITY #1-4

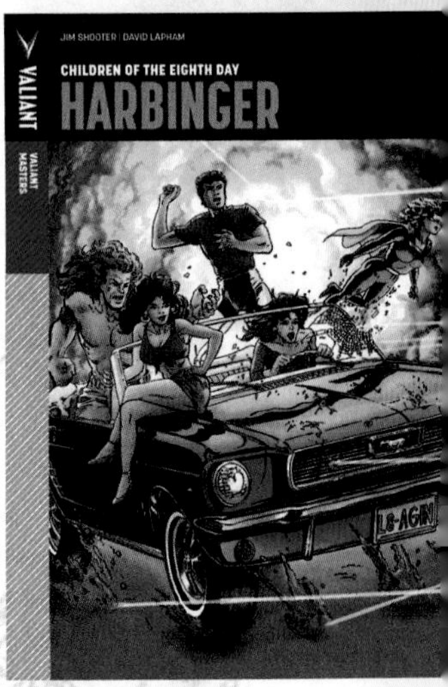
VALIANT
JIM SHOOTER | DAVID LAPHAM
CHILDREN OF THE EIGHTH DAY
HARBINGER
VALIANT MASTERS

VALIANT MASTERS

Bloodshot Vol. 1 - Blood of the Machine
ISBN: 9780979640933

H.A.R.D. Corps Vol. 1 - Search and Destroy
ISBN: 9781939346285

Harbinger Vol. 1 - Children of the Eighth Day
ISBN: 9781939346483

Ninjak Vol. 1 - Black Water
ISBN: 9780979640971

Rai Vol. 1 - From Honor to Strength
ISBN: 9781939346070

Shadowman Vol. 1 - Spirits Within
ISBN: 9781939346018

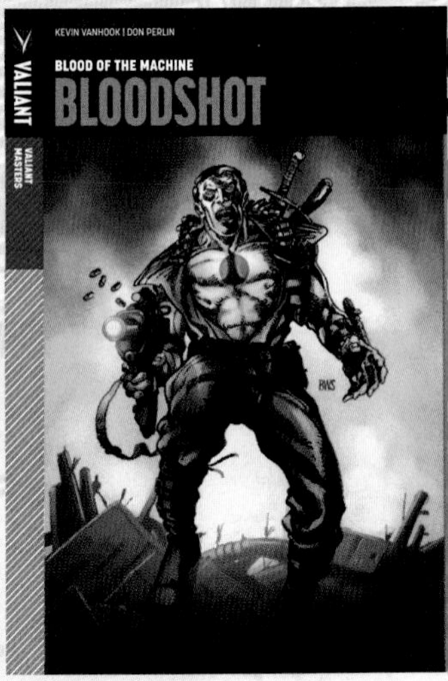
VALIANT
KEVIN VANHOOK | DON PERLIN
BLOOD OF THE MACHINE
BLOODSHOT
VALIANT MASTERS

VALIANT
JOSHUA DYSART | DOUG BRAITHWAITE
COLLECTING MONSTERS
インペリアム
IMPERIUM

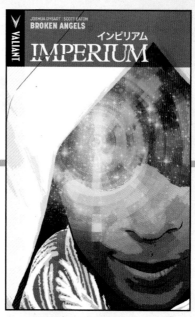

Imperium Vol. 1: Collecting Monsters

VALIANT
JOSHUA DYSART | SCOTT EATON
BROKEN ANGELS
インピリアム
IMPERIUM

Imperium Vol. 2: Broken Angels

Before the fight for utopia, Toyo Harada waged his war in the shadows... and only the teen-aged psiot Peter Stanchek and his band of Renegades stood in his way. See where the saga began in the Harvey Award-nominated series, HARBINGER!

VALIANT
OMEGA RISING
HARBINGER

Harbinger Vol. 1:
Omega Rising

VALIANT
RENEGADES
HARBINGER

Harbinger Vol. 2:
Renegades

VALIANT
HARBINGER WARS
HARBINGER

Harbinger Vol. 3:
Harbinger Wars

VALIANT
PERFECT DAY
HARBINGER

Harbinger Vol. 4:
Perfect Day

VALIANT
DEATH OF A RENEGADE
HARBINGER

Harbinger Vol. 5:
Death of a Renegade

VALIANT
HARBINGER
ΩMEGAS

Harbinger Vol. 6:
Omegas

LIANT

IMPERIUM®

VOLUME TWO: **BROKEN ANGELS**

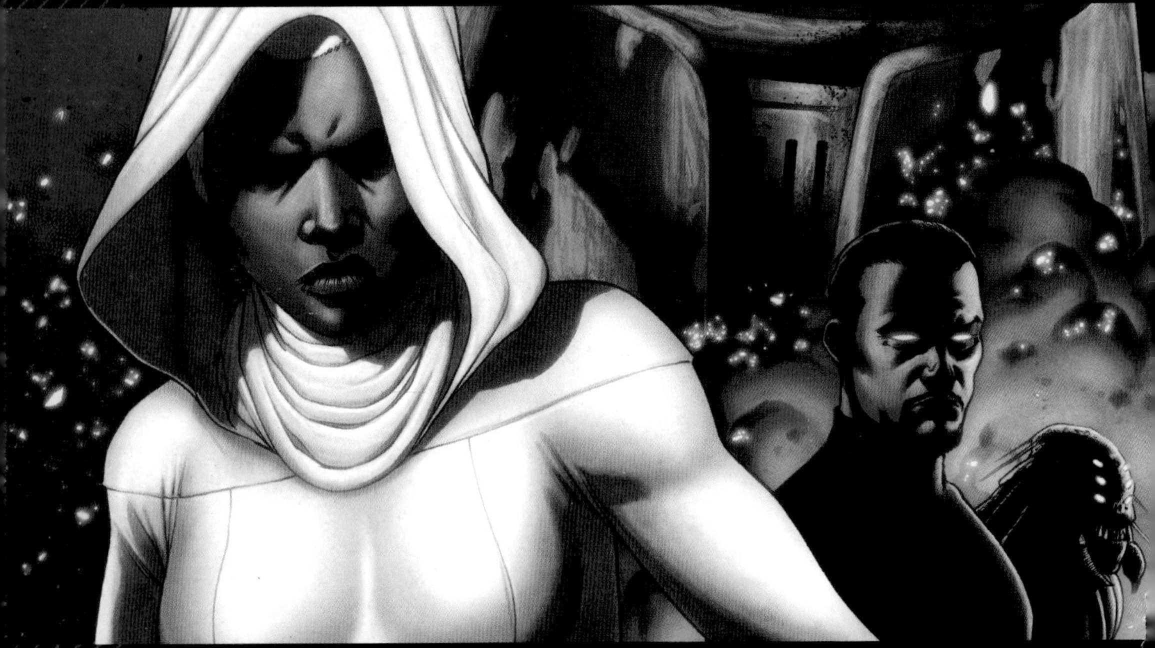

The telepathic mastermind. The alien assassin. The mercenary super-soldier. The mad scientist. And the killer robot with a soul. Toyo Harada has collected the monsters that will make his vision of world peace a reality. Now he pursues the most difficult and desirable asset of all - the spaceman with all the powers of a god - the outcast who can rewrite reality with a thought - the man who is no longer a man - the all-powerful being who is simply called Divinity.

From New York Times best-selling writer Joshua Dysart (HARBINGER) and veteran artist Scot Eaton (*X-Men: Legacy*, *Battle Scars*) Toyo Harada's mission to shape the future of humanity - by any means necessary - continues right here! Collecting IMPERIUM #5-8.

TRADE PAPERBACK
ISBN: 978-1-939346-89-6

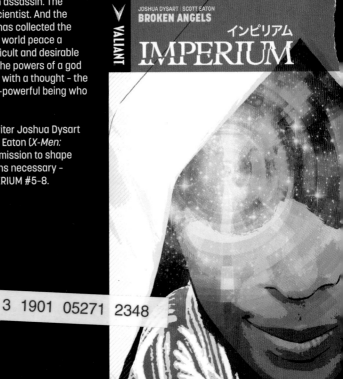

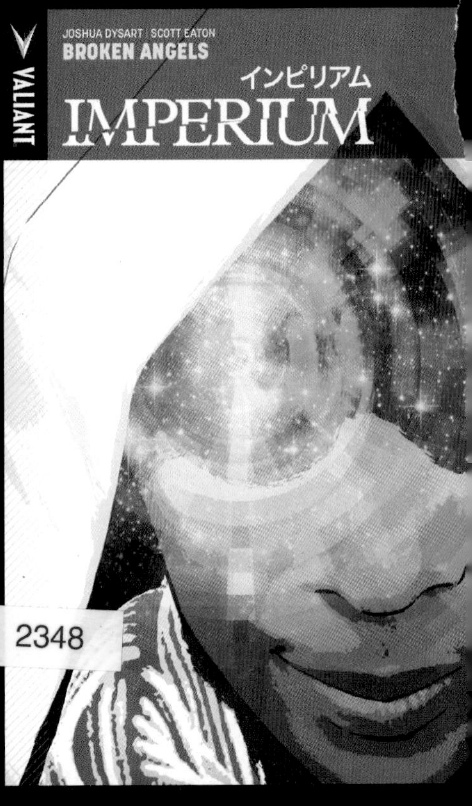
VALIANT
JOSHUA DYSART | SCOTT EATON
BROKEN ANGELS
インペリアム
IMPERIUM